Practical Ethics
for Psychologists

Practical Ethics for Psychologists

A POSITIVE APPROACH

Samuel J. Knapp
Leon D. VandeCreek

AMERICAN PSYCHOLOGICAL ASSOCIATION • WASHINGTON, DC

First Printing, September 2005
Second Printing, October 2006

Published by
American Psychological Association
750 First Street, NE
Washington, DC 20002
www.apa.org

To order
APA Order Department
P.O. Box 92984
Washington, DC 20090-2984
Tel: (800) 374-2721; Direct: (202) 336-5510
Fax: (202) 336-5502; TDD/TTY: (202) 336-6123
Online: www.apa.org/books/
E-mail: order@apa.org

In the U.K., Europe, Africa, and the Middle East, copies may be ordered from
American Psychological Association
3 Henrietta Street
Covent Garden, London
WC2E 8LU England

Typeset in Goudy by Stephen D. McDougal, Mechanicsville, MD

Printer: Port City Press, Baltimore, MD
Cover Designer: Mercury Publishing Services, Rockville, MD
Technical/Production Editor: Devon Bourexis

The opinions and statements published are the responsibility of the authors, and such opinions and statements do not necessarily represent the policies of the American Psychological Association.

Library of Congress Cataloging-in-Publication Data

Knapp, Samuel.
    Practical ethics for psychologists : a positive approach / Samuel J. Knapp and Leon D. VandeCreek. — 1st ed.
        p. cm.
    Includes bibliographical references and index.
    ISBN 1-59147-326-8
    1. Psychologists—Professional ethics. 2. Psychology—Standards. I. VandeCreek, Leon.
II. Title.

    BF76.4.K64 2006
    174'.915—dc22   2005008957

British Library Cataloguing-in-Publication Data
A CIP record is available from the British Library.

Printed in the United States of America

To Janemarie Heesen Knapp
Samuel J. Knapp

To Barbara VandeCreek
Leon D. VandeCreek

IMPORTANT NOTICE

The statements and opinions published in this book are the responsibility of the authors. Such opinions and statements do not represent official policies, standards, guidelines, or ethical mandates of the American Psychological Association (APA), APA's Ethics Committee or Office of Ethics, or any other APA governance group or staff. Statements made in this book neither add to nor reduce requirements of the APA "Ethical Principles of Psychologists and Code of Conduct" (2002a), hereinafter referred to as the APA Ethics Code or the Ethics Code, nor can they be viewed as a definitive source of the meaning of the Ethics Code Standards or their application to particular situations. Each ethics committee or other relevant body must interpret and apply the Ethics Code as it believes proper, given all the circumstances. Any information in this book involving legal and ethical issues should not be used as a substitute for obtaining personal legal and/or ethical advice and consultation prior to making decisions regarding individual circumstances.

CONTENTS

ACKNOWLEDGMENTS

We thank the Pennsylvania Psychological Association and its executive officer, Thomas DeWall, for allowing us to adapt the article entitled "Ethics of Advocacy" that was written by Samuel J. Knapp and Thomas DeWall and previously published in the *Pennsylvania Psychologist*.

We express our appreciation to the American Psychological Association (APA) Practice Directorate, which trained Samuel J. Knapp and other state directors of professional affairs on the Health Insurance Portability and Accountability Privacy Rule.

We also express our appreciation to the reviewers of the manuscript, including Lindsay Childress-Beatty, Alan Nessman, Stanley Jones, and Stephen Behnke of the APA.

We thank Mitchell Handelsman and Michael Gottlieb who, among many contributions, developed the acculturation model for training students, collaborated on expanding the implications of positive ethics, and refined concepts related to patient-centered decision making. In addition, I (Knapp) have a special debt to many individuals who have instructed me and clarified my thinking on ethics, including Rachael Baturin, Patricia Bricklin, Constance Fischer, Peter Keller, Linda Knauss, Richard Small, Alan Tepper, and Allan Tjeltveit. Linda Knauss also assisted in the development of the five-step ethics-decision-making model.

Of course all of the errors and shortcomings are ours.

Practical Ethics for Psychologists

1

REMEDIAL AND POSITIVE ETHICS

Ethics is a general term that refers to values, how we ought to behave, and what constitutes proper conduct. *Practical* or *applied ethics* refers to the application of ethics to specialized areas or professions, such as psychology (Beauchamp & Childress, 2001). The purpose of this book is to help psychologists clarify what they value, consider how they should behave, and determine what constitutes proper professional conduct. Our goal is to help psychologists reach a higher level of service by attending to the practical ethical issues that arise as they deliver health care, teach, conduct research, or engage in other professional activities.

Psychologists use the word *ethics* to refer both to the mandatory floor or minimum standards adopted by the profession (i.e., *remedial ethics*) as well as to voluntary efforts to live out moral ideals. The remedial approach focuses almost exclusively on the laws or standards designed to protect the public from harmful actions by psychologists (i.e., state and federal laws regulating the practice of psychology, the regulations of state licensing boards, and the enforceable standards of the American Psychological Association's (APA) "Ethical Principles of Psychologists and Code of Conduct," (hereinafter APA Ethics Code or the Ethics Code; 2002a; www.apa.org/ethics/code2002.html).

However, ethics can also be viewed as a voluntary effort to "do the right thing," motivated by deeply held moral principles. This approach is reflected in the aspirational principles of the APA Ethics Code and in writings on positive or active ethics (Handelsman, Knapp, & Gottlieb, 2002). Although psychologists may be motivated by different religious or philosophical sources, most ethical systems reflect a "common morality" or shared core of aspirational beliefs.

The remedial approach reflects an incomplete view of ethics. Most psychologists want to do more than just avoid being punished; they want to have a positive impact on others and to excel in their profession. Being technically legal is not the same as being morally sensitive (Bricklin, 2001). For example, conscientious psychologists not only ensure that they meet minimal standards of competency but also want to excel in their ability to help others. Ethical standards forbid psychologists from discriminating unfairly, especially against persons who belong to groups that have historically experienced discrimination. However, most psychologists also ask themselves how they can be affirmative of these individuals. Although psychologists want to meet the "letter of the law" on informed consent, they also want to meet its spirit as well and ensure that their patients participate in treatment decisions as fully as possible.

The disciplinary and aspirational aims of ethics are interactive. Psychologists can better fulfill their minimum professional responsibilities if they understand and can apply the moral principles that underlie the disciplinary codes. In addition, psychologists can better fulfill their highest ideals if they learn the disciplinary codes that establish minimum standards of conduct.

However, disciplinary codes are not sufficient in and of themselves to guide psychologists in all of their professional decisions or to prescribe conduct for all situations or contingencies. Psychologists often face problems in which they need to interpret and apply ethical standards or to rely on their personal ethical code to guide their actions.

In this book, we review the disciplinary codes as they apply to psychologists who deliver health care, teach, conduct research, or otherwise engage in professional activities. Although we recognize the need for disciplinary codes, we keep sight of the benefits of studying ethics as a way to help psychologists fulfill their highest ethical ideals.

THE REGULATION OF PSYCHOLOGY

Psychology is both a scientific discipline and a profession. In everyday usage, the word *profession* refers broadly to any occupation, and the term *professional* is sometimes used for a member of any occupation who practices conscientiously. However, especially in the health care arena, the term *traditionally* has been restricted to occupations whose members have mastered a body of specialized knowledge, must use their judgment in the application of that knowledge, commit themselves to the public welfare, and agree to adhere to specific standards of conduct.

According to these criteria, attorneys belong to a profession because they must acquire extensive legal training to enter the field, use judgment in advising their clients, and agree to follow the rules of the court and their profession. Legal clerks, however, do not need extensive education, apply only predetermined or routine knowledge, and are not, at least by these criteria, members of a profession.

Accountants are professionals; bookkeepers are not. Veterinarians are professionals; veterinary assistants are not. Physicians are professionals; medical clerks are not. Historically nursing would not be considered a profession because licensing laws for nurses require them to act under the supervision of physicians, and therefore, nurses are not permitted to exercise their full professional judgment. However, some states have recently revised nurses' practice laws to give nurse midwives, nurse anesthetists, and advance practice nurses greater autonomy, and it could be argued that those nurses are professionals (Knapp & VandeCreek, 2003b).

In addition to advanced training, ethical standards help distinguish professionals from businessmen and businesswomen. Professionals have a fiduciary relationship (or a relationship of trust) with concurrent responsibilities to promote the public welfare and avoid or minimize conflicts of interests with their clients or patients.

Psychology is a profession, and as such, has an agreed-upon standard of conduct to guide its members. It is not a coincidence that the code of ethics for psychologists was originally published by APA in 1953, or soon after the movement for licensing psychology as an independent profession began to gain momentum.

Psychologists, like all health care professionals, are regulated by other controls, both from inside and outside the profession. Some of these controls are designed to prevent psychologists from harming their patients or violating the APA Ethics Code and other standards (i.e., *before-the-fact controls*). Other controls are designed to discipline psychologists after they have harmed patients or violated the Ethics Code and other standards (i.e., *after-the-fact controls*). The demarcation between the before-the-fact and the after-the-face controls is not absolute. The mere knowledge that after-the-fact controls exist can act as a before-the-fact control (Knapp & VandeCreek, 2003b).

In addition to being a profession, psychology is also an academic and research discipline whose members teach and conduct research. Recently, more attention has been given to the rights of students and research participants. Academic and research psychologists do not have the same set of controls as professional psychologists, but nonetheless, they are subject to external controls of their own such as grant funding agencies and academic institutions.

Before-the-Fact Controls

Before-the-fact controls attempt to prevent misconduct or harm to the public. Before-the-fact controls include the requirements of training programs, licensing requirements, and mandatory continuing education (CE). All things being equal, the preference is for before-the-fact controls because they have the potential to prevent harm (Knapp & VandeCreek, 2003b).

Theoretically at least, training programs only graduate those who have adequate academic credentials and make progress in graduate school, including acceptable performance in practica and internships. Presumably, training programs screen out applicants who do not have the potential to acquire the information and skills or do not demonstrate the character necessary to become competent psychologists.

Licensing boards require that applicants obtain the appropriate education, receive supervision, show acceptable moral character, and pass an examination on the content of psychology (and some states require an examination on state law or an oral examination). Furthermore, most licensing boards require licensees to acquire CE as a condition of licensure renewal (many require ethics as part of those CE requirements).

After-the-Fact Controls

After-the-fact controls are activated when professionals have harmed the public or violated a standard of the profession. After-the-fact controls include disciplinary actions by licensing boards and ethics committees, various civil and criminal statutes that empower lawsuits against psychologists, and if applicable, institutional oversight (Knapp & VandeCreek, 2003b).

Licensing boards may discipline their licensees who have violated the licensing law or its regulations. Typically, licensing boards adopt the APA Ethics Code entirely or modify it in their regulations. Offending psychologists can receive letters of reprimand or censure, or if the offense is especially severe, be suspended or have their licenses revoked. In addition, licensing boards may fine licensees or require them to take additional CE courses, receive supervision from another professional for a period of time, or take other steps to ensure their competence.

Complaints before a licensing board fall under the general category of administrative law. Because such complaints do not fall within the purview of criminal law (psychologists cannot be imprisoned as a result of prosecution before a licensing board), the civil liberty protections found in criminal court do not apply to proceedings before licensing boards. For example, licensees do not have a constitutional right to be represented by counsel, to confront their accusers, or to have a speedy trial. Investigators may accept (and sometimes appear to encourage) self-incriminating statements. The standard of proof may be "clear and convincing" or "preponderance of evidence," both of which are lower than the standard of "beyond a reasonable doubt" required in criminal cases.

Professional organizations can also provide after-the-fact controls. The APA Ethics Code has been adopted as binding on its members by APA and most of its state affiliates. Members of APA or its state affiliates may be disciplined if they violate the Ethics Code (although currently only a minority of state psychological associations have ethics committees authorized to discipline members). Associations have jurisdiction only over their members, however. Offending members can receive letters of reprimand or censure, or if the offense is especially severe, be suspended or expelled from the association. Although they cannot fine a member, they can, as a condition of membership, require that the psychologist take additional CE courses, submit to supervision, or take other steps to ensure his or her competence.

Malpractice courts act as another after-the-fact control. In order for malpractice to occur, the actions (or lack of actions) of the professional must have deviated from acceptable standards of care and directly damaged a patient with whom he or she had a professional duty. The four criteria for malpractice complaints all begin with the letter D: duty (a professional duty has been established), deviation (the professional deviated from acceptable standards of conduct), damage (the patient or third party was harmed), and direct (there was a direct relationship between the deviation from professional standards and the damage to the patient or third party; Simon, 1992). Plaintiffs in a malpractice suit must prove harm to the patient. In contrast, complainants before an ethics committee or a licensing board only need to prove that the accused psychologist violated an ethics code, licensing law, or board regulation. Also, malpractice courts, unlike ethics committees or licensing boards, may grant monetary awards to patients.

A variety of criminal laws also apply to psychologists. These include laws against insurance fraud, mandatory reporting provisions in child protective service laws, and sexual contact between patients and psychotherapists (in some states).

Finally, psychologists who work in institutions such as hospitals, schools, or public mental health centers are regulated by their employers. Often these institutions require their psychologist employees to adhere to the APA Ethics Code or licensing board regulations.

These various disciplinary mechanisms interact with each other in complex ways. For example, a finding that a psychologist violated the licensing law may be a crucial piece of evidence in a malpractice case. The mere fact that a licensee violated the APA Ethics Code or the licensing law or its regulations may be sufficient to prove one of the important Ds in a malpractice case: deviation from acceptable standards of care.

Academic and research psychologists also have before-the-fact and after-the-fact controls, although they differ somewhat from those of their professional colleagues. The before-the-fact controls for academic and research psychologists include training programs and institutional review boards, and the after-the-fact controls include ethics committees, institutional employers, and funding agencies (Knapp & VandeCreek, 2003b).

The extent to which these mechanisms are effective and the degree of fairness in how disciplinary bodies fulfill their mission are sources of controversy. Some claim that licensing boards are overly aggressive in prosecuting licensees (Williams, 2000), whereas others claim that they use considerable restraint (Van Horne, 2004).

Unfortunately, no standardized set of data identifies the most common infractions of psychologists. Data can be obtained from a variety of sources, such as licensing board complaints through the data bank of the Association of State and Provincial Psychology Boards (ASPPB), complaints before the APA Ethics Office, and information from malpractice carriers (their data are proprietary, but sometimes they disclose general trends concerning complaints). However, these sources do not categorize complaints in the same manner. A recent effort by ASPPB to refine data collection may eventually result in the development of a standardized data bank, at least for licensing board complaints (Kirkland, Kirkland, & Reaves, 2004).

Additional information can come from studies on the perceptions of psychologists on the most salient ethical issues that they encounter. For example, VandeCreek, Knapp, and Rosas (2003) asked psychologists involved with ethics training and education to identify the most important ethical issues. Other data can be obtained on the self-reports of psychologists (see, e.g., Pope, Tabachnick, & Keith-Spiegel, 1987). However, the self-reported concerns of psychologists do not necessarily match the most frequent causes of disciplinary actions.

Because of the incompleteness of these multiple sources of data, it is impossible to create a definitive ranking of the areas in which psychologists are most likely to be disciplined. Nonetheless, an "eyeball" analysis shows that common sources of complaints are multiple relationships (sexual and nonsexual), alleged incompetence in diagnoses or treatment, disputes arising out of child custody evaluations, fee disputes, and premature termination or abandonment. Other complaints include inadequate supervision, breach of confidentiality, inadequate record keeping, impairment, and failure to acquire required CE for licensure renewal. Also, academic or research psychologists tend to deal with more concerns about authorship, plagiarism, and informed consent.

Similarly, it is impossible to compile the exact number of psychologists who have been disciplined by a licensing board or ethics committee, found liable by a malpractice court, or convicted of violating a criminal statute related to the practice of psychology. Both Schoenfeld, Hatch, and Gonzalez (2001) and Montgomery, Cupit, and Wimberly (1999) found that 11% of the psychologists in their surveys had responded to a complaint before a licensing board at some time in their career, but states vary widely in the frequency with which they discipline psychologists. The annual report of the APA Ethics Committee also has shown that few psychologists are disciplined by the APA Ethics Office (APA Ethics Committee, 2004). Data are not available on the number of malpractice complaints because these are propriety data from several different insurers, and data on violations of criminal statues are not uniformly reported. However, Montgomery et al. reported that 6% of the psychologists in their survey had been sued for malpractice. Nonetheless, many of these disciplinary venues overlap. For example, a crime in the practice of psychology may be grounds for a disciplinary complaint, or if it involved harm to a patient in the context of a professional relationship, it could also be grounds for a malpractice suit. Furthermore, some complainants seek redress against psychologists in a variety of venues, such as a licensing board complaint, an ethics committee complaint, and a malpractice lawsuit for the same act of alleged misconduct.

Although disciplinary complaints against psychologists are relatively rare, they are high-impact events. Even professionals who have violated no rule may have to spend thousands of dollars and dozens (or hundreds) of hours defending themselves. Professionals who have prided themselves on the quality of their services risk great public humiliation as a result of a charge against them, even if the complaint is eventually dismissed. Psychologists who have had to respond to these complaints often feel depressed, angry, and anxious (Montgomery et al., 1999; Schoenfeld et al., 2001).

POSITIVE (ACTIVE) ETHICS

Many psychologists construe ethics primarily or exclusively in terms of the laws regulating psychology, the enforceable ethics codes, and the adjudicatory procedures of disciplinary bodies (Handelsman et al., 2002). Although the number of psychologists who are disciplined by a regulatory body is small, the study of ethics, defined in terms of punishment, often becomes anxiety producing. According to the remedial approach, ethics represents a fixed entity of prohibitions or commandments that must be followed.

This limited view of ethics minimizes the spirit or underlying philosophy behind these commandments, deprecates the significance of the subtle ways in which patients can be harmed, ignores the positive contributions of ethics, and fails to consider the ways in which ethics can uplift the many psychologists who try to function effectively. Furthermore, it presents ethics in an unnecessarily unpleasant manner. In reality, disciplinary codes represent only the ethical "floor" or minimum standards to which psychologists should adhere. They are the standards by which psychologists may be disciplined for misconduct.

As stated by Handelsman et al. (2002),

[T]he current notions of professional ethics focus too heavily on avoiding or punishing misconduct rather than promoting the highest ethical conduct. . . . [S]imilar to the pathology perspective, the prevailing models of ethics often are too rule-bound or defensive. (p. 732)

Ethics could also be viewed as a way to help psychologists fulfill their highest potential as psychologists. It could mean relying on an underlying philosophical system to help psychologists think through complex ethical dilemmas. Ethics should focus not only on how a few psychologists harm patients but also on how all psychologists can do better at helping them. This view of ethics is called *positive* or *active ethics*. The concept of positive ethics is consistent with the comments of bioethicists Beauchamp and Childress (2001) to focus on moral excellence and not just the minimal obligations found in the disciplinary codes of the health care professions.

Positive or active ethics is similar to the General (aspirational) Principles found in the APA Ethics Code in that positive ethics encourages psychologists to live up to their highest ethical standards. However, positive ethics differs from aspirational ethics in that it encourages psychologists to integrate personal ideals into their professional lives. Also, it recognizes that the ethical foundations of psychologists may differ from the principle-based ethics found in the aspirational section of the Ethics Code.

Positive ethics requires a fundamental philosophical underpinning, although it does not specify what that philosophical underpinning should be. It could be virtue ethics, deontological (Kantian) ethics, utilitarianism, principle-based ethics, or another philosophical system. We briefly review these ethical systems in chapter 2 (Foundations of Ethical Behavior). Often it is a system based on or influenced by religious convictions or personal upbringing. The goal is for psychologists to consider their vision of the good life and "formulate ways of translating these visions into action" (Prilleltensky, 1997, p. 518).

This development of positive ethics parallels the development of *positive psychology* as a scientific endeavor. According to positive psychology, the goals of psychology need to shift from an almost exclusive focus on pathology and healing to a science that helps "to articulate a vision of the good life" (Seligman & Csikszentmilhalyi, 2000, p. 5). Positive psychology focuses on positive individual traits (competence, courage, interpersonal skills, etc.) as well as how institutions can promote civic virtues (responsibility, altruism, civility, etc.).

Similarly, a goal of positive ethics is to shift the emphasis of professional psychologists away from an almost exclusive focus on wrongdoing and disciplinary actions toward an articulated vision of high ethical standards. Positive ethics can focus on individual conduct (whether articulated as virtues such as generosity or ethical principles such as beneficence) as well as on how institutions can promote high standards. Remedial ethics focuses on how disciplinary bodies react to misconduct. Positive or active ethics also considers how individual psychologists or institutions can actively promote exemplary behavior.

This is not to say that remedial ethics has no place in ethics education. It is important to know the laws that govern the practice of psychology. It is also important for psychologists to appreciate risk management principles. Risk management programs identify ways that patients can be harmed (or at least perceive themselves to be harmed) and how psychologists can protect themselves from unfounded or frivolous complaints. Risk management principles or recommendations go beyond or expand on the minimum standards of conduct. Although they are not enforceable as legal standards of conduct, good risk management programs are generally consistent with good ethical practice. However, education about disciplinary codes, risk management principles, and disciplinary boards and their procedures are not sufficient for ethics education in and of themselves.

A complete education in ethics requires consideration of the perspectives or processes by which psychologists can maximize their adherence to moral principles. It means going beyond the minimal standards found in the APA Ethics Code and trying to uphold the moral principles that form the foundation of the Ethics Code.

It means, for example, taking special effort to ensure that patients understand the treatment process, rather than just trying to get their signatures on an informed consent form. It means taking a special effort to ensure that the debriefing of research participants is truly helpful, as opposed to a perfunctory formality. Table 1.1 shows the contrast between the remedial and positive approach in several moral domains.

Precursors of Positive Ethics

It could be argued that we are creating a straw man with our characterization of the remedial approach. In reality we know of no leading scholar in the field of ethics who adopts that approach. Nonetheless, we believe that many individual psychologists equate professional ethics with the remedial approach. In addition, all psychologists (including the authors) may allow a remedial mode of thinking to drift into their conception of ethics.

Furthermore, the terms positive or active ethics only place a general label on similar perspectives already articulated by other scholars in the field of professional ethics. Brown (1994) commented that many psychotherapists have mistakenly conceived of ethics as "a concrete wall hemming us in, forbidding us from human connections" (p. 276). Bricklin (2001) stated that being ethical means more than just obeying the law. "All ethical issues are not legal issues. To treat them as if they are, creates confusion" (p. 195). Kitchener (2000b) noted the limitations of the APA Ethics Code and urged psychologists "to turn to the foundational ethical principles and theories"

TABLE 1.1
A Comparison of Remedial and Positive Ethics

Moral domain	Remedial approach	Positive ethics
Nondiscrimination	Avoiding discrimination	Promoting understanding and appreciation of traditionally disenfranchised groups, such as developing a "gay affirmative" orientation
Competence	Acquiring and maintaining minimal formal qualifications	Striving for highest standards of competence, including self-awareness and self-care
Boundaries	Avoiding boundary violations, especially sexual exploitations	Striving to enhance the quality of all professional relationships
Informed consent	Fulfilling legal responsibilities such as ensuring that patients sign an informed consent form	Striving to maximize patient participation in development of the goals of the evaluation or therapy
Confidentiality	Avoiding prohibited disclosures	Striving to enhance trust

(p. 20). Prilleltensky (1997) encouraged psychologists to articulate a lucid set of guiding ethical principles.

Many of the specific applications of positive ethics in this book have been identified by previous authors. In chapter 5 (Competence), we note the importance of emotional competence, a concept that has been advanced by Pope and Brown (1996). In chapter 6 (Multiple Relationships and Professional Boundaries), we argue that psychologists should try not only to prevent the sexual exploitation of patients by a few psychologists but also to uplift the quality of treatment to all patients by asking psychologists to be sensitive to the sexual feelings that may arise during therapy. These concepts were presented in the landmark book, *Sexual Feelings in Psychotherapy*, by Pope, Sonne, and Holroyd (1993). In chapter 7 (Informed Consent or Shared Decision Making), we argue that informed consent should maximize patient participation in the therapeutic process. This concept was presaged by Handelsman (2001), who encouraged psychologists to maximize patient understanding of the treatment process; by Prilleltensky, Rossiter, and Walsh-Bowers (1996), who urged a participatory framework for psychologist–patient relationships; and by Pope and Brown, who endorsed "empowered consent." In chapter 12 (Assessment), we reference Brenner (2003), who urged the coparticipation of evaluated persons in the assessment process. In chapter 16 (Research and Scholarship), we cite Fisher (2000b), who suggested that psychologists adopt a "duty-based" perspective toward research participants and treat them as moral agents with intrinsic worth and helpful perspectives, instead of as simply the means by which investigators can reach their research goals. Other examples can be identified, such as when scholars adopt perspectives consistent with positive ethics. We present only a general conceptual framework for these perspectives.

Throughout this book we have identified several instances in which a positive approach would alter the manner in which psychologists conceptualize their relationships to patients and others. However, we make no pretense of having the last word on positive ethics. Instead, we hope that others will identify additional ways that psychologists can implement a positive approach and improve on the suggestions contained in this book. These continual revisions will help ensure that positive ethics does not get frozen into its own set of formulas and shibboleths.

We can enhance the clarity of our moral vision by studying the literature on philosophical ethics and accounts from persons who have traditionally been marginalized in society. Although feminists represent diverse philosophical perspectives, they share common ground in identifying how societal structures contain power dynamics that tend to disenfranchise women and other groups. Attending to these perspectives may help psychologists see ways in which they may unknowingly minimize the perspectives of others. Similarly, culturally diverse psychologists have identified ways that majority psychologists have failed to appreciate the unique life situations of culturally diverse patients, and as a result, have provided less than optimal treatment. Much can be learned by reading and trying to understand first person accounts of mental patients. The most important step is to include all affected parties in the dialogue.

Benefits of Positive Ethics

A positive approach to ethics can have several benefits. It can sensitize psychologists to the ethical implications of the decisions they face in their daily practices. For example, they may have to decide whether to accept a particular patient, how to balance the apparently competing needs of family members and patients, or how much to support their patients' desires for freedom from or dependence on their families (see Tjeltveit, 1999; Richardson, Fowers, & Guigon, 1999, for discussions of many ethical issues faced in the daily practices of psychologists).

Positive ethics also may help psychologists appreciate the moral values on which the APA Ethics Code and other ethics codes are based. Many rules such as those prohibiting sexual contact with patients, respecting patient confidentiality, and avoiding harmful multiple relationships are designed to avoid harming patients. Appreciating the moral basis of these rules will help psychologists feel greater support for and commitment to upholding them.

Currently many psychologists feel alienated from the APA Ethics Code. Insofar as the Ethics Code ceases to reflect the values of psychologists, its perception as a legitimate authority is diminished. Psychologists who can connect the specific standards of the Ethics Code with their own beliefs are less likely to feel alienated. However, part of the alienation occurs because of the idiosyncratic manner in which licensing boards and ethics committees interpret the Ethics Code. When licensing boards or ethics committees engage in bizarre and unfair interpretations of the Ethics Code, they lead psychologists to question the benefit–cost valence of these disciplinary bodies.

Positive ethics will also assist psychologists in their ethical decision making, especially when that decision making requires balancing the competing ethical demands in a given situation. Although some ethical rules for psychologists are absolute (e.g., do not have sex with patients, do not gossip about patients, do not falsify insurance forms), psychologists encounter many gray areas in which they need to exercise substantial judgment. These ethical dilemmas can be stressful for psychologists who sincerely want to do the right thing but can find no clear-cut answer in the APA Ethics Code. Psychologists who are more aware of the moral principles that underlie the Ethics Code should become more effective at identifying ethical issues, thinking through their implications, and following the optimal course of action.

In addition, many psychologists aspire to address systemic social problems. By working through their professional organizations in psychology or through other collaborative efforts, psychologists can collectively apply scientific information or a scientific perspective to social problems.

2

FOUNDATIONS OF
ETHICAL BEHAVIOR

People become psychologists for many reasons. Career choice, like many other choices, is probably overdetermined. Certainly psychologists want employment that is interesting, pays enough, and has adequate working conditions. Nonetheless, another major reason for choosing any career is the opportunity to live out important ethical ideals (Martin, 2000). The same applies to psychology. Most psychologists want a profession that allows them to live out their values. They want to integrate their personal commitments into their professional lives.

Like others, psychologists have asked themselves, What is the good life? How should we live? What should be our obligations to others? and What principles should guide our lives? Although few psychologists have taken up a comprehensive study of philosophical ethics, most have deliberated conscientiously on their personal ethical positions. Often their values are influenced by their religious or cultural backgrounds, guided by parents and other caregivers, and altered through personal experiences. These values can become central to their self-concepts.

These value systems generally correspond to a *common morality* or an intuitive sense of what is honest, helpful, trustworthy, or civil. As it applies to their personal lives, individual psychologists may disagree about certain ethical issues, such as whether membership in a religious organization is important. Nonetheless, they share a core set of values, such as that people should generally be honest, help each other, and follow through with commitments. As it applies to their roles as psychologists, individual psychologists may disagree about certain technical practices, such as when to allow secrets while conducting family therapy or the desirability of using deception in research. Nonetheless, they share a core set of values, such as that all psychologists should generally be honest with patients, work to promote their well-being, and avoid gossiping about them.

Formal philosophical systems have a place in the discussion about ethics because they can help to increase ethical acuity (or our ability to identify and clarify ethical issues; Tjeltveit, 1999), ground or justify ethical positions, or help psychologists make good decisions in situations in which their ethical obligations are not clear. Understanding moral foundations is necessary for psychologists who desire to reach high standards of conduct (Tjeltveit, 1999). Psychologists who have a clear sense of what they believe and why they believe it are more likely to make good ethical decisions. A well-trained psychologist can produce empathy statements even under considerable stress. Similarly, a well-trained psychologist can call on deeply held ethical schemas, even during periods of considerable personal turmoil.

We briefly review four philosophical systems (*virtue ethics*, *utilitarianism*, *deontological ethics*, and *principle-based ethics*) that appear particularly helpful to psychologists. Although academic philosophers have considered these systems in detail, they have more than theoretical or historical importance. Many of the terms and assumptions of these ethical systems have seeped into common culture and influence how people interpret everyday ethical situations. Although all ethical systems have their weaknesses, these systems have endured because of their coherence and usefulness in addressing ethical problems. This brief review can only touch the surface of these major philosophical traditions because each tradition has numerous subthemes, variations, and branches to it.

These philosophical systems have important differences, but the differences should not be overemphasized. The philosophical systems often start in different places on an issue but end up in a similar location. They may appear highly dissimilar on the surface, but they lead to similar conclusions on most of the common ethical issues facing psychologists. That is to say, they are consistent with the common morality. Only on the more technical or specific issues do they lead to differences in conduct.

Self-interest is not one of the philosophical systems reviewed here because it has never attracted a substantial following among philosophers or even in the public in general. Respect for legitimate self-interest is an integral part of all of the philosophical systems reviewed. Certainly pursuing one's enlightened self-interest, if conducted appropriately, usually contributes to overall social welfare.

But self-interest as an overarching and comprehensive philosophical perspective appears to lack internal consistency. Persons who believe in self-interest as a comprehensive philosophy believe that the primary ethical obligation of all individuals is to promote their own welfare. However, to promote their own welfare to the fullest, they would have to argue that others should be altruistic toward them. In other words, they must argue against their own philosophical system to promote it.

Most contemporary thinkers agree that *feminism* has a substantial influence on important current ethical issues, although not all would recognize it as a separate ethical system. Rather, adherents of feminism can be found among those who advocate virtue ethics or other philosophical systems. Feminism's influence is especially important when considering ethical issues dealing with fairness and abuse of power. Consequently, we do not discuss feminism as a separate ethical system but refer to feminist influences on ethical thinking as appropriate throughout this book.

In the discussion that follows we show an inclination toward principle-based efforts, but we rely on perspectives from other ethical theories when it appears useful.

VIRTUE ETHICS

Whereas most ethical theories focus on a dominant principle of moral behavior, virtue ethics focuses on individual character. Virtues are character traits that have moral value. Aristotle was the first major Western philosopher to emphasize virtues in the conceptualization of morality, although a virtue-oriented approach to ethics is found in writings of non-Western philosophers as well, such as Master Kong-Fut-zi (Confucius).

According to virtue ethics, an ethical professional has the right mixture of motives, knowledge, and character. Adherents of virtue ethics may disagree about the exact list of these virtues, but Meara, Schmidt, and Day (1996) have included the following: (a) prudence (demonstrating planned, appropriate forethought and good judgment), (b) integrity (adhering to an internally consistent code of conduct), (c) respectfulness (considering others worthy of high regard or special attention), and (d) benevolence (acting to help others). Feminists may expand on these virtues. For example, Kitchener (2000b) has noted that respectfulness from a feminist perspective requires listening to the perspectives of other persons, especially those who come from populations that have traditionally been underrepresented or oppressed.

Proponents of virtue ethics claim that ethics codes can never cover every fact that psychologists need to know or cover all situations that psychologists may encounter. Instead, ethics codes require psychologists and other moral agents to use judgment in implementing moral principles in novel or ambiguous situations. Indeed, it would not be appropriate to try to replace the judgment of virtuous psychologists with an exhaustive list of rules calculated to predict every possible situation. Such a system of rules, even if it could be comprehensive, would risk becoming so complex that it would be unmanageable and risk missing nuances of the individual situation that can undercut goals.

Furthermore, it could be claimed that other systems of ethics risk turning ethical dilemmas into intellectual puzzles that are solved through the application of specific rules. However, virtue ethics forces individuals to see ethical dilemmas as human activities that sometimes involve strong and competing motives and emotions.

On the whole, virtue ethicists argue that we are better off emphasizing character building in psychologists rather than just trying to enforce conformity to rules. The virtuous psychologist chooses the virtuous act because it is the right thing to do, not because of any anticipation of personal gain. Over time, a psychologist who acts virtuously will cultivate a steady state of character whereby virtuous actions become more automatic and eventually become nurtured habits.

Critics of virtue ethics are not opposed to such attributes as benevolence and integrity but believe that these may not be the optimal basis on which to formulate an ethical theory. They may claim that these virtues strongly resemble the ethical principles articulated by others (benevolence corresponds to beneficence; respectfulness corresponds to respect for patient autonomy, etc.), but they see no merit in conceptualizing these virtues in terms of personality traits as opposed to more abstract moral principles (Bersoff, 1996). Furthermore, the virtue ethics perspective does not naturally lead to an ethical decision-making formula, as do some systems of ethics.

DEONTOLOGICAL (DUTY-BASED) ETHICS

Immanuel Kant (1724–1803) is the leading figure in the history of deontological (duty-based) ethics. The primary goal of ethical behavior according to Kant (1785/1988) is for individuals to fulfill their duties. Happiness is only a fortuitous by-product of doing one's duty. Being happy is not necessarily immoral; it is possible to be happy while doing one's duty. However, happiness is not an end in and of itself. Moral actions do not occur out of spontaneous emotions but out of an intention to fulfill one's responsibilities. "An action done from duty must wholly exclude the influence of inclination" (Kant, p. 25).

According to Kant (1785/1988), people can do the right thing for the wrong reasons. The consequences of an action are irrelevant for determining the morality of an action. For example, three psychologists may waive the copayment for a patient who is unable to afford the full cost of therapy. The first psychologist may believe that she has a duty to provide some services to those who otherwise cannot afford them. The second psychologist would rather fill up his empty time slot with a partial payment patient than to leave it empty. The third psychologist may be moved by the plight of a patient and act out of a spontaneous moment of sympathy. According to Kant, the first psychologist would be acting ethically; whereas the second and third psychologists would not. Although all performed the same outward act, they are not morally equal. One is fulfilling an obligation to help others; the second is promoting self-advantage; and the third is responding to a spontaneous emotion.

Kant (1785/1988) distinguished between *hypothetical (conditional) imperatives* and *categorical (universal) imperatives*. The hypothetical imperative can be expressed in the form of an "if–then" statement. A hypothetical or conditional imperative tells us to act in a certain way if we want to achieve a certain result. An example of the hypothetical imperative might be, "If I want to become licensed as a psychologist, then I need to pass the licensing examination." The categorical imperative applies to all persons even if there is no "if." A categorical imperative commands individuals to act a certain way at all times. Obedience to a categorical imperative is a duty; whereas obedience to a hypothetical imperative is only a matter of prudence.

Kant (1785/1988) established several versions of the categorical imperative, and the two most familiar ones are repeated here. Kant's first formulation of the categorical imperative was to "act only on that maxim whereby thou canst at the same time will that it should become a universal law" (p. 49). Kant's second formulation was to "act as to treat humanity, whether in thine own person or in that of any other, in every case as an end withal, never as means only" (p. 58). These formulations have a not coincidental similarity to the "golden rule" of Christianity. Although Kant was influenced by the Christian tradition, similar golden rules have been found in Judaism, Buddhism, Confucianism, and other religions.

The categorical imperative does not state that one cannot use other people as a means; it states that one cannot use other people only as a means. For example, it is appropriate to charge patients for health care services. In that sense, psychologists are using them as a means to promote their self-interest. However, such actions are moral if the patients get something in exchange for the money (e.g., health care services). Similarly, it would be appropriate to use research participants to gain information. In that sense, researchers are using them for their own purposes. However, such actions are moral if the research participants get something in return, such as course credit, insight into the research process, or payment.

A feminist perspective could complement the Kantian perspective by giving special emphasis to the intrinsic worth of all individuals regardless of social rank and the need to "hear their voices" (to avoid using them as a means only and not as an end in themselves).

UTILITARIANISM

Although seeds of utilitarianism can be found in the writings of some early philosophers, it was more fully developed by the English social reformer Jeremy Bentham (1748–1832) and was best articulated by John Stuart Mill (1806–1873). According to utilitarianism, the moral value of an act is determined by the consequences (i.e., the sum of happiness and unhappiness) to everyone involved. According to Mill (1861/1987), "the creed which accepts as the foundation of morals, Utility, or the Greatest Happiness Principle, holds that actions are right in proportion as they tend to promote happiness, wrong as they tend to produce the reverse of happiness" (p. 278). Utilitarianism, therefore, is concerned with benefit maximization for all relevant parties.

The three essential features of utilitarianism theory are that it is *consequential, hedonistic,* and *universal* (Knapp, 1999). It is consequential in that the litmus test of morality depends on the consequences or outcomes of behavior. This contrasts to deontological theory, in which the intentions of the actor are important but the consequences are incidental to the morality of the action. Utilitarianism is hedonistic in that happiness, pleasure, or well-being is the goal of behaviors. It is universal in that the happiness, pleasure, or well-being of others (i.e., generalized benevolence) is just as important as the happiness of the individual in determining the morality of an action.

According to early formulations of utilitarianism (i.e., *act utilitarianism*), it would be necessary to calculate the consequences of all of a person's actions through an extensive happiness (i.e., felicific or hedonic) calculus with myriad projections and assumptions. It would be necessary to estimate the happiness that would derive from each possible action, estimate the unhappiness that would derive from each of those possible actions, and then decide in favor of the action that promises the maximum of happiness or the minimum of unhappiness for all of the persons involved. Accurately predicting the consequences of every alternative action necessarily involves much uncertainty and requires much effort.

A later formulation of utilitarianism, *rule utilitarianism,* focused on middle-range, intermediary, or instrumental principles that generally lead to happiness or well-being. Rule utilitarianism does not require a detailed happiness calculus to predict the outcome of all possible alternatives. It is assumed that certain acts, such as murder, stealing, lying, or deceit, which generally produce unhappiness, may be considered immoral without the need to do a happiness calculus. Other acts, such as respecting the property of others or telling the truth, which generally produce happiness, may be considered moral without doing a happiness calculus. These general happiness rules should not be compromised except in very unusual circumstances.

Consequently, rule utilitarianism applies the principle of utility to the intermediary or instrumental moral rules, not to every specific action. In summary, rule utilitarianism asks, What intermediary or instrumental rules produce the greatest happiness for all persons? This contrasts with act utilitarianism, which asks, What specific actions produce the greatest happiness for all persons?

PRINCIPLE-BASED (PRIMA FACIE) ETHICS

Principle-based, or prima facie, ethics was developed by the Oxford philosopher Sir William David Ross (1877–1940). Ross wanted an ethical theory that could address the shortcomings of both deontological and utilitarian theories (Knapp & VandeCreek, 2004). The major characteristic of ethical behavior in deontological ethics is that the actors are attempting to fulfill their duties. The outcomes of the action are not important, but the intentions of the actor are. Deontological theory is absolute in that it allows no exceptions to its absolute or categorical imperatives. However, Ross (1930/1998) argued that sometimes the most moral action requires breaking absolute rules. For example, according to Ross, at times it may be more moral for a psychologist to slant or withhold information if doing so upholds another important moral principle, such as protecting the patient from great harm.

The major characteristic of ethical behavior in utilitarianism is that the actors are considering the consequences of their behavior on all affected persons. No special consideration is given to the impact of behavior on personalized relationships, such as the impact of behavior on one's family or close friends. Utilitarianism judges ethical behavior according to the standard of utility: the greatest good for the greatest number. However, at times moral agents have obligations to specific individuals (e.g., family members or close friends) that transcend their obligations to the society in general. For example, according to Ross (1930/1998), the obligations that psychologists have to family members may require them to restrict the amount of their pro bono services, even though the psychologist could assist more people and improve the overall good of the community.

According to Ross (1930/1998), the best ethical theory rests on several moral principles referred to as *prima facie duties*, meaning an obligation that holds unless it is overridden by a superior obligation. These duties are sometimes referred to as *ethical intuitions*. They may be seen in the prereflective immediate reactions of individuals when they see an injustice. For example, most individuals would not think twice or engage in the steps of moral decision making when they see a gross injustice. Ross identified several prima facie duties, such as fidelity, gratitude, justice, beneficence, self-improvement, and nonmaleficence, but acknowledged that there may others as well.

According to Beauchamp and Childress (2001), four moral principles are especially important in the field of biomedical ethics (i.e., *respect for patient autonomy, nonmaleficence, beneficence,* and *justice*), and Kitchener (1984) and Bersoff and Koeppl (1993) have also identified *fidelity* as a fifth moral principle applicable to psychologists. We suggest that *public responsibility* (or *general beneficence*) is a sixth moral principle applicable to psychologists.

Beneficence means working to help others. "Morality requires not only that we treat people autonomously and refrain from harming them, but also that we contribute to their welfare" (Beauchamp & Childress, 2001, p. 165). Psychologists have a positive obligation to help patients by conscientiously implementing appropriate services for them.

"Nonmaleficence asserts an obligation not to inflict harm on others" (Beauchamp & Childress, 2001, p. 113). Although many psychologists remember this moral principle through the phrase *primum non nocere* (i.e., *above all, do not harm*), Ross does not suggest that this moral principle always trumps or takes priority over other moral principles. Given the right circumstances, nonmaleficence may be trumped by another moral principle.

Different theorists conceptualize justice differently. However, from the perspective of principle-based ethics as described by Beauchamp and Childress (2001), justice has two major aspects. *Distributive justice* refers to the equitable distribution of resources. *Formal (procedural) justice* refers to equal treatment either before the law or by others. We would argue that procedural justice is a prima facie obligation within the professional activities of psychologists. That is, psychologists have an obligation to treat all individuals fairly. This principle can be manifested in such obligations as refraining from discrimination against persons because of race, religion, national background, or sexual orientation (Knapp & VandeCreek, 2004).

Respect for autonomy means respecting the freedom of others to do as they choose as long as they do not infringe on the rights of others. "Personal autonomy is, at a minimum, self-rule that is free from both controlling interference by others and from limitations, such as inadequate understanding, that prevent meaningful choice" (Beauchamp & Childress, 2001, p. 58). Under this principle, psychologists should treat patients as autonomous and independent agents who can participate as full partners in determining treatment goals and methods.

According to the principle of fidelity, psychologists should be faithful to their obligations and promises. According to Kitchener (1984), fidelity means truthfulness, faithfulness, promise keeping, and loyalty. Psychologists show fidelity when they protect patient confidentiality and avoid harmful conflicts of interests.

Responsibility to the public at large, citizenship, or general beneficence is a sixth moral virtue that corresponds closely to "responsibility to society," one of the principles identified in the Canadian Psychological Association *Code of Ethics* (Canadian Psychological Association, 1986). For example, psychologists may have a responsibility to act to protect the public when one of their patients presents an imminent danger to harm an identifiable third party (see chap. 9, this volume). In another example, psychologists have a responsibility to protect future consumers of psychological services by protecting the integrity of psychological tests.

Furthermore, *moral principles* are generally to be followed. Nonetheless, at times it may be impossible to follow one moral principle without violating another. One moral principle may override another moral principle in some situations. According to Ross (1930/1998),

> When I am in a situation . . . in which more than one of these prima facie duties is incumbent on me, what I have to do is to study the situation as fully as I can until I form the considered opinion (it is never more) that in the circumstances one of them is more incumbent than any other. (p. 268)

Beauchamp and Childress (2001) identified six conditions that must be met before infringing on a moral principle. First, "better reasons can be offered to act on the overriding norm than on the infringed norm." Second, "the moral objective justifying the infringement must make a realistic prospect of achievement." Third, "no morally preferable alternative action can be substituted." Fourth, "the infringement selected must be the least possible infringement, commensurate with achieving the primary goal of the action." Fifth, "the agent must seek to minimize any negative effects of the infringement." Sixth, the "agent must act impartially in regard to all affected parties; that is, the agent's decision must not be influenced by morally irrelevant information about any party" (pp. 19–20).

For example, professional psychologists generally show full respect for patient autonomy by acknowledging patient control over the direction and major events of psychotherapy. However, under rare circumstances, such as when a patient presents an imminent danger of self-harm, psychologists have to consider whether to temporarily invoke the principle of beneficence (and, e.g., break confidentiality and notify a family member of the serious suicidal threat) to override the principle of respect for patient autonomy.

Using the six conditions previously identified with a suicidal patient, psychologists would ask themselves, Is protecting the life of the patient more important than ensuring his or her autonomy? Will breaking confidentiality have a realistic chance of protecting the life of the patient? Is there any other alternative to breaking confidentiality? Can I infringe on confidentiality as little as possible to ensure the safety of the patient? and Can I minimize the harm caused by the breach of confidentiality? Finally, psychologists should ask themselves whether their decision is influenced by any morally irrelevant information. Morally irrelevant information might include minor inconveniences to the psychologist in implementing measures to protect the patient.

Even though beneficence may trump respect for patient autonomy, the psychologist can minimize the infringement of autonomy and involve the patient as much as possible in selecting the intervention designed to reduce the likelihood of self-harm (VandeCreek & Knapp, 2001). For example, if the desired intervention requires notifying the spouse of the patient, then the psychologist can ask the patient, How should we go about informing your spouse? Do you want to be present when I share the information about your needs? If the psychologist speaks to the spouse directly, then the psychologist should give only the minimal amount of information necessary to achieve the goal.

SUPEREROGATORY OBLIGATIONS[1]

The laws and enforceable standards of the Ethics Code (American Psychological Association [APA], 2002a) can be justified by the moral theories presented here. For example, virtuous psychologists do not lie to their patients, and the standards in the after-the-fact controls can be found largely on the basis of a utilitarian analysis of the greatest good for the greatest number of persons. However, do the ethical theories reviewed have any relationship to positive ethics? That is, do psychologists have supererogatory obligations (obligations that exceed the minimum laws and ethical standards)?

It appears that followers of Ross (1930/1998) would argue that the principle of beneficence would obligate psychologists to act to their highest level of ability (such as striving for the high levels of competence or donating services), subject to the limitations placed on them by other obligations. According to principle-based ethics, those supererogatory obligations should (a) not divert us from our obligation to those with whom we have special relationships (family, friends, or current patients), (b) be moderate and not cause us more suffering than they produce relief to others, and (c) be thought out deliberately and done selectively (Beauchamp & Childress, 2001).

According to the first point, Ross (1930/1998) might have criticized the actions of Mohandas Gandhi when, in his efforts to ensure justice and well-being for India, he failed to attend to the needs of his family and refused to pay (or allow his friends to pay) for the education of his children (L. Fischer, 1983). Similarly, psychologists may have obligations to their own family members that require them to restrict their working hours, even though more people would be assisted and the overall good of the community would be improved if they worked more hours.

According to the second point, psychologists ought not to donate time and resources if doing so causes them as much suffering as they would relieve through their giving. Also, giving to others to the point of personal exhaustion would result in the loss of the gift in the first place. Competence as a

---

[1]This section is an adaptation of "Do Psychologists Have Supererogatory Obligations?" by S. Knapp and L. VandeCreek, 2003, *Psychotherapy Bulletin, 38*(3), pp. 29–31. Copyright 2003 by Division 29. Adapted with permission.

psychologist requires emotional competence. Effective psychologists need to balance their personal and professional lives and cultivate outside sources of social support and strength. These outside activities distance psychologists from their professional lives and give them a breadth of life experiences that enrich their experiences as psychologists. Those psychologists who fail to care for their personal needs risk compromising their effectiveness and their ability to perform their minimum professional obligations.

We could conduct similar analyses of supererogatory behaviors from the standpoint of other ethical theories as well. According to virtue ethics, the goal of behavior is moral excellence (Meara et al., 1996). However, it is hardly moral excellence to be guided only by a desire to avoid sanctions for violating a professional standard of conduct.

According to Kant's duty-based ethics, behavior needs to conform to the categorical imperative ("act only on that maxim whereby thou canst at the same time will that it should become a universal law" [Kant, 1785/1988, p. 49]). Because we would wish other professionals to show high levels of concern for us and competence if we were patients or clients, we should show high levels of concern for others and competence, even if that concern exceeds the minimum required in the disciplinary codes.

According to utilitarianism, the rightness of an action is determined by the principle of utility or the greatest amount of good for the greatest number of persons (Mill, 1861/1987). The standard of producing the greatest good for the greatest number would require actions exceeding the minimum required by legal standards. However, rule utilitarians would not endorse complete subjugation of personal needs and obligations to friends or family (Knapp, 1999).

It appears that the ethical systems reviewed here have standards of conduct higher than the minimum found in the disciplinary codes of the profession and consistent with the goals of positive ethics (Knapp & VandeCreek, 2003a). Consequently, the question that should be asked is not, What must I do to fulfill the minimum requirements of the APA Ethics Code? Instead it should be, What must I do to fulfill my ethical ideals? If psychologists strive to become moral maximalists, instead of moral minimalists, they will still follow the disciplinary codes but only as the beginning of their ethical responsibilities. According to Beauchamp and Childress (2001), the "concentration on minimal obligations has diluted the moral life. . . . If we expect only the moral minimum, we have lost an ennobling sense of excellence in character and performance" (p. 44).

INTEGRATING PERSONAL AND PROFESSIONAL ETHICS

One important feature of positive ethics is that it encourages psychologists to integrate their professional ethics with the ethical beliefs that guide their personal lives. Psychologists do not approach the practice of psychology in a moral vacuum. They have a background of personal beliefs that they bring to their professional duties.

Generally speaking, the moral foundations of one's personal ethics should be consistent with the moral foundations of one's professional ethics. Psychologists will show more commitment to their professional ethics if they can appreciate the connection between the moral standards underlying professional ethics and the moral standards underlying their personal ethics.

However, the manner in which professional ethics are implemented differs from how ethics are implemented in one's personal life. For example, beneficent behavior among friends may involve mutual self-disclosure, the exchange of gifts, touching, exchanging favors, and the possibility that a sexual relationship may develop given the willingness or availability of the other person. In contrast, beneficent behaviors between psychologists and patients involve primarily one-way self-disclosure, restrictions on gift giving and touching, and no sexual relationship. Friends may loan each other money or set up dating relationships. Psychologists do neither of these with their patients.

One of the goals of psychology training programs is to help students understand the differences in how moral principles are actualized or implemented in personal and professional lives. Psychology students bring a set of habits or perceptions of how to implement their personal value systems without understanding how those same behaviors could harm patients or themselves when implemented within the unique role of a psychologist.

Handelsman, Gottlieb, and Knapp (2005) have described this socialization process in terms similar to those used by Berry and Kim (1988) in describing *acculturation*. Just as recent immigrants to a foreign country bring their distinct cultural background to the United States, psychology students bring their distinct value systems to psychology. Just as recent immigrants vary in the extent to which and the speed at which they acculturate themselves to the United States, students vary in the extent to which and the speed at which they acculturate themselves to the unique ethical demands found in psychology.

Acculturation is a complex process, and immigrants typically fall along a continuum of acculturation. They may be very acculturated in some parts of their lifestyle, but not in others. It is also a process that may continue throughout their lifetimes.

The model by Handelsman et al. (2005) is a metaphor that helps explain how to integrate personal and professional ethics. Psychology students who are not acculturated to the roles of their future profession may be more willing to get involved, as a friend would, and loan money, give advice, self-disclose personal information, and give or receive gifts. Students who are well acculturated to the roles of the profession would be less likely to cross those boundaries.

This does not mean that psychologists lose the capacity to feel compassion. However, psychologists understand that the manifestation of compassion in friendships differs from the manifestation of compassion in a professional relationship. In the long run, psychologists know that they can best promote the welfare of their patients by adhering to certain norms of behavior.

Berry and Kim's (1988) model describes acculturation as a 2 × 2 design, with the recent immigrant being high or low in the degree of identification with the culture of origin and high or low in the degree of identification with the host culture. Similarly, the acculturation process for psychology students (or psychologists) can be described as being high or low in their degree of identification with their personal value system, and high or low in the degree of identification with the value system of psychology. This classification is shown in Table 2.1. Students who are low on personal ethics but high on professional ethics may attempt to follow the letter of the code but fail to understand the meanings behind it. They are at risk to develop a legalistic stance. Handelsman et al. (2005) would identify these as the *assimilated group*.

Students who are low on personal ethics and low on professional ethics present the greatest risk of harming others. They are at risk of being motivated primarily by self-interest and not by concern for their patients. Furthermore, they lack an appreciation of professional ethics. Handelsman et al. (2005) would identify these as the *marginalized group*.

Students who are high in personal ethics but low on professional ethics have strong personal values. However, they fail to see how the unique roles of psychologists direct the implementation of those values. They risk allowing spontaneous impulses of compassion to override good professional judgment. Handelsman et al. (2005) would identify these as the *separated group*.

Finally, students who are high on personal ethics and high on professional ethics understand how to implement their personal values in the context of a professional role. Handelsman et al. (2005) would identify them as the *integrated group*.

The evolution of an integrated professional corresponds closely to the description of a virtuous professional by Jordan and Meara (1990). According to Jordan and Meara, professional training introduces a new context for defining and developing virtues.

> People socialize one another into a professional culture that they continually construct and shape and from which they seek inspiration and support. As time passes, certain shared assumptions and values are "taken for granted" and form the character of the profession and are part of the individual characters of the professionals. (p. 110)

Here is an example of how people using assimilation, marginaliation, separation, and integration strategies might respond to a clinical situation.

TABLE 2.1
Ethics Viewed From an Acculturation Model

| Personal ethics | Professional ethics | |
	High	Low
High	Integrated	Separated
	Professionally informed; guided by personal compassion; highly effective psychologist	Personal compassion not restrained by professional ethics; may get overinvolved (runaway compassion)
Low	Assimilated	Marginalized
	Adopted professional standards, but lacks compassion; may become rigid and legalistic	Low professional and personal standards; risks becoming exploitative

A psychologist is working at a mental health center for adults with developmental disabilities. One day a patient who usually is driven to work by his mother arrived by taxi. Minutes later, the psychologist received a phone call from the mother who wanted to know if her son had arrived safely. The patient was relatively new to the program, and a release of information form for the mother had not yet been signed.

A psychologist using a marginalization strategy (low personal ethics and low professional ethics) would say whatever was convenient without concern for the mother, the patient, or professional rules.

A psychologist using an assimilation strategy (low personal ethics and high professional ethics) would be at risk for taking a rigid stance and stating, "I am sorry, but laws forbid me to disclose information about patients without a release signed ahead of time." Although the psychologist has followed the rules, he or she has failed to show compassion for the mother and does not search for an approach to address her legitimate concerns.

A psychologist using a separation strategy (high personal ethics and low professional ethics) would risk reacting spontaneously and stating, "Yes, he arrived here." The psychologist has allowed the genuine concern for the mother to override respect for the confidentiality rules.

A psychologist using an integration strategy (high personal ethics and high professional ethics) would seek a way to show compassion for the concerns of the mother while at the same time to follow the rules of the profession. She might respond by stating, "Sometimes I forget to tell my patients that they need to call home to verify that they arrived safely. Give me your phone number so I can do that." Here the psychologist has respected the laws of confidentiality but still has addressed the mother's concern.

Integration can best occur when instructors take a positive approach to ethics. Ideally, instructors create a supportive environment in which students reflect on their implicit ethical assumptions in a supportive environment. Instructors are able to identify the adaptive strategy of the students and move them closer to integration. Just as clinical supervisors are more effective when they know their supervisees, ethics educators are more effective when they understand how their instructions fit within the values and skills of their students.

3

APPLYING ETHICAL THEORIES TO PROFESSIONAL STANDARDS OF CONDUCT

The minimum standards of professional conduct are found in the Ethics Code (American Psychological Association [APA], 2002a), licensing laws and regulations, standards of malpractice courts, and other laws. However, consistent with our focus on positive or active ethics, we hope psychologists do more than just identify the obligations of psychologists. It is important for psychologists to understand the moral principles on which the standards of the Ethics Code are based. We begin with a review the Ethics Code from the standpoint of principle-based ethics and then review risk management principles from an ethical perspective.

AN OVERVIEW OF THE APA ETHICS CODE

The APA Ethics Code contains three major parts: Introduction and Applicability, the aspirational Preamble and General Principles, and the enforceable Ethical Standards. The Introduction and Applicability section briefly describes the purposes of the Ethics Code and its applicability. Among other things, it explains that there are three major parts of the Ethics Code, that psychologists who belong to APA are obligated to adhere to the Ethics

Code, and that the Ethics Code applies only to the work-related roles of psychologists. Purely private personal conduct is not governed by the Ethics Code. The aspirational principles encourage psychologists to strive for the ethical ceiling. In addition, psychologists can use these aspirational principles to assist them in ethical decision making. However, psychologists should not be disciplined only because they failed to uphold any one of the aspirational principles.

The aspirational principles are roughly modeled on principle-based ethics. However, principle-based ethicists do not necessarily agree on the optimal manner to define or categorize the prima facie principles. Ethics codes may categorize these principles slightly differently, but these differences have more to do with wording and emphasis than with substance.

The third part of the APA Ethics Code contains the enforceable standards. Psychologists who do not comply with these standards risk disciplinary sanctions by the APA Ethics Committee or by other organizations, such as licensing boards, to the extent that they adopt the Ethics Code.

Before 1992, the APA Ethics Code combined aspirational principles and enforceable standards. Although aspirational and enforceable standards are separated in the Ethics Code, it is impossible to separate them completely on a day-to-day basis. Psychologists attempting to provide the highest level of services should also ensure that they fulfill the minimum standards of the profession.

Ideally, the ethics codes of professionals are based on ethics theories and moral principles. Of course, no ethics code exists in a legal or social vacuum. In reality, federal laws (e.g., the Privacy Rule of the Health Insurance Portability and Accountability Act), previous negotiations with the Federal Trade Commission, case law, and other factors influenced the final wording of the APA Ethics Code. Nonetheless, a very real attempt was made to base the Ethics Code on moral principles and to focus on public welfare. The Ethics Code largely succeeded in reaching that ideal (Knapp & VandeCreek, 2004).

The standards of the APA Ethics Code are distinct from guidelines that are approved by the APA Council of Representatives and inform psychologists about conduct in certain practice areas (e.g., child custody evaluations, services to linguistic or cultural minorities). Guidelines are not enforceable except to the extent that they reiterate standards in the Ethics Code. Also, entities other than APA may attempt to use guidelines as if they were enforceable standards.

A PRINCIPLE-BASED INTERPRETATION OF THE APA ETHICS CODE

As noted in the previous chapter, the responsibilities of psychologists can be viewed in terms of their prima facie moral obligations (beneficence, nonmaleficence, respect for patient autonomy, justice, fidelity, and general beneficence). These prima facie principles can be linked to standards in the APA Ethics Code. For example, it would be impossible for psychologists to show beneficence if they did not have the competence to fulfill their professional responsibilities (Standard 2.01a, Boundaries of Competence). It could violate the principle of nonmaleficence if psychologists entered into harmful multiple relationships with their patients (Standard 3.04, Avoiding Harm). Psychologists demonstrate respect for patient autonomy when they engage their patients in meaningful informed consent procedures (Standard 3.10a, Informed Consent; Standard 10.01, Informed Consent to Therapy). Psychologists fulfill their ethical ideals of justice when they avoid unfair discrimination against members of minorities. Psychologists who keep the confidences of patients (Standards 4.01, Maintaining Confidentiality; 4.02, Discussing the Limits of Confidentiality) are upholding the principle of fidelity. Psychologists who act to correct problematic ethical conduct by their peers (Standards 1.04, Informal Resolution of Ethical Violations; 1.05, Reporting Ethical Violations) are demonstrating the principle of general beneficence.

Some of the standards in the APA Ethics Code reflect more than one moral principle. For example, informed consent procedures demonstrate respect for patient autonomy. However, these informed consent standards could also be based partially on the principle of beneficence, as research suggests that psychologists who use comprehensive informed consent procedures may be viewed more positively by their patients (Sullivan, Martin, & Handelsman, 1993).

The standards of the APA Ethics Code can be classified into those that are key or foundational (i.e., closely reflect a prima facie moral principle); those that clarify, amplify, or apply the key standards; and those that are exceptions to the key standards. Consequently, each of the standards in the APA Ethics Code can be linked to a prima facie moral principle (Knapp & VandeCreek, 2004).

Key or Foundational Standards

Certain standards,[1] such as 2.01a, Boundaries of Competence; 3.04, Avoiding Harm; 3.10a, Informed Consent; and 3.01, Unfair Discrimination, can be considered key or foundational standards. These standards closely reflect the application of prima facie moral principles to the practice of psychology. For example, Standard 2.01 is a key or foundational standard that requires psychologists to work within their areas of competence.

---

[1]Unless specified differently, the word *standard* refers to a standard in the APA Ethics Code.

Clarification, Amplification, or Application of Key Standards

Other standards clarify, amplify, or apply these key or foundational standards. For example, Standard 3.10a, Informed Consent, is a key or foundational standard that requires psychologists to obtain informed consent. However, this standard is amplified in other standards that deal with informed consent in forensic work (Standard 3.10c), with organizational clients (Standard 3.11, Psychological Services Delivered to or Through Organizations), in therapy (Standard 10.01, Informed Consent to Therapy), with assessments (Standard 9.03, Informed Consent in Assessments), and in research (Standard 8.02, Informed Consent to Research). For example, all psychologists must meet the informed consent standard found in 3.10a. However, Standard 3.10c expands on the informed consent obligations of psychologists when services are court ordered or otherwise mandated.

Some standards apply a key standard to specific types of professional activities. For example, Standard 2.01a, Boundaries of Competence, is a key or fundamental standard that requires all psychologists to be competent. Standard 2.01b applies that general standard of competence to working with diverse populations. Technically, Standard 2.01b should not be necessary because it could be logically inferred that the requirement to be competent includes the requirement to be competent when dealing with diverse populations. Nonetheless, the standard was added because it applies the standard in a situation in which historically there has been a potential for harm. To their credit, the framers of the APA Ethics Code properly determined that the Ethics Code should provide clear direction to psychologists, and the framers wanted to alert psychologists to an area to which the competence section might not be applied appropriately.

Exceptions to Key Standards

Some standards provide exceptions to the key or foundational standards. For example, Standard 8.02, Informed Consent to Research, requires researchers to obtain informed consent from prospective research participants. However, Standard 8.07, Deception in Research, allows for the dispensing of informed consent in certain types of research involving deception. Consistent with principle-based ethics, a principle can only be overridden if there is justification for doing so. As it applies to Standard 8.07, the assumption is that the promotion of public welfare through deceptive research can sometimes take a higher precedence than the moral obligation to be fully honest and accurate in dealing with research participants.

Consistent with principle-based ethics, the exceptions to any fundamental or key standard should be narrowly drawn. According to principle-based ethics, when one moral principle is trumped, efforts should be made to minimize the harm to the offended moral principle. When deception is used, the offense to the rule of honesty needs to be minimized by debriefing the participants and allowing them to withhold their data from the research. Furthermore, no one may deceive participants about research that is likely to cause pain or serious emotional distress.

For example, as it applies to competence, Standard 2.01a (a subsection of Boundaries of Competence) is the fundamental standard. Standards 2.01b (applying competence to services to diverse populations); 2.03, Maintaining Competence; and 2.04, Bases for Scientific and Professional Judgment clarify, amplify, or apply the fundamental standard. Finally, Standards 2.01d (exceptions for underserved populations); 2.02, Providing Services in Emergencies; and 9.01b (under Bases for Assessment, permitting limited comments on persons not directly evaluated) are exceptions to the fundamental standard. A similar analysis can be done with each of the key or foundational standards in the APA Ethics Code.

A VIRTUE-BASED INTERPRETATION OF RISK MANAGEMENT PRINCIPLES

Risk management principles are designed to minimize the legal risks to psychologists by identifying ways in which patients have been injured and ways in which psychologists can protect themselves from allegations of misconduct. There is no predetermined agreement on a fixed set of risk management principles, as many authors or lecturers on the topic have unique perspectives and terminology. Nonetheless, it is often useful to look at the causes of problematic behavior from the standpoint of both proximal (immediate or close in time) and distal factors (more removed or further away in time). The vignette that follows provides an example:

An Avoidable Error
A psychologist's office did not adequately prevent sound from seeping from the secretarial area into the patient waiting area. One day, while a secretary was talking to an insurance company, a patient in the waiting room overheard the secretary repeat another patient's name, diagnosis, prognosis, and elements of the treatment plan. The inadvertent disclosure caused the patient to lose faith that her information would be kept confidential.

The proximal factor in the misconduct was the failure of the secretary to notice that a patient had entered the waiting room. However, the distal factor was the failure of the psychologist to listen to staff who had previously expressed concerns about "noise seepage" in the waiting room.

No psychologist can eliminate all risks. However, the general goal is to establish a "culture of safety" whereby the distal causes of problems are anticipated and protective actions are taken ahead of time. The culture of safety requires psychologists to be alert to subtle cues that problems may be present or are developing and take steps to address them and to ensure that high quality services are being provided.

Also, the culture of safety suggests that psychologists should monitor their own behavior. Although some psychologists do have serious character flaws, it is inaccurate to attribute most of the infractions of psychologists to some defect or disorder within the psychologist. "Any psychologist, given the right circumstances, might make an ethical mistake" (Knapp & VandeCreek, 2003b, p. 36). The goal is to create a culture of safety whereby the risk of making those mistakes is minimized, and the possibility of living up to the highest ethical ideals is maximized.

An effective culture of safety requires some personal introspection. Bricklin, Knapp, and VandeCreek (2001) identified six Is of negligence: ignorance, incompetence, impulsiveness, insensitivity, impairment (incapacity or lack of insight), and incomplete documentation (although in this discussion we are subsuming incomplete documentation into incompetence). In our experiences serving on ethics committees and consulting with psychologists, these traits or habits commonly appeared among psychologists who were charged with ethical or legal infractions. These Is are not empirically based, and the concepts overlap. Nonetheless, they are a useful mnemonic to remember basic risk management principles. For example, the psychologist in the vignette was incompetent (because he failed to take special steps to prevent noise leakage) and insensitive (he failed to respond when staff complained about information leaks).

These Is can be transformed into risk management virtues (informed, competent, emotionally balanced, sensitive, and personally insightful) that have counterparts similar to the traits that Meara, Schmidt, and Day (1996) associated with virtuous psychologists. To that extent, these virtue-based risk management principles reflect good clinical practice. It is the proper goal of risk management principles to enhance the quality of care and the quality of relationships between psychologists and their patients. An overly legalistic approach to risk management is contrary to the humane values that psychologists want to espouse. Any purported risk management principle that compromises patient welfare needs to be reconsidered.

We suggest that psychologists who have best integrated strong personal ethics with strong professional ethics are most able to exemplify these virtues. For example, the psychologist who shows the most therapeutically indicated sensitivity will be able not only to be sensitive but also to keep the appropriate professional distance necessary for effective therapy.

Psychologists who are informed can identify the laws and codes that apply to them. They will, among other things, only release information when they should, keep patient records for the length of time required by their state law, and in other ways act with awareness of the laws or their professional responsibilities.

Competent psychologists can perform services at a minimally acceptable level or skill. For example, a psychologist who conducted a neuropsychological examination used the proper tests, scored it accurately, and used acceptable standards in establishing the diagnosis. In addition, adequate documentation can be considered part of competent practice. Certainly from a risk management perspective, it is essential to document carefully. Courts give great deference to professional records. The general assumption is that if it is not written in the record, then it did not occur.

A Careful Psychologist

A psychologist was falsely accused of engaging in a sexual relationship with a patient. However, he was aware of his patient's tendency to "push" boundaries and he carefully documented her advances and his responses. The judge exonerated him from any charge of malpractice.

Good psychologists show emotional balance. They are neither too involved nor too distant with their patients. At times, psychologists get themselves into trouble by acting impulsively. A male psychologist spontaneously announced to his female patient that he found her very attractive and had erotic dreams about her. He later defended his actions by stating he made the comment in a therapeutic attempt to bolster her self-esteem. Nonetheless, his actions gave the appearance that he had unresolved emotional needs that were expressed inappropriately. Psychologists who are more aware of their personal needs should be less likely to respond to impulses in this way.

Sometimes psychologists act impulsively in response to negative feelings elicited by their patients. Those patients who are needy, demanding, engage in "splitting," or otherwise have troubled interpersonal relationships may act out against or attempt to provoke their psychologists. Ideally, the responses of psychologists are based on a therapeutic model and rationale, not on unproductive emotional reactions.

Although it is poor practice for psychologists to act impulsively, it also would be poor practice for psychologists to be too restrained so that they can express no spontaneous emotion. According to Guthiel (1994), "The only sound and valid risk management principles rest upon a rock-solid clinical foundation. . . . sound risk management is also not antithetical to spontaneity, warmth, humanitarian concerns, or flexibility of approach" (p. 295).

Sensitivity is an important virtue. Tactful and responsive psychologists are better able to create a sound therapeutic relationship that facilitates effective treatment and is also one of the best protectors against a malpractice complaint. Data gathered from the experiences of physicians may be instructive for psychologists. Physicians who spend more time with patients, explain things in more detail, and use humor have significantly lower frequencies of malpractice charges (Levinson, Roter, Mullooly, Dull, & Frankel, 1997). Although the risk of receiving a patient complaint does not correlate with technical skill among physicians, it does correlate with their ability to establish rapport and communicate effectively (Hickson et al., 2002). The patients of physicians with the highest number of lawsuits were more likely to say that their physicians did not listen, return telephone calls, or treat them courteously.

A Considerate Psychologist

A psychologist treated her patients with great courtesy. She made certain that the waiting room and chairs were comfortable and that the rest rooms were always clean. Coffee and tea were available in the waiting room. She said, "I treat my patients as important guests." Her considerate manner was also reflected in her genuinely kind and professional demeanor toward them.

The delivery of psychological services requires insight into one's abilities and weaknesses. Prudent psychologists know to withdraw from treatment or at least seek consultation when they are not helping or are unlikely to help certain patients. For example, a psychologist who was a survivor of a severe trauma declined to treat patients known to have similar traumas because the status of his own trauma resolution was likely to impair the quality of his treatment.

4

ETHICAL DECISION MAKING

Ethical behavior requires the ability to solve ethical problems. Although it is important for psychologists to understand the standards in the Ethics Code (American Psychological Association [APA], 2002a), licensing law regulations, and salient court cases, these rules by themselves cannot address all of the ethical concerns that psychologists face. Instead, psychologists need to think through ethical issues such as when laws or ethics codes do not provide clear direction (or provide conflicting directions). Psychologists need to make decisions almost daily about how to interpret or apply ethical rules.

In this chapter, we review the areas related to ethics in which psychologists need to apply their decision-making skills. We then present the five-step ethical-decision-making process (five-step model), which can be used for most ethical dilemmas. Specific examples that apply the five-step model appear in later chapters.

AREAS IN WHICH PSYCHOLOGISTS NEED TO APPLY ETHICAL-DECISION-MAKING SKILLS

Psychologists need to use ethical-decision-making skills when (a) an applicable ethical or legal standard requires them to use their professional judgment, (b) the APA Ethics Code or laws are silent, (c) the Ethics Code conflicts with the law or organizational policies, and (d) they need to decide what supererogatory obligations to assume. Each of these areas is discussed in detail.

Professional Judgment

Many standards require the use of professional judgment in implementing the standards. This is particularly true when the APA Ethics Code uses modifiers such as *reasonably*, *appropriately*, or *potentially*. For example, Standard 10.01a, Informed Consent to Therapy, states that "psychologists inform clients/patients as early as is feasible in the therapeutic relationship about the nature and anticipated course of therapy, fees, involvement of third parties, and limits of confidentiality." Consequently, psychologists have to determine when it is feasible to reach that agreement. Although the decision is routine in most situations, there are times, such as when patients are in severe distress, when psychologists may elect to delay the informed consent process.

APA Ethics Code or Legal Standards are Silent

At times the APA Ethics Code or other legal standards are silent on a particular issue. For example, the 1992 Ethics Code (APA, 1992) made no reference to the transmission of information through e-mail or conducting health care services through electronic means. Although the APA Ethics Office issued a policy statement concerning ethical standards that psychologists should use when conducting telephone therapy, this general policy left much discretion on the part of psychologists as to how to apply these standards to telephone therapy and the extent to which those standards would apply to the use of e-mail for therapy. Furthermore, state licensure boards of psychology have been slow to develop regulations to address these issues.

Fortunately, commentaries have appeared recently in the professional literature to guide psychologists when they transmit information or deliver health care services electronically. However, until recently psychologists who used electronic transmissions for professional purposes had to decide for themselves whether or how to use them. Of course, the commentaries in the professional literature are not binding on the APA Ethics Office or licensing boards, which can adopt their own standards. Furthermore, future developments in electronic communications may create situations not anticipated by the current literature.

The 2002 APA Ethics Code makes no explicit mention of "e-therapy," although it does address the necessity of informing clients about the limits of confidentiality of electronic communications (Standard 4.02c Discussing the Limits of Confidentiality), the need for accuracy in public statements made through electronic means (Standard 5.01, Avoidance of False or Deceptive

Statements), and the importance of security when records are transferred in electronic formats (Standard 6.02, Maintenance, Dissemination, and Disposal of Confidential Records of Professional and Scientific Work). The ethical standards relating to competence, informed consent, research, and other aspects of psychological work apply to electronic communications in the same ways in which they apply to other forms of communication or information storage.

Conflicts With Laws or Organizational Standards

At times a law (i.e., a statute or regulation) or court order may conflict with the APA Ethics Code. According to the Ethics Code, when its standards create obligations greater than those found in the law, psychologists must follow the Ethics Code. If the Ethics Code conflicts with a particular law, however, then psychologists "make known their commitment to the Ethics Code and take steps to resolve the conflict" (Standard 1.02, Conflicts Between Ethics and Law, Regulations, or Other Governing Legal Authority). The Ethics Code does not necessarily require a psychologist to follow a particular law. That is, the APA Ethics Committee should not find psychologists in violation of the Ethics Code only for failure to obey a particular law, although those psychologists may face sanctions from other bodies. Nonetheless, psychologists often have to decide if they should follow a specific law or if they can identify some creative solution that will allow them to fulfill both their obligations to the law and to the Ethics Code.

At times, organizational policies conflict with the APA Ethics Code. If the Ethics Code conflicts with an organizational policy, then psychologists "make known their commitment to the Ethics Code, and to the extent feasible, resolve the conflict in a way that permits adherence to the Ethics Code" (Standard 1.03, Conflicts Between Ethics and Organizational Demands). The Ethics Code does not require a psychologist to follow the rules of an organization. That is, the APA Ethics Committee should not find psychologists in violation of an enforceable standard only because they failed to comply with a particular organizational policy. Nor should the Ethics Code hold psychologists who complied with an organizational policy in violation if they took reasonable means to attempt to redress the incompatibility between the organizational policy and the Ethics Code. What constitutes a reasonable action depends on the circumstances and options available. Again, psychologists often have to decide if they should follow the organizational demand or if they can identify a creative solution that will allow them to fulfill both the organizational demand and the Ethics Code.

Supererogatory Obligations

The APA Ethics Code primarily focuses on the minimum responsibilities of members of the profession. However, the Ethics Code provides limited guidance for those who aspire to be the best that they can be. Consequently, the Ethics Code should not be viewed as the sum of all that is known or worth knowing about ethical conduct.

Fortunately, many psychologists rely on a personal ethics code that compels them to do more than just avoid being disciplined. For example, although the APA Ethics Code requires psychologists to be minimally competent, most psychologists want to go beyond this basic standard and become very skilled at what they do. Many times, circumstances force psychologists to make ethical decisions. However, when psychologists determine their supererogatory obligations, they actively seek out the ethical dilemma themselves.

THE FIVE-STEP MODEL

The five-step model increases the likelihood that a good decision can be reached. Also, because it is easy to learn and overlearn, it may be used during periods of crisis or emergency. Furthermore, psychologists may incorporate other more specific decision-making models into the five-step model.

The five steps of this model are (a) to identify or scrutinize the problem, (b) to develop alternatives or hypotheses, (c) to evaluate or analyze options, (d) to act or perform the best option, and (e) to look back or evaluate the results. Similar five-step models have been systematized in the IDEAL system (identify, develop, explore, act, and look back; Bransford & Stein, 1993) and SHAPE system (scrutinize, develop hypothesis, analyze proposed solution, perform, and evaluate; Härtel & Härtel, 1997). These decision-making models were not designed especially for ethics but appear applicable to ethical issues. Indeed, variants of the five-step model seem quite pervasive (see, e.g., *problem-solving therapy*, Heppner & Lee, 2002).

The five-step model can be used to implement ethical decision making using different philosophical models. We describe it from the standpoint of principle-based ethics. The goal in a principle-based model is to reach a "good decision," which has the following features: (a) it is consistent with the values or moral principles of the psychologist in that there is sufficient reason to justify acting on behalf of one moral principle or norm rather than another; (b) the action has a realistic chance of success; (c) no morally preferable alternative is available; (d) the infringement of the offended norm is the least possible, consistent with the primary aims; (e) the psychologist seeks to minimize any negative effects of infringing on the offended norm or moral principle; and (f) the decision must be made impartially without regard for extraneous information (Beauchamp & Childress, 2001).

In the five-step model, the psychologist will (a) identify or scrutinize the problem to determine which moral principles appear threatened; (b) develop alternatives or hypotheses that are based on, or at least can be consis-

EXHIBIT 4.1
Incorporating Principle-Based Ethics Into the Five-Step Model

1. *Identify or scrutinize the problem.* Activities that violate or threaten to violate one of the moral principles are identified as moral concerns.
2. *Develop alternatives or hypotheses.* The alternatives should be based on, or at least be consistent with, general moral principles.
3. *Evaluate or analyze options.* The option chosen depends on which one strikes the optimal balance or ranking of moral principles.
4. *Act or perform.* Although one moral principle may be violated, efforts are taken to minimize the harm to the offended principle.
5. *Look back or evaluate.* The activities are evaluated according to the extent to which they fulfill, balance, or minimize harm to offended moral principles.

tent with, general moral principles; (c) evaluate or analyze options according to a balancing or ranking of moral principles; (d) act or perform in a manner to minimize the harm to the offended principle; and (e) look back or evaluate the extent to which the actions balanced or fulfilled moral principles. Exhibit 4.1 summarizes the relationships between the five-step and principle-based models.

Identify or Scrutinize the Problem

In the first step, psychologists identify the ethical dilemma or conflict. It is important for psychologists to know the APA Ethics Code so they know when it requires them to use their professional discretion or to know when it conflicts with the law or organizational policies.

However, for many psychologists the first indication of a problem comes from their own "gut" reactions or the reactions of a patient. That is, a strain in interpersonal relationships or a feeling of emotional uneasiness is often the first indication of an ethical problem. Here is an example of an ethical dilemma.

A Problem Intern
A supervising psychologist heard a credible report that a predoctoral intern had alcohol on his breath while at work. Other evidence pointed to an alcoholic intern. The intern's patient evaluations were not good; the intern was sometimes late for work, especially on Monday mornings; and once, while on call, he could not be reached until the next day.

The first step is to identify or scrutinize the problem. According to the principle-based process, the relevant moral principles will be identified. The supervising psychologist has moral obligations to the patient (i.e., to protect the welfare of the supervisee's patients), the supervisee (i.e., to enhance the professional development of the supervisee), the employer, the student's training program, and society in general (i.e., not to promote the career of an individual who is incompetent, and therefore, to report accurately any substantial problems with the supervisee on forms to the licensing board).

Develop Alternatives or Hypothesize Solutions

The second step involves the generation of alternative solutions. To a large extent, the ability to reach the best decision requires the development of a wide range of useful alternatives. Psychologists who are more aware of the cognitive and emotional influences on their decision making can improve their ability to generate useful solutions.

Cognitive Factors That Decrease Solution-Generating Abilities

A factor that may decrease the ability of psychologists to generate solutions is *cognitive rigidity*, the tendency to fixate on one possible solution. Cognitive rigidity causes people to view a problem as having only one solution (or one kind of solution) without allowing for alternative strategies and explanations. For example, when dealing with life-endangering patients, psychologists sometimes jump immediately to the conclusion that they have to warn the identified victim. However, it would be more desirable for those psychologists to get out of the dichotomous thinking of "either warn" or "do nothing" and to consider other ways to diffuse the danger. To a certain extent the cognitive rigidity or fixation may be due to lack of knowledge; however, it also may be due to emotional interference.

Emotional Factors That Decrease Solution-Generating Abilities

Although the five-step model involves rational processes, the quality of ethical decision making improves when the emotional aspects of human behavior are considered. Although feelings motivate people to solve problems, the quality of problem solving tends to decline when individuals are in crisis or in emotional turmoil. Intense emotions appear to interfere with the cognitive processes necessary to generate or evaluate solutions.

This high anxiety may cause a psychologist to select the first or one of the first solutions that come to mind, only because having a solution temporarily reduces anxiety. However, the first halfway reasonable ("just-good-enough") solution to come to mind may not be the optimal solution. It may be prudent to consider the Aristotelian "golden mean" when it comes to emotions and decision making. Too little, as well as too much, emotion can undermine the quality of the decision-making process (Ziegler, 1999).

Cognitive Factors That Increase Solution-Generating Abilities

Some ideas may occur through an apparently random flow of ideas. However, other potential solutions may be generated by systematic strategies. Two such strategies are to look for alternatives "within" the problem (such as looking at the situation as a "problem within a problem") and to look for alternatives outside of ("without") the problem (i.e., viewing the problem as a subset of a larger or more general problem).

At times, reliance on a specialized domain of information can help identify potential alternatives. For example, Gottlieb (1993) described decision-making steps when dealing with multiple relationships. He described factors to consider when determining risks to patients or ex-patients. Because they include information within the context of the decision-making process, this is called *within decision making.*

Also, it may help to view the problem from without, or as a subset or specific example of a more general problem. In other words, the psychologist may be able to develop an analogy between this and similar problems. Information and strategies that are useful for other problems may also be useful for this problem as well.

For example, consider the specific case described earlier in this chapter of the psychologist with an intern who is probably an alcoholic. This case represents a variant of a more general problem of how supervising psychologists should enforce professional standards on interns or how psychologists should respond when they learn of a colleague who is impaired or acting in a manner harmful to the public. A knowledgeable consultant may be able to give information about the patterns of alcoholics and about the options available. For example, perhaps the state has an impaired psychologist program sponsored by its state psychological association. Volunteer psychologists working for that program could provide information on how the psychologist could proceed.

Emotional Factors That Increase Solution-Generating Abilities

Sensitivity to emotional discomfort may facilitate ethical decision making. A sense of uneasiness may indicate an underlying or unarticulated moral qualm or concern about a situation. To that extent, self-awareness can help facilitate ethical responses. At first glance, a particular alternative may seem logical but somehow "feel" wrong. Careful reflection may help the psychologist to articulate the cause of the emotional qualm.

Benefits of Consultation

Consulting with others often improves the quality of decisions. Consultants can help psychologists address both the cognitive and the emotional aspects of decision making. From a cognitive perspective, consultants may be able to identify sources of knowledge, types of interventions, or resources that could be useful to the psychologist. In addition, the consultation may help reduce strong emotional affect and allow psychologists to process the information more clearly. Finally, the very process of describing the dilemma may help psychologists to clarify and think through the dilemma themselves.

Perhaps the most effective consultants challenge psychologists to explore their perceptions, intuitions, assumptions, and logic. Everyone has blind spots, and the effective consultant may be able to gently nudge the psychologist to identify feelings and balance options.

Evaluate or Analyze Options

The third step includes evaluating or analyzing options. Part of generating the optimal solution is to identify the advantages and disadvantages of each potential solution. A general strategy may be to select a solution that combines the best elements of the different solutions proposed through a process akin to *theory knitting*. In experimental psychology "theory development progresses through the integration of the strongest features of the alternative theories with one's own ideas about the phenomenon under investigation" (Sternberg, Grigorenko, & Kalmar, 2001, p. 107). Similarly, psychologists can "knit together" solutions by integrating the best aspects of possible alternatives. The previous strategies could be compared and the conflicting properties of the alternatives evaluated.

In the case of the intern with alcohol on his breath, there are advantages to each of three possible alternatives: (a) ignore the problem, (b) fire the intern, or (c) just talk to him. Ignoring the problem would relieve the supervisor of the risk of violating procedural justice for the intern, especially if the intern is not an alcoholic. Firing the intern for this (and other misconduct) would relieve the supervisor of the immediate problem and fulfill the obligations of nonmaleficence in that it would protect current patients from this intern and put a serious impediment in his ability to become licensed and run the risk of harming future patients. Talking with the intern might provide an opportunity for the intern to admit to a problem and prompt the intern into a higher level of conduct. It would show respect for procedural justice toward the intern.

However, each of these possible solutions has disadvantages. Ignoring the problem would violate the principle of nonmaleficence because it would not address the risk to the public (i.e., current and future patients) if an alcoholic were to become licensed as a psychologist. Firing the intern might appear to solve the immediate problem, but it would not fulfill the demands of justice, especially because there still is a possibility, albeit remote, that the intern is not abusing alcohol. Nor would ignoring the problem fulfill the obligation of the supervisor to the supervisee if he actually did have a problem with alcohol. Also, it might not promote general beneficence or protection of the public in the long run. Furthermore, it might deprive the psychologist of leverage needed to get the supervisee into treatment and would leave current patients without a chance for closure. Merely talking to the intern about the problem would probably not be sufficient to fulfill the obligations of beneficence to either the public or the intern. It might be unlikely for the intern to acknowledge a problem, especially because denial is very common among persons with alcoholism.

In the example used here, the supervising psychologist concluded that protection of the public (and protection of the intern) mandated that affirmative action be taken to confront the intern about his drinking (and possible termination). Fortunately, there is a body of specialized knowledge concerning the process of confronting impaired professionals. Reliance on that body of literature (as well as consultation) helped reduce the problems associated with implementing the decision. Consultation helped the supervisor moderate her anger at the supervisee and knit a response that balanced her moral obligations.

In this case, firmness was mixed with sensitivity. Although confronting individuals about their drinking is unpleasant, the supervising psychologist tried to minimize the degree of distress in the supervisee by expressing concern for his welfare and allowing time for the supervisee to ventilate. However, the sensitivity to the feelings of the supervisee was balanced with a firm commitment to the welfare of the public to ensure that the drinking would be stopped.

This solution knitted together the advantages of the alternatives. It included procedural justice in that it only required the intern to be evaluated; such an evaluation might clear the intern of the possibility of alcoholism. Also, it disciplined the intern in accordance with preestablished agency rules. Finally, it fulfilled the obligations of beneficence to the intern in that it provided a mechanism for the intern to seek treatment and protected current and future patients from harm from an alcoholic professional.

Act or Perform

The fourth step involves acting on or performing the option selected. It should not be assumed that psychologists who reach a solution will necessarily act on that solution. Bernard and Jara (1986) found that many psychology graduate students who reached the "right" solution to an ethical dilemma did not intend to act on that solution. The reasons for this finding are not clear. On the one hand, it could perhaps indicate lack of moral courage on the part of the psychologist. On the other hand, it could be that the right solution that they reached was not really the right solution. That is, their response reflected what they thought the APA Ethics Code, law, or risk management guidelines required of them but did not reflect what they truly believed was the most moral or ethical response. Betan and Stanton (1999) opined that the failure to consider emotional reactions could be responsible for a failure to follow through with the "ethical" solution.

In addition, the manner in which a decision is implemented can be as important as the decision itself. The ideal solution to a moral dilemma requires that the actor try to minimize harm to the offended moral principle. This may require considerable tact, sensitivity, and social skills. The morality of the specific behaviors is often context dependent. This is another area in which the emotions of the psychologist become important. A psychologist who is motivated by beneficence is more likely to show kindness, consideration, and courtesy in implementing that decision.

Look Back or Evaluate

The fifth step is to look back and evaluate the problem-solving intervention. In the case of the intern with suspected alcoholism, a question arises as to whether the decision (a) is consistent with the values or moral principles of the psychologist in that there is sufficient reason to justify acting on behalf of the overriding norm (i.e., patient welfare) rather than the offended norm (i.e., supervisee welfare or autonomy), (b) has a realistic chance of success, (c) is made with no morally preferable alternative available, (d) infringes on the offended moral principle in the least possible manner consistent with the primary aims, (e) seeks to minimize any negative effects of infringing on the offended moral principle, and (f) is made impartially without regard for extraneous information.

In this situation, the supervisee initially reacted badly, denied everything, threatened a lawsuit, and stormed out of the office. The supervisor anticipated the possibility of such a response and (with the support of the facility director) instructed him to get an evaluation or he would be fired and a letter would be sent to the state board of psychology stating that he should not be allowed to sit for the licensing examination. The supervisee eventually admitted a problem, entered an inpatient facility, and enrolled in an impaired psychologist program that required, among other things, attendance at 12-step meetings and random drug screens for 3 years.

The short- and long-term goals of the psychologist were to stop the drinking of the intern, get treatment for the intern, and protect current and future patients. The intervention was consistent with the values of the psychologist. She placed beneficence (i.e., promotion of the welfare) of the patients (including current and future) and the intern as the highest priority. This was appropriate given the substantial harm that can occur when alcoholism among professionals is left untreated. Although this meant overriding respect for the autonomy of the intern, it was necessary to do so to achieve her goals. As much as possible, the supervising psychologist showed respect for the intern by allowing him the option of declining the evaluation (although there were serious consequences for failing to do so).

Although looking back or evaluating is the fifth step in the five-step model, it may or may not be the final step in the process. In many cases, the five-step process results in a solution that essentially ends the ethical dilemma. In other cases, it is appropriate to look back, evaluate the effectiveness of the intervention, and determine whether another intervention might be warranted.

The five-step model is not necessarily linear. That is, the five steps should be viewed as dynamic and not fixed. For example, the resolution of one dilemma may give rise to subsequent dilemmas, or it may provide more information that causes psychologists to alter their previous interpretation of the problem and return to previous steps of the five-step model. For example, work on the second and third steps (i.e., develop alternatives or hypothesize solutions and evaluate or analyze options) may lead a psychologist to go back to Step 1 (i.e., identify or scrutinize the problem). Also, sometimes it is not until the fourth or fifth steps (i.e., act or perform and look back or evaluate) that the psychologist becomes aware of contextual factors that would have modified the options generated in Steps 1 and 2.

EMERGENCY OR CRISIS DECISION MAKING

At times, psychologists will have time to go through the five-step model carefully. They will have time to identify the problem, develop alternatives, consult with others, or do some detailed reading in the problem area. For example, psychologists who are considering their supererogatory obligations can discuss their plans with friends, family, and professional colleagues; generate a list of alternatives; and carefully plan their decisions.

At other times, psychologists will suddenly become aware of an ethical problem (such as an action or statement by a patient) that requires an immediate response. For example, if a patient unexpectedly expresses a serious homicidal threat in the middle of a psychotherapy session, psychologists need to act without the option of carefully deliberating.

Emergency situations require immediate decisions. These need to be distinguished from crises in which psychologists have a high degree of emotional arousal and feel a need to resolve the situation quickly to reduce their emotional discomfort. Here, however, circumstances may not demand an immediate response.

Nonetheless, psychologists can increase the likelihood of making reasonable decisions in emergencies or crises if they know the APA Ethics Code and other disciplinary codes. Knowing the Ethics Code well should help psychologists be alert when an ethical dilemma has arisen. Also, psychologists who practice with some awareness of their own emotional states should be better able to detect the nagging doubts and begin their ethical-decision-making response.

Often psychologists can anticipate the kinds of problems that could occur in their type of practice. For example, psychologists who work with families can anticipate problems when dealing with confidentiality with adolescents, when keeping family secrets, or with potential conflicts of interest. Therefore, family therapists should be prepared to respond when their patients offer "secret" information about another family member. Ideally, psychologists will have thought out, consulted on, and formulated possible responses.

Finally, psychologists can overlearn the five-step model and use it even during periods of stress. That is, psychologists should be immediately able to outline the steps of the decision-making process. Although other decision-making models may be thorough and have numerous substeps, we think they may be too complex for psychologists to rely on during crises.

5

COMPETENCE

The standards of competence are based on the moral principles of beneficence and nonmaleficence. That is, psychologists should work to benefit and to avoid harming those with whom they work. In a broad sense, other moral principles (e.g., respect for patient autonomy, justice, and integrity) also are essential for competence, insofar as psychologists who adhere to these moral standards will be delivering services in accord with acceptable standards of practice. Competence was also one of the traits we identified in virtue-based risk management (see chap. 3, this volume).

Although scholars still debate the specific skills that define competence, we describe it as a three-part process involving technical knowledge, social skills, and emotional well-being. The importance of *emotional competence* should not be underestimated (Pope & Brown, 1996). Emotional competence refers to psychologists' ability to withstand the emotional difficulties associated with professional practice. Pope and Brown (1996) described emotional competence in the context of delivering health care services, especially to patients who are "despairing, terrified, sexually aroused, enraged, violent, frantic, or experiencing other intense feelings or impulses" (p. 121). However, we suggest that the term could also apply to the ability to feel and express compassion, empathy, and other qualities related to good interpersonal relationships. In that sense, emotional competence is also important for psychologists who serve as teachers, researchers, and consultants.

Psychologists who demonstrate emotional competence are more likely to make prudent decisions. *Prudence* means carefully thinking through complex situations by attending to factual information, social cues, and personal feelings. At times, psychologists will be faced with difficult dilemmas that have no clear answer. Psychologists are better able to make appropriate decisions if they are able to identify and modulate their emotional reactions to events.

Lack of competence could result in a disciplinary action from the Ethics Committee of the American Psychological Association (APA), a state ethics committee, or a state licensing board (many of which adopt the Ethics Code [APA, 2002a] or a variation of it). A charge of incompetent practice is implicit in malpractice cases because the plaintiff argues that the psychologist failed to perform at an adequate level of professional care and that this deviation from a minimum standard of care caused harm. The courts determine competent practice after hearing testimony from expert witnesses who comment on the acceptable standard of care.

From a practical perspective, allegations of incompetence are more frequent during the delivery of forensic services because the services of the psychologist are under greater scrutiny and because disgruntled clients[1] are more willing to file complaints if they believe they were harmed.

In this chapter, we review essential information about competence, including competence with cultural, sexual, and religious minorities. We also discuss exceptions to the general rules of competence, which include emergencies and providing services in underserved areas. Finally, in this chapter we review emotional competence and impairment.

PRACTICING WITHIN AREAS OF COMPETENCE

In the APA Ethics Code, the key or foundational standard dealing with competence states, "Psychologists provide services, teach, and conduct research with populations and in areas only within the boundaries of their competence, based on their education, training, supervised experience, consultation, study, or professional experience" (Standard 2.01a, Boundaries of Competence). The related key or foundational standard dealing with nonmaleficence states, "Psychologists take reasonable steps to avoid harming their clients/patients, students, supervisees, research participants, organizational clients, and others with whom they work, and to minimize harm where it is foreseeable and unavoidable" (Standard 3.04, Avoiding Harm).

---

[1]We are using the term *client* here instead of *patient* because the individuals receiving services from forensic psychologists are often not receiving treatment for mental disorders.

A general rule is that psychologists can ascertain whether they are competent or proficient in a certain area of practice after colleagues evaluate their work and determine that they have reached acceptable standards of practice. The most obvious example of external feedback is when students attend training programs in psychology and submit their performance to the feedback of faculty and supervisors.

The standards for competence as a teacher can sometimes be less clear. The hiring institution provides the primary oversight for teachers. It is sometimes difficult to determine how direct the link should be between the formal academic training of psychologists and their teaching responsibilities. Sometimes, because of sudden vacancies in the department, faculty members are pressed into teaching courses for which they did not have the optimal academic preparation. Nonetheless, those psychologists should be able to fulfill their obligations under the APA Ethics Code if they undertake appropriate study or consultation (Knapp & VandeCreek, 2003b).

Good researchers know the literature in a particular area of psychology, research design skills, statistics, and research ethics. However, no predetermined sequence of courses or examinations qualifies an individual to conduct research. Consequently, most of the responsibility for the quality of research rests with each individual and peer reviewers. Instructors or advisors are responsible for the research conducted by their psychology students. Of course, if the research entails the delivery of services, then researchers are held to the standards of minimal competence required of practitioners who deliver such services.

Standard 2.04, Bases for Scientific and Professional Judgments, requires that the work of psychologists be based on the knowledge foundation of the discipline or profession of psychology. Although psychologists would like to have a scientific basis for all of their decisions, gaps in the scientific literature require them to also rely on clinical intuitions or tradition.

In his advice to psychology trainees, Plante (1996) focused on the need for students to stay current and competent in their professional skills because psychology has an ever-expanding knowledge base. Such efforts are required by Standard 2.03, Maintaining Competence. Past training, in the absence of ongoing readings, study, experience, or workshops, is not sufficient to maintain competence if the standard of practice in a particular area has shifted. Although many state boards of psychology now require continuing education (CE) as a condition of licensure renewal, these requirements only represent the minimum of professional education that psychologists should receive.

Many psychologists maintain competence by receiving consultation. No psychologist is knowledgeable about all areas of practice, and all psychologists benefit from discussions with others from time to time. Sometimes the consultation is done on an as-needed basis. Other consultations occur through *peer consultation* or *mutual consultation* groups in which participants share information about treatment plans and techniques.

A Group of Thoughtful Psychologists

Five psychologists in solo practice belonged to a "journal club," which met once a month for many years. Each participant brought an article to discuss at each meeting. However, the group involved more than just discussions of the articles and provided an opportunity for these psychologists to share perspectives on difficult cases and reflect on their day-to-day practices.

These psychologists knew that they performed at their best when they had an opportunity to share ideas and regularly seek consultation. One group member said, "My colleagues saved me from a couple of clinical mistakes that could have had tragic consequences." Others noted that the group led them to a higher level of professional services.

Psychologists are responsible for the quality of the work of their supervisees. The supervisory relationship is a hierarchical one. Supervisees have no independent authority to make decisions regarding patient care or any other professional responsibility. Psychologists commonly supervise unlicensed psychology trainees who are receiving experience to qualify to sit for the licensing examination and other unlicensed employees. The same obligations to ensure quality applies to all employees, even those who are not undergoing the supervision required for licensure or another credential and those who are not providing services directly (e.g., administrative support staff or interpreters).

Clearing Up a Misunderstanding

A psychologist was contacted by a young social worker who wanted supervision. Upon further discussion, it was clear that the social worker wanted to retain his independent practice but only have the psychologist sign insurance forms for some patients.

The social worker did not understand the meaning of the word *supervision*. The social worker could not both have an independent practice and be under supervision. Furthermore, it was not entirely clear that insurance companies would have reimbursed for services provided with this level of supervision. Supervision differs from consultation. In consultation, one mental health professional provides expertise to other professionals who still retain control over the final work product. In supervision, the supervisor retains all authority over and responsibility for the services delivered by the supervisee. More information on supervision is found in chapter 15 (Clinical Supervision).

Competence With Cultural and Linguistic Minorities

Effective treatments consider the unique needs of each patient. Although each patient has unique strengths, concerns, and attitudes, certain themes are commonly found among members of different cultural groups, and ignorance of them could compromise the quality of treatment. European Americans who do not have routine encounters with members of cultural minorities on a daily basis may fail to appreciate the experiences of persons of color.

Concern has been expressed about the effectiveness of psychotherapy with cultural, linguistic, or ethnic minorities (Lam & Sue, 2001). One extreme position is that only persons from certain backgrounds can work effectively with persons from the same background (e.g., only African American therapists should work with African American patients). The other extreme position is that background has no impact on treatment. Although outcome data alone suggest that these demographic variables are not always crucial in treatment outcomes, anecdotal evidence continues to suggest that they are, at least for some persons. Standard 2.01b, Boundaries of Competence, adopts a middle position that requires psychologists to be competent, refer, or obtain supervision when special knowledge "is essential for effective implementation of . . . services or research." Exceptions are permitted for emergencies (Standard 2.02, Providing Services in Emergencies) or when services are not otherwise available (see Standard 2.01d).

Although the APA Ethics Code establishes the minimal standards for the profession, we encourage psychologists to strive to go beyond the minimum. The goal is not so much how to avoid being disciplined but how to ensure a high level of skill when working with diverse populations. Although few psychologists are bigots, it may be helpful for psychologists to consider ways in which they are inadvertently distancing themselves from patients from different cultural backgrounds. Although psychologists may not be culturally competent with every ethnic group in the United States, they can make special efforts to be culturally competent with ethnic groups with whom they expect to have frequent contact, and they can develop sensitivity to the fact that unique issues may arise when they treat any individual from a different cultural background.

The need for cultural sensitivity can be based on several moral principles. For example, the moral principles of beneficence and nonmaleficence require psychologists to be competent when they provide services to individuals of diverse backgrounds. In addition, the key or foundational principle of procedural justice may be applicable here as well. That key principle (Standard 3.01, Unfair Discrimination) prohibits psychologists from engaging in unfair discrimination based on race, ethnicity, culture, or other factors. Finally, the moral principle of distributive justice applies as well in that, all things being equal, it is desirable to ensure equal assess to high-quality psychological services for all individuals.

Studies have not yet established the necessity to match psychotherapists or treatments to patients on the basis of their ethnicity, culture, national origin, or language. However, it is also not known the extent to which outcome studies with predominately European American patients generalize to ethnic minority populations. Indeed, determining the external validity of these studies is complicated because of the diversity within ethnic minority populations (e.g., individuals who fit into the broad category of Native Americans may represent widely diverse tribal backgrounds), the variation with which individuals have been acculturated to American society, the possibility that the individual has a bicultural identity, or the interaction of several factors, such as an African American man with sexual orientation concerns (Knapp & VandeCreek, 2003b).

Also, from a cultural perspective, a demographic match may not be meaningful. For example, an American of Hispanic background who came from one of the landed Spanish families that predated the American Revolution may have little in common with a recent immigrant from Cuba. Nonetheless, cultural background may be relevant to treatment planning. Psychologists who are unfamiliar with ethnic minority cultures are likely to overlook or misinterpret important facts about an individual from a minority culture (Hall, 2001).

Determining Cultural Competence

A doctoral intern at the counseling center was from a Chinese American background, but her family had lived in the United States since the 1850s. Because of her appearance and Chinese name, the supervisor assumed that she was especially competent to work with the Asian students who came to the counseling center. This assumption was not always warranted as she had little in common with Asian students whose families had only recently immigrated to the United States.

What is the level of education, awareness, or skills needed to be competent to treat an individual from a cultural or linguistic minority? Certainly, basic therapeutic skills, such as ability to form relationships and diagnostic skills, are needed; but are they sufficient? Competence means more than memorizing a list of stereotypes about particular cultures; it means being able to think in cultural terms and focus on process as well as content (Lopez, 1997).

Here are some conditions for cultural competence that we have adapted and modified from the APA (2003); Cardemil and Battle (2003); Hansen, Pepitone-Arreola-Rockwell, and Greene (2000); La Roche and Maxie (2003); Stuart (2004); and Vasquez (1998).

Background Preparation

Psychologists can work more effectively with persons from different cultural backgrounds if they recognize the impact of their own cultural heritage on their values and assumptions. For example, compared with many other cultures, American culture tends to give more emphasis to individuals and less to group or family identity. The individualistic American standard is not better or normative; it is just different. Although patient autonomy is considered an important ethical principle in the delivery of health care in North America, it might not be equally important to other cultures. In the

Confucian tradition, dutifulness (i.e., obedience to the family hierarchy) is one of the cardinal virtues (Stevenson & Haberman, 1998).

Contemporary American culture views people as basically good, and it values high self-esteem. However, other cultures may view people as possessing a great potential for evil and value hard work at correcting individual flaws and tendencies to violate moral principles (Dowd, 2003).

Psychologists are likely to be effective in their work with persons from different cultural backgrounds when they understand the psychological sequelae produced by a history of oppression, prejudice, and discrimination. This knowledge may help European Americans to understand the wariness with which some members of minorities approach them.

Assessment

Care needs to be taken when making a diagnosis. A consultation program funded by the Canadian government found that about one third of the cases reviewed had involved an inaccurate diagnosis because the treating professional did not understand the culture of the patient (Lehman, 2002). The evaluation process often requires the services of a mental health professional with knowledge of the cultural background of the patient. An accurate diagnosis may require knowledge of culture-specific diagnoses. Some of these include amok (i.e., a murderous frenzy occurring mainly in Malaysia), religion-induced trances (Latino spiritualists), Shin-byung (i.e., Korean beliefs about spirit possession), or coraje (i.e., psychosomatic manifestations of emotional upset among native Mexican tribes).

Accurate diagnoses may require culturally appropriate assessment instruments, or at least the knowledge of how to adapt them. A literal translation of the words on a psychological test may not result in testing the equivalent domain. For example, the literal translation of the proverb "Shallow brooks are noisy" does not have the same meaning in Spanish. That phrase is a metaphor for the concept that sometimes people who talk a lot have little to say. Another Spanish proverb may be better at expressing that concept (Dattilio, 2000).

Effective psychologists are sensitive to cultural differences, including the degree of assimilation into mainstream culture. The length of time a family has stayed in the United States may be positively correlated to degree of assimilation, but it is not the only determinant. Also, psychologists should be aware of the interaction of gender and culture.

Many recent immigrants to the United States have *bicultural identities*. That is, they identify both with Western or global cultures and with their local culture. Inuit children may, for example, go ice fishing during the day and watch their favorite NHL hockey team in the evening. A young adult from India may have advanced computer skills but still expect his parents to arrange his marriage (Arnett, 2002). La Roche and Maxie (2003) urged psychologists to be flexible in how they treat different patients who appear to be from the same cultural background. More information on cultural factors in assessment can be found in chapter 12 (Assessment).

Intervention

When possible, psychologists should honor patient requests or preferences for a patient–therapist match. Although no data suggest that such matches are essential for an effective outcome, it shows respect for patient autonomy when such requests can be honored.

It is also ideal when psychologists use the language preferred by the patient. If this is not possible, it is desirable to refer the patient to those who can use that language or to use an appropriately trained interpreter. Professional interpreters understand the basic rules and technical issues of translation, which untrained individuals would not necessarily know (Bradford & Muñoz, 1993). In urban areas, commercial interpreter services are common. However, in rural areas, or if the patient speaks a less common language, it may be necessary to use another fluent person such as an instructor of the foreign language (Fortuny & Mullaney, 1998). Because of the risk of conflicts of interest and their potential to contaminate information, friends or relatives of family members should be used only as a last resort.

Psychological services can be delivered more effectively when psychologists understand cultural factors that influence the attitudes of patients toward mental health care. This includes normative health-seeking behaviors and attitudes toward health professionals. It may affect patient willingness to seek help or continue in treatment or the manner in which the patient relates to the psychologist. Also, effective psychologists understand the patient's family structure, worldviews, and values and how they may affect the relationship and treatment. For example, Meer and VandeCreek (2002) described how the failure to include or consider the impact of family dynamics impaired the ability of psychologists to develop relationships with or conduct successful therapy with individuals from South Asia.

Similarly, Latino patients often have close relationships with their families, which could be misconstrued as being "enmeshed" (La Roche, 1999). Latino girls may experience greater pressures than European American girls to stay at home and care for family members rather than pursue higher education (Vasquez, 2002).

By understanding the cultural perspectives of their patients, psychologists are better able to work collaboratively to determine treatment goals and measure success from the patient's standpoint. Miscommunications can be reduced through the use of frequent clarifications and nonjudgmental acceptance.

Culturally competent psychologists have the ability to form relationships in which they convey empathy in culturally appropriate ways and explore differences between cultures and ask for guidance in a helpful manner. No fixed set of rules can be given for addressing cultural issues with every patient (La Roche & Maxie, 2003). Therapeutic discretion may be required here, as patients vary in the degree of comfort they have in discussing ethnic issues (Cardemil & Battle, 2003; Thompson, Bazile, & Akbar, 2004).

Thompson et al. (2004) noted how subtle cues can convey the cultural attitudes of the psychologist. Readings in the waiting room of special interest to persons from minorities, ethnically diverse artwork, and the presence of persons from ethnic minorities who work for or with the psychologist can do much to increase confidence in the psychologist.

Finally, when working with culturally diverse populations, it is desirable for psychologists to document culturally relevant variables such as the number of generations (and number of years) the patient has lived in this country. If the patient is an immigrant, then psychologists should note any change in mental health status as a result of the immigration. If the patient lived in a country characterized by civil violence, then psychologists should screen for posttraumatic stress disorder. Psychologists should also note the language proficiency, including English fluency; extent of support (or disintegration) among family, extended family, or community; and acculturation and acculturation stress. Broad categories such as "first generation Asian American" fail to identify the myriad factors that influence a person's degree of acculturation (Stuart, 2004).

Competence With Sexual Minorities

Sexual minorities include lesbians, gay men, bisexual people, or transgendered (LGBT) people. Although persons who are LGBT struggle with many of the same issues as heterosexuals, they have unique issues as well. Throughout their lives, many persons who are LGBT have been physically or sexually assaulted or have been alienated from their families (Goldfried, 2001). Years of legal and social stigmatization have left most members of sexual minorities with an emotional legacy of distrust and fear. They appear to be at a higher risk than heterosexuals to develop depression, personality disorders, or other mental illnesses. Suicidal risk is especially high among adolescents who are LGBT (Cochran, 2001).

Of course, psychologists should avoid prejudice and discrimination against persons of other sexual orientations (APA, 2000). However, being effective with patients who are LGBT involves more than just refraining from overt discrimination. Even psychologists who do not believe that homosexuality is a form of pathology and would strongly defend the rights of individuals who are LGBT may view alternative lifestyles as less desirable than heterosexual lifestyles and be less effective in their therapeutic encounters. In contrast, being gay affirmative means having special knowledge of the population and the unique stressors they face, knowledge of LGBT issues, understanding of how to handle emotional reactions to patients who are LGBT, and comfort dealing with explicit sexual issues (Liddle, 1997). It also means understanding the importance of LGBT relationships and the ways in which family is defined (APA, 2000).

Readers are referred to *Guidelines for Psychotherapy With Lesbian, Gay, and Bisexual Clients* (APA, 2000) for more details on these general principles. For example, Guideline 1 states that "psychologists understand that homosexuality and bisexuality are not indicative of mental illness" (p. 1441). Consequently, it would not be appropriate for psychologists to assume that sexual orientation itself is the presenting problem.

However, at times confusion about sexual orientation is a presenting problem for the patient. In those situations, psychologists should have enough information so they can correct misconceptions on the part of the patients (Schneider, Brown, & Glassgold, 2002). Also, psychologists can be most effective when they consider the role that cultural beliefs systems have in the development of any homophobic feelings on the part of the patient or by considering therapy from a developmental perspective whereby the needs of the patient may vary over time (Lasser & Gottlieb, 2004).

A question, therefore, arises as to whether *reparative therapy* or *reorientation therapy* (i.e., therapy focused on changing the sexual orientation of the patient) constitutes competent professional behavior. On the one hand, anecdotal evidence suggests some success in changing sexual orientation with highly motivated individuals. Furthermore, it can be argued that competent individuals should be able to make an informed decision to reorient their sexual orientation so that it will be consistent with their religious beliefs (Yarhouse & Throckmorton, 2002).

On the other hand, no controlled studies attest to the effectiveness of reorientation therapy, and there are concerns about the selection criteria for the interventions. Shidlo and Shroeder (2002) found that 87% of the survey respondents who participated in sexual conversion therapy perceived themselves as failing, and many reported that the process was harmful. Furthermore, some individuals who choose reparative therapy may be unduly influenced by exaggerated claims of success or because they hold ego-dystonic beliefs about their sexual orientation (i.e., *internalized homophobia*). Finally, unless the participants are screened carefully, any benefit to those few who are "repaired" may be counterbalanced by the harm that comes to those who participate in sexual reorientation therapy but do not change their sexual orientation. The APA Council of Representatives has passed the Resolution on Appropriate Therapeutic Responses to Sexual Orientation (APA, 1998), which does not ban or condemn reorientation therapy but affirms the need for competent practitioners to ensure informed decisions on the part of consumers.

Competence With Religious Minorities

Religious beliefs sometimes have a profound influence on the thoughts, feelings, and behaviors of believers. A large percentage of Americans believe in God and attend church regularly. In addition, the lifestyle of some religious Americans diverges substantially from that of mainstream America. For example, Amish and Old Order Mennonites withdraw from "English" society, avoid the use of technology, and have strict codes of conduct (Cates & Graham, 2002). Other patients may not fall into the Judeo-Christian religious tradition. Specific competencies are often needed when treating religiously committed patients from unique backgrounds.

A Respected Psychologist

The local bishop of the Amish community sometimes referred parishioners for counseling to a local Mennonite psychologist. (Mennonites have theological and historical links with the Amish, although they are more "worldly"; most own cars and other modern appliances, permit higher education, and some even vote.) The psychologist understood the Amish worldview and was able to help most of her Amish patients.

At other times religiously committed patients may initially appear highly acculturated to mainstream culture. Nonetheless, many of these patients hold their religious beliefs and affiliations at the core of their identity. These beliefs influence how they think about the roles of husband and wife (e.g., hierarchical rather than egalitarian), child-rearing practices (e.g., emphasis on corporal punishment rather than positive reinforcement and modeling), or same-sex orientation (e.g., homosexuality is a sin rather than homosexuality is a lifestyle choice).

Some patients from religious groups outside the mainstream of American society look askance on psychologists and even when they participate in therapy need more time to develop trust. An accepting attitude and a willingness to learn and listen can be very helpful in establishing rapport. Many secular psychologists find it practical to leave the use of religious language to the patient. Referrals to clergy for adjunctive counseling on religious issues can be helpful, although clergy vary considerably in their sophistication on integrating psychology and religious issues.

A Cleric Psychologist

A Roman Catholic priest who was also a licensed psychologist accepted a patient who presented his concerns in highly religious language. The patient reported substantial marital discord prompted largely by his almost continual praying. Further inquiry suggested that this behavior was a manifestation of obsessive–compulsive disorder. The psychologist priest knew that "over scrupulousness" has been recognized by Roman Catholic authorities for centuries and that it must be distinguished from piety.

For psychologists who practice a religious-based form of psychotherapy, informed consent is especially important. Explicit integration of religion into psychotherapy should be done only with a clear understanding on the part of the patient before psychotherapy begins. Some of the ways that religion could be integrated into psychotherapy include the use of prayer, teaching spiritual concepts, encouraging forgiveness, or using a religious community for support (Richards & Potts, 1995). This would probably mean that the public announcements of the psychologist should indicate "Christian counseling" or other denominational or religious identification (Richards & Bergin, 2004; Sperry & Shafranske, 2005).

MOVING INTO NEW AREAS OF COMPETENCE

The APA Ethics Code also contains standards for psychologists who retrain themselves to work with techniques or populations that are new to them and for psychologists who are moving into areas in which generally recognized standards of practice do not yet exist. These topics have special relevance for psychologists who engage in alternative or complementary medicine or who communicate electronically with patients.

New Areas of Practice

Competent psychologists may want to develop proficiency in areas of practice in which they did not receive formal doctoral-level training. In some domains of practice, it is possible for psychologists to ensure their competence by working for a proficiency credential, such as a diplomate in forensic psychology or a proficiency certificate in the treatment of persons addicted to alcohol or other drugs.

In other domains of practice, no such credentials exist. Moreover, experts may not agree on a uniform sequence of experiences, course of study (i.e., set of readings, workshops, or classes), or examinations to ensure proficiency. Furthermore, there is no guarantee that psychologists have actually acquired the knowledge and skills found in the books or workshops. Finally, competent performance in a new domain may require actual skills as opposed to just factual knowledge. For example, individual work with children requires psychologists to have a personal style appropriate for children. It may require nuances of body language, tone of voice, and choice of vocabulary that are best acquired through direct contact with children, as opposed to just reading about them. Psychologists should not consider themselves competent in a new domain until they have had another psychologist who is proficient in that field monitor or supervise them.

Psychologists who intend to move into a new domain of practice ask themselves if they are current with the scientific basis in the relevant domain, have mastered the needed clinical skills, understand the treatment milieu, and appreciate any ethical or legal issues involved (Belar et al., 2001). They also encourage psychologists who are entering new fields of practice to apprentice themselves to an experienced psychologist. Submitting one's work product to external control, whether through seeking a credential or through an apprenticeship, is part of the "culture of safety" whereby psychologists take reasonable steps to ensure their competence and ability to help others.

Moving Into a New Area of Practice

A psychologist in independent practice wanted to develop proficiency in working with older adults. He read several professional books on geropsychology, subscribed to and read two peer-reviewed professional journals in geriatrics, took several CE courses in geropsychology, and then hired a geropsychologist as a consultant for his work.

Fortunately, in this case the consultant established a set of proficiencies that every psychologist working with older adults should have. The consultant graded the psychologist on each of these domains, and at a certain point, determined that regular consultation was no longer required. However, they continued to consult as needed for several more years.

Emerging or Experimental Treatments

Psychologists use the scientific method to improve their ability to serve others. Engaging in the systematic search for knowledge is a defining characteristic of the profession. This scientific enterprise could occur through a well-considered protocol for a specific condition developed by a team of researchers, approved by a panel of experts, and subjected to institutional review board standards. Or, it could be based on single-subject designs, case studies, or qualitative research that involves systematic reflections on experiences.

Before agreeing to use an experimental technique, psychologists need to ask themselves numerous questions. Does empirical evidence support the use of these techniques? If it does support their use, for what populations and under what conditions can they be of benefit? Do other treatments have a greater likelihood of success? Could the treatment be iatrogenic?

Has the psychologist consulted with peers about the use or application of this technique? Are patients informed about the innovative nature of the treatment? Will the psychologist monitor the progress and welfare of patients throughout the course of treatment? Is the psychologist sufficiently trained in the technique? Will the patient be discouraged from trying more conventional approaches if the experimental one fails? Ineffective treatments are not morally neutral if they discourage patients from taking advantage of more acceptable treatments (Knapp & VandeCreek, 2003b).

Alternative or Complementary Treatments

Alternative treatments refer to those treatments that are not taught regularly in professional programs. *Complementary treatments* are the same as alternative treatments except that they are used in conjunction with instead of in place of traditional treatments. What is or is not an alternative or a complementary treatment may vary according to the nature of the disorder being treated. Relaxation exercises might not be an alternative or a complementary treatment for an anxiety disorder, but they could be for a personality disorder. Common alternative or complementary treatments include herbal supplements and massage therapy.

Psychologists who recommend these options need to balance the benefit to the patient with the cost in terms of money, time, and any possible iatrogenic effects. However, some patients initiate such treatments before they enter therapy. In these situations, psychologists who refuse to respect the wishes of their patients may risk having them drop out of treatment. Compromise may be clinically indicated in some situations. Nonetheless, psychologists should not blindly acquiesce to the treatment theories of their patients, especially when they involve herbal or dietary supplements. Patients may not be aware of the toxic effects of some "natural" remedies or potential interactions with some prescription medications. Furthermore, the efficacy of any herbal remedy may be difficult to measure because of the lack of standardization in herbal content across product brands. Before deciding on nonprescription medications or herbal remedies, it is generally best for psychologists to confer with the patient's physician.

Therapy by Telephone or Other Electronic Means

The use of telephone or e-mail therapy creates the potential for some ethical problems. Proponents of telephone therapy claim that it is a useful intervention for persons with transportation limitations. However, telephone therapy raises the question of whether the psychologist can do an adequate assessment and intervention without the benefit of visual cues. Furthermore, it is unclear if telephone therapy can be construed as practicing psychology without a license if the patient lives in a state where the psychologist is not licensed.

Only a few years ago, no one would have seriously considered the feasibility of doing e-mail therapy. However, in the last 10 years, e-mail has become an accepted part of everyday life. In addition, e-mail has become the mode of communication for many business transactions and a way to keep up personal relationships.

To date, research on online therapy is limited. Although there are isolated case examples of patient satisfaction, the data do not support the use of online therapy as a preferred mode of treatment. One of the considerations when conducting online therapy is whether confidentiality can be maintained. Although confidentiality of the communications can never be entirely achieved, A. Ragusea and VandeCreek (2003) believe that with proper safeguards a reasonable degree of confidentiality can be ensured.

Other concerns with online therapy are that psychologists can never be entirely certain that the individual who is sending the communication is indeed the person he or she claims to be. Also, the therapist may not know the physical location of the patient and may not know how to reach the patient in an emergency. Finally, online communication lacks the nonverbal cues that are often necessary for effective communication.

As with telephone therapy, it could be argued that treating a patient who lives in another state may constitute practicing psychology in that state. At present, it may be best to use confidential electronic communications with patients as a supplement to face-to-face communications, just as therapists often use telephone communications (A. Ragusea & VandeCreek, 2003).

EXCEPTIONS TO COMPETENCE

The APA Ethics Code makes exceptions to the general requirements of competence when services are not otherwise available (e.g., in rural or other underserved areas) or in an emergency. Some psychologists work in geographical areas where mental health services are not readily available. In those circumstances, "services referred often means services denied" (Knapp & VandeCreek, 2003b, p. 58). For nonemergency services in underserved geographical areas, psychologists can make a "compassionate exception" (Koocher & Keith-Spiegel, 1998) and deliver services if they are competent in closely related areas and make reasonable efforts to obtain the necessary competence.

It is difficult to give fixed rules for determining how much psychologists can stretch their competence in providing services outside of their areas of expertise. It may be necessary to do a utilitarian calculus and determine whether patients are better off with the not-yet-competent psychologist or better off to wait until a more qualified professional is identified.

Of course, psychologists may provide services to anyone in an emergency. However, after the emergency is over, they should refer the patient elsewhere if necessary to ensure an adequate level of ongoing care.

EMOTIONAL COMPETENCE

Standard 2.06, Personal Problems and Conflicts, requires psychologists to "refrain from initiating an activity when they know or should know that there is a substantial likelihood that their personal problems will prevent them from performing their work-related activities in a competent manner." In addition, it requires psychologists to "take appropriate measures, such as obtaining professional consultation or assistance, and determine whether they should limit, suspend, or terminate their work-related duties" when they become aware that personal problems might limit their professional effectiveness.

Maintaining competence means more than just keeping up-to-date with the changing knowledge base and standards of care. Maintaining competence also requires *self-care* (i.e., protection of one's physical or mental well-being). From a deontological perspective (see chap. 2, this volume), self-care is important because care of oneself reflects something that should be a universal law. The same moral principle that requires psychologists to promote the welfare of their patients also requires psychologists to promote their own welfare. Feminist writers have emphasized self-care, and it is mentioned specifically in the Feminist Code of Ethics (Rave & Larsen, 1995).

The utilitarian perspective holds that the morality of an act or a rule is determined by whether it promotes the well-being of all the parties affected by that act or rule. Therefore, it assumes that the well-being of the psychologist should be included in the calculus used to determine the morality of an act or a rule.

Furthermore, from a practical perspective, psychologists who do not show sufficient concern for their own well-being risk losing or limiting their ability to help others. Psychologists need to function well themselves to help others (Lambert & Barley, 2001). Improved self-knowledge may help psychologists become more effective in identifying their own emotional reactions and sensitivity to patient information (Wiseman & Schefler, 2001). This relationship of self-care to competence is found in the aspirational section of the APA Ethics Code, which states that "Psychologists strive to be aware of the possible effect of their own physical and mental health on their ability to help those with whom they work" (Principle A, Beneficence and Nonmaleficence). As noted by Zeddies (1999),

> One of the most challenging aspects of clinical work is the necessity at times for the therapist to understand how his or her own psychological and emotional dynamics—including personal values, beliefs, theories, and commitments—influence the therapeutic approach with clients. (p. 229)

The factors that could impair the emotional competence of psychologists include personal stressors (e.g., problems in a marital relationship and stressful life events such as the illness of a loved one) and professional stressors (e.g., a difficult managed care patient and stressful life events such as a patient suicide). We look at those stressors and discuss ways to prevent them or minimize their negative impact.

Personal Stressors

The quality of psychological work is affected by personal factors. Psychologists can better identify and understand the emotional nuances of psychotherapy when they can identify and understand their own emotions. The emotional health of the psychologist can be influenced by personal predispositions to mental illnesses or by reactions to chronic stressors or stressful life events.

Psychologists appear to have no more emotional problems than others in comparable professions. Nonetheless, many students entering psychology come from dysfunctional families of origin (Brems, Tryck, Garlock, Freemon, & Bernzott, 1995; Elliott & Guy, 1993; Feldman-Summers & Pope, 1994; Murphy & Halgin, 1995), although many may have already resolved personal issues that could impair professional performance. Many psychologists also report mental illnesses or addictions to alcohol or other drugs (Thoreson, Miller, & Krauskopf, 1989), although the rates are probably no higher than those found in the population in general. Distress and impairment do occur among psychologists, and a degree in psychology provides no vaccination against mental disturbances.

Unfortunately, some of the personality traits that helped psychologists get through their doctoral programs may undermine their satisfaction with their personal lives and their long-term professional success. To get through or succeed in graduate school, students need to defer gratification, put in long exhausting hours (often to the point of impairing physical well-being), and place their careers above their personal lives. For most students, this is a temporary sacrifice until they can get their professional careers started; for a few others, it starts or reinforces a lifestyle that places them at risk for burnout or depression.

Personal Stressful Life Events

Of course, psychologists, like other persons, are influenced by personal stressful life events such as divorce or illness of a loved one.

A Careful Decision
A psychologist underwent a series of personal tragedies. Within a 3-month period, his father died (leaving substantial estate problems that needed to be handled), his wife underwent taxing cancer treatments, and his oldest son was hospitalized as a result of a serious traffic accident.

These events strained the time commitments of the psychologist and also exacted a substantial emotional toll. The psychologist appropriately reduced his workload so that he could meet these domestic responsibilities. He entered short-term personal therapy; received antianxiety medication from his family physician; and made a list of obligations, prioritized them, and took "one day at a time."

The steps for stress management for psychologists do not differ substantially from those that psychologists recommend to their patients: Take regular vacations, separate professional from private life, exercise, eat properly, get medical attention, and so forth. Another underlying principle is for psychologists to develop social relationships and interests outside of their professional work. Many personal needs cannot be met through relationships with patients or even professional colleagues. "Within a comprehensive self-care program for psychologists, it is best to deliberately maintain healthy ways to satisfy our longing for respect and nurturance within a network of vibrant relationships with loved ones and friends" (Guy, 2000, p. 352).

It is never too late to learn self-care strategies, but they are best taught in graduate school. Ideally these stressors are discussed openly and students are taught coping and prevention strategies in graduate schools. Graduate students and interns need to see coping models of mature professionals who acknowledge that they have problems dealing with the emotional reactions generated in the process of therapy, occasionally experience concern about their own abilities, and sometimes take their problems home with them. The ideal model is not a psychologist who is free of stress or negative life events but a psychologist who knows how to handle them.

Of course, the goal should not just be to minimize the harmful effects of stress. The goal should be to optimize well-being in a manner consistent with ethical principles. Psychologists (and others) do not always agree on the optimal definition of well-being or the paths to get there. We are not presenting a definition of well-being or recommending a specific wellness program ourselves, but we are suggesting that psychologists consciously attempt to apply their own notions of well-being to themselves.

Professional Stressors

Psychologists often have chronic life hassles, such as working with difficult patients, having too much paperwork, having inadequate time for obligations, and dealing with restrictions imposed by managed care companies (Sherman & Thelen, 1998). However, these all occur against the backdrop of the continual stress of dealing with the emotional pain of others.

Psychologists need to be especially aware of *compassion fatigue*. Psychologists are trained to pay attention to and give primary concern to the welfare of their patients. Indeed, one of the moral bases of our profession is beneficence or the active work to help others. According to Guy (1987), individuals who tend to be overly idealistic or dedicated are at risk of burning out. Psychologists run the risk that their caring for others becomes so ingrained that they do not take care of themselves. One of the traits of virtue-based risk management is insight that includes the ability to identify emotional fatigue (see chap. 3, this volume).

According to the professional acculturation model presented in chapter 2 (Foundations of Ethical Behavior), those psychologists who are separated (i.e., those with strong personal ethics but weak professional ethics) may be more vulnerable to compassion fatigue than those who are integrated (i.e., those with strong personal ethics and strong professional ethics). Although the psychologists who are separated have strong feelings of compassion based on a personal code of morality, they may not have internalized the therapeutic detachment needed for effectiveness as a psychotherapist.

The possibility of compassion fatigue can also be addressed. Psychologists may feel responsibility to take on more patients or to take on patients with special needs that tax their resources. Another professional risk is that of *vicarious traumatization*, whereby trauma therapists risk compromises to their well-being as a result of continual contact with trauma survivors (Pearlman & MacIan, 1995). The risks are especially high for those psychologists who have a personal history of trauma. The training and supervision for trauma therapists should include attention to countertransference issues (Pearlman & MacIan, 1995). However, psychologists need to ensure that their exposure to exhausting or draining patients does not prevent them from meeting their primary obligations to friends, family, or other patients.

Not all of these profession-specific hassles affect all psychologists equally. Ackerly, Burnell, Holder, and Kurdek (1988) found that self-reported burnout was more common among psychologists who were young, had a low income, experienced lack of control in their therapeutic setting, felt overcommitted to patients, and engaged in little personal psychotherapy. Some of these feelings of burnout may occur because of external factors. Younger psychologists are more likely to have institutional jobs in which they have less control over their employment situation and have more demanding caseloads. However, some feelings of burnout may be the result of a lack of self-knowledge or an inability to establish appropriate boundaries.

It is important to anticipate the chronic work stressors and develop strategies for handling them. Sherman and Thelen (1998) found that the most common behaviors of psychologists for preventing impairment were either personal (e.g., participating in non-work-related activities, exercising regularly, and engaging in church-related activities) or professional (e.g., seeking periodic vacations, scheduling breaks in the day, using stress management techniques, keeping caseloads at manageable levels, refusing to accept certain types of patients, and limiting work hours). Other helpful behaviors include keeping a sense of humor, perceiving patient problems as interesting, diversifying tasks, and getting peer consultation even if it means having one's case analyses or methods of intervention challenged (Kramen-Kahn & Hansen, 1998).

Professional Stressful Life Events

The careers of psychologists place them at risk to experience certain stressful life events (e.g., patient suicides or egregious boundary challenges). For example, Kleespies and Dettmer (2000) found that sometime during their careers, one in four psychologists is likely to have a patient commit suicide.

"Therapists uniformly experienced these suicides as stressful and . . . patient suicide[s] had a significant acute impact on the professional and personal lives of a substantial number of therapists" (Chemtob, Bauer, Hamada, Pelowski, & Muraoka, 1989, p. 297). The suicide of a patient can have an especially substantial impact on trainees, who may feel sadness, self-blame, guilt, shame, or depression as a result of the suicide (Kleespies, Penk, & Forsyth, 1993).

Ellis and Dickey (1998) found that many training programs did not have clear administrative procedures to follow when the patient of an intern commits suicide. Nor did they always train supervisees in interventions with suicidal persons or provide adequate emotional support when a suicide did occur. Kleespies and Dettmer (2000) recommended that training programs prepare interns for dealing with suicidal patients, including didactic and supervised experience in the management of suicidal states and assistance in dealing with the aftermath of a suicide.

Assaults against health professionals do occur, especially in inpatient facilities or prisons in which the population as a whole tends to be more violent. Guy, Brown, and Poelstra (1990) found that almost 40% of psychologists reported being attacked by a patient at least once in their careers. Two thirds of the attacks occurred against psychologists working in hospitals, and about 23% of the attacks resulted in physical injury to the psychologist.

Guy, Brown, and Poelstra (1992) showed that either a history of being assaulted or a history of receiving threats was related to worry about future assaults. The protective measures taken by psychologists included refusing to treat certain patients, refusing to disclose personal data to patients, prohibiting patients to appear at the psychologist's home, locating the office in a "safe" building, specifying intolerable patient behaviors, and having an unlisted phone number.

deMayo (2000) found that many psychologists-in-training had been sexually harassed by their patients who had made sexual remarks, asked for a date, brushed up against them, touched or grabbed them, exposed themselves, or solicited sexual activity. Most of the events involved male patients and female psychologists or interns. In addition, about 10% of psychologists reported being stalked (Gentile, Asamen, Harmell, & Weathers, 2002). Whereas a majority of the stalking victims in the general population are female, only half of the stalking victims among psychologists were female.

A Frightening Situation

The female patient of a psychologist was furious when she was referred to another provider. Although the referral was therapeutically indicated and handled tactfully, the psychologist found that his car was vandalized, a rock was thrown through his office window, and his wife received a letter falsely accusing him of having an affair with another woman.

Upon consultation with an expert, the psychologist changed his daily routine, installed an alarm in his house, notified family members to be wary of this woman, and had his attorney send a strong letter threatening legal action. In this case the stalking stopped. However, stalkers represent a heterogeneous group, and no one set of solutions is appropriate for all stalkers (Kamphuis & Emmelkamp, 2000).

These profession-specific life events need to be put in perspective. In spite of these occasional threatening events, most psychologists have rewarding careers. On the whole, older psychologists experience greater satisfaction with their work. Perhaps less satisfied psychologists have found other vocations or have modified their work responsibilities to be more compatible with their interests. Or perhaps older psychologists have acquired greater skills and abilities to deal with work-related problems that occur. Nonetheless, younger psychologists who are starting their careers should expect a certain level of stress from both professional and personal chronic stressors or negative life events. Psychologists who are aware of the potential of professional specific stressors or events can take steps to prevent them or minimize their harmful impact.

An underlying principle in reducing the impact of environmental stressors or negative life events is for psychologists to place themselves in an environment that reinforces behaviors that promote personal and patient welfare. "Make your environment work for you, not against you" (Norcross, 2000, p. 711). The environment should provide a feedback loop whereby psychologists continually reflect on their procedures and outcomes. The various forms of external feedback include, but are not limited to, consultation, study groups, and gathering systematic data on patient outcomes or satisfaction. Other forms of feedback include reviews of professional notes, informal conversations with colleagues, and CE programs.

Social support appears especially important when working in a career such as professional psychology. If upsetting patient behaviors occur, then it is important for psychologists to receive emotional support or even enter into psychotherapy. When in difficult situations, it is important to "share the burden" or involve others in the critical decision making. Clinically, those psychologists who receive regular consultation from others benefit from their shared clinical expertise and are able to deliver a high standard of care. Also, sharing the burden has psychological benefits as well. Just the opportunity to express one's dismay can have healing effects and reduce stress. Indeed, Coster and Schwebel (1997) found that social support was rated as one of the key components of success among psychologists who were nominated by their peers as being "well-functioning," and Dlugos and Friedlander (2001) found that peer-nominated, passionately committed psychologists continually sought feedback and supervision.

One way to look at self-care is to assume that there should be no such thing as a completely independent practice. A license only allows the opportunity to select the means of regulation, not to avoid regulation altogether.

IMPAIRED PSYCHOLOGISTS

At its extreme, these personal or professional stressors or life events can result in impairment or loss of the ability to fulfill the minimum responsibilities of the profession. Impairment needs to be distinguished from distress in which individuals have subjective pain but still perform their jobs responsibly. Impairment also differs from technical incompetence or the lack of knowledge or technical skills necessary to perform the functions of a psychologist.

The estimates of impairment among psychologists vary because of the differing ways researchers have defined and operationalized the term. However, we argue that at least 3% of psychologists will, at some time in their careers, have a mental or physical disability that prevents them from adequately performing the functions of their profession (other researchers have suggested higher rates; see, e.g., Thoreson et al., 1989). The issue of impairment is of concern to all health care professions. Some anecdotal data suggest that those health care professionals who can prescribe or have easy access to drugs (e.g., physicians, nurses, pharmacists, podiatrists) have higher rates of polysubstance abuse, whereas psychologists are more likely to have uncomplicated alcoholism. Of psychologists who rated themselves as impaired, Wood, Klein, Cross, Lammers, and Elliott (1985) found that almost 50% had referred themselves for treatment. Fortunately, data suggest that recovering psychologists do extremely well in treatment (Thoresen, Budd, & Krauskopf, 1986).

According to Standard 2.06a, Personal Problems and Conflicts, of the APA Ethics Code, psychologists refrain from work activity when "they know or should know that there is a substantial likelihood that their personal problems will prevent them from performing their work-related activities in a competent manner." In addition, provisions of some state licensing laws make impairment, in and of itself, grounds for disciplinary actions. Psychologists who know or should know that they are impaired must withdraw from their work or seek supervision to ensure the quality of their work. Moreover, according to Koocher and Keith-Spiegel (1998), about one half of the psychologists who were disciplined by the APA Ethics Committee appeared to have committed their misdeed in the context of some personal crisis or stress. Perhaps they did not meet a formal criterion of impairment, but these data suggest that some ethical violations by psychologists could be prevented if psychologists engaged in adequate self-care.

Fortunately, many state and provincial psychological associations have created programs to help distressed or impaired psychologists (Barnett &

Hillard, 2001). In addition, some associations may offer CE programs, publish articles, present workshops, and otherwise disseminate information on how psychologists can help reduce distress and prevent impairment. These efforts encourage psychologists to focus on general self-care, which means anticipating and learning to handle these stressors and to focus on positive self-care.

A Positive Outcome

A psychologist received two DUIs within a year and was sentenced to prison for 30 days (suspended if he entered treatment). Upon an agreement with the impaired professional program, the psychologist was allowed to continue to practice under supervision if he attended AA meetings, participated in psychotherapy, took medications, and underwent periodic drug monitoring. After 3 years of sobriety he returned to fully independent practice. He has been sober for the last 15 years and publicly speaks about his addiction and recovery.

Procidano, Busch-Rossnagel, Reznikoff, and Geisinger (1995) found that in the last 5 years, 34% of the graduate departments of psychology had students with personality or other problems that indicated impairment. Ideally, graduate programs monitor their students closely enough so they can identify those students who show signs of impairment, help them address their problems, or remove them from the training program. Standard 7.04, Student Disclosure of Personal Information, specifically permits training programs to require personal disclosures on the part of students who appear to be impaired.

6

MULTIPLE RELATIONSHIPS AND PROFESSIONAL BOUNDARIES

Boundaries refer to the rules of the professional relationship that set it apart from other relationships. They clarify which behaviors are appropriate and inappropriate in therapy as compared with those behaviors that are appropriate or inappropriate in other settings (Sommers-Flanagan, Elliot, & Sommers-Flanagan, 1998). Boundaries set limits, provide structure, and thereby prevent harm to patients (Borys, 1994). They create an atmosphere of safety that allows a relationship to develop so the patient can reflect on personal experiences without worrying about the needs of the psychologist. Boundaries support the notion that the primary purpose of therapy is to promote the welfare of the patient.

Guthiel and Gabbard (1998) distinguish between *boundary crossings* and *boundary violations*. A boundary crossing occurs whenever a professional deviates from a strictly professional role. A boundary violation is a boundary crossing that creates a reasonable risk of harming or exploiting a patient.

Some boundary crossings, such as sex with a patient, are always boundary violations. Other boundary crossings, such as therapist *self-disclosure*, may be violations, benign, or even helpful to the patient, depending on the circumstances. To a certain extent, the decision on how to handle these boundary crossings may reflect the theoretical orientation of the psychologist, because humanistic or eclectic therapists may allow themselves more flexibility in their boundaries (Baer & Murdock, 1995; Williams, 1996). The challenge to the psychologist is to determine when the circumstances warrant bending or holding firm on boundaries (Sommers-Flanagan et al., 1998). Consequently, education about professional boundaries needs to be more than just learning a list of "thou shalt nots." Instead, it requires a consideration of the purposes and goals of general rules and an understanding of how they are implemented in the context of good clinical judgment to meet the needs of a patient.

Small boundary crossings may be the first step down a "slippery slope" to a highly exploitative relationship. However, the fact that exploitative psychologists may cross boundaries does not mean that all boundary crossings are harmful, unethical, exploitative, or the first step down a slippery slope. It may be therapeutically indicated for a psychologist to talk about sports to a treatment resistant male adolescent to help him feel comfortable in therapy or to accept Christmas or Hanukkah cookies from a patient. Psychologists need not develop rigid stances, but they should use their clinical judgment to determine when such boundary crossings may be therapeutically indicated (Guthiel & Gabbard, 1993, 1998).

Boundary crossings need to be considered carefully because of the power differential inherent in the psychotherapist–patient relationship. Several factors contribute to this power differential. Psychologists have professional status, knowledge of interpersonal influences, and personal knowledge of the patient. Patients may be emotionally dependent or vulnerable as a result of a mental illness or situational stresses.

The current standards for therapeutic boundaries have evolved over time. During the early days of psychoanalysis, Freud expressed concern when he learned that some analysts were getting romantically involved with their analysands. He doubted the wisdom of such involvement and was concerned about scandals harming the public acceptance of psychoanalysis (Baur, 1997). Over the years, clinical lore and empirical data have informed standards on proper professional boundaries.

The rules regarding boundaries can be found in the Ethics Code (American Psychological Association [APA], 2002a), in the regulations or ethics codes of state boards of psychology, and decisions issued by malpractice courts. In addition, several states have criminalized sexual contact between psychotherapists and their patients.

Boundary violations represent about half of the disciplinary actions of the APA Ethics Committee (APA Ethics Committee, 2004). Most of the violations involved sexual contact between a psychologist and a patient (about 80% of these involved contact between a male psychologist and female patient). However, nonsexual multiple relationships were the cause of numerous other complaints. Boundary violations are a common source of complaints before disciplinary boards and are sometimes found in malpractice complaints.

The moral principles guiding decisions about boundaries are nonmaleficence (i.e., do no harm) and beneficence (i.e., work to promote the welfare of others). In addition, respect for patient autonomy is also relevant because psychologists should not undercut patient autonomy by creating dependency or exploiting the power differential inherent in the professional relationship.

Virtue-based risk management principles can help psychologists make decisions about boundary crossings. Wise psychologists are informed (i.e., they understand the legal and disciplinary standards governing multiple relationships), competent (i.e., they show competence in handling their emotional reactions to therapy and document important boundary issues clearly), sensitive (i.e., they show sensitivity to the needs of patients), balanced (i.e., they guide their actions by therapeutic rationales and not momentary urges or anger or compassion), and insightful (i.e., they are aware of the ways that personal vulnerabilities may limit their effectiveness with certain patients).

In this chapter, we review the definitions of boundaries in concurrent and consecutive relationships, subtle boundary issues (e.g., self-disclosure, gift-giving, touching, and hugging), patient challenges to boundaries, unavoidable multiple relationships, role conflicts, multiple relationships with students and supervisees, and sexual relationships. Forensic multiple relationships are mentioned briefly but considered in more detail in chapter 11 (Forensic Psychology).

CONCURRENT OR CONSECUTIVE MULTIPLE RELATIONSHIPS

Standard 3.05, Multiple Relationships, defines a multiple relationship as occurring

> when a psychologist is in a professional role with a person and (1) at the same time is in another role with the same person, (2) at the same time is in a relationship with a person closely associated with or related to the person with whom the psychologist has the professional relationship, or (3) promises to enter into another relationship in the future with the person or a person closely associated with or related to the person.

In a concurrent multiple relationship, psychologists have social or business relationships with patients at the same time as they have professional relationships. In a consecutive multiple relationship, psychologists have social or business relationships with patients either before or after the professional relationships.

Concurrent Relationships

Standard 3.05a, Multiple Relationships, explicitly states that not every multiple relationship is necessarily harmful. "Multiple relationships that would not reasonably be expected to cause impairment or risk exploitation or harm are not unethical." The issue is whether a reasonable psychologist would be aware of factors that would make harm or exploitation foreseeable.

Self-interest can blind psychologists to the dangers of entering into a multiple relationship. All persons run the risk of minimizing the impact of their own welfare or self-interests on interpersonal relationships. "One must always assume that a compromise in one's objectivity might reach beyond one's awareness" (Younggren & Gottlieb, 2004, p. 257). Nonetheless, the welfare of patients comes first, and psychologists should not objectify patients or to treat them only as objects to gratify their own needs (Brown, 1994).

Even if psychologists are able to discern and control their self-interests, they need to monitor certain behaviors that in and of themselves appear harmless but that could be misinterpreted by patients. Even if psychologists are able to be completely objective with their patients, they might not have patients who are able to reciprocate (Knapp & VandeCreek, 2003b).

A multiple relationship combined with harm to the patient can result in a claim of misconduct in a malpractice court. For example, one malpractice court found a psychiatrist guilty of misconduct when, among other things, she used the therapy to discuss her own legal and emotional problems, discuss treatment issues with other patients (who were named), and solicit assistance in performing custodial work in her office, such as moving furniture and performing office chores (*Hamanne v. Humenansky*, 1995).

Patients or prospective patients may push boundaries out of ignorance, pathology, or both. This finding should not be surprising because nonsexual, dual relationships are common among clients or patients of physicians, accountants, lawyers, etc. Popular television shows (e.g., *Frasier*) and movies (e.g., *Good Will Hunting*) reflect this misunderstanding when the plot lines require psychotherapists to cross boundaries with their patients.

Positive limit setting may be beneficial for these patients. Positive limit setting refers to "responding to the client's request while, at the same time, reframing the response in a way that meets a legitimate underlying need" (Koocher & Keith-Spiegel, 1998, p. 177). That is, a psychologist may decline a patient's social invitation but recognize the legitimate need for the patient to develop other social relationships.

Some patients push boundaries as a function of their pathology. They may view psychologists as rescuers or potential lovers. When boundaries are set, these patients may retaliate with irrational and primitive anger. However, they are better off with psychologists who maintain boundaries than with ones who are intimidated into breaking them.

Of course, sometimes contacts with patients outside of the office are clinically indicated. For example, it could be appropriate for psychologists to use treatment procedures such as in vivo desensitization outside of the office. Sometimes cleaning obsessions and compulsions are best treated when some of the sessions occur in the patient's home. In addition, it may be acceptable for psychologists to accept invitations from patients for certain special events such as weddings or funerals.

Consecutive Relationships

Other multiple relationships are consecutive in that a social or business relationship developed before the professional relationship started or after the professional relationship ended. Lamb et al. (1994) reported that psychologists had serious reservations about the appropriateness of developing business relationships with former patients (i.e., they rated business relationships with former patients a 4.5 on a scale of 1 to 5 on inappropriateness).

In an exploratory nonrandom survey, Anderson and Kitchener (1996) identified numerous posttherapy contacts between psychologists and patients. These involved personal friendships, incidental social contacts, business or financial contacts, workplace–professional contacts, professional and collegial plus social contacts, supervisory or evaluative relationships, and participation in the same religious organization. Generally, psychologists who had brief unintended contacts with their patients were less likely to view the situation as ethically problematic. However, psychologists who initiated social or business contacts with former patients were more likely to see ethical problems. Some of the ethical concerns identified by psychologists included threats to confidentiality, the inappropriateness of the patient to return to treatment with the same professional, a power differential in the relationship, and overlooking the emotional reactions generated by the relationship.

Psychologists should weigh several factors when considering posttherapy relationships, including the power differential (from the standpoint of the patient), which may be influenced by the duration of treatment and the clarity of the termination (Gottlieb, 1993). They should also consider the possibility that the patient may need to return to therapy. Some patients remain vulnerable to exploitation even after termination; the patient or psychologist may have strong feelings generated by therapy; psychologists may not retain objectivity in the posttherapy relationship; the trustworthiness of psychologists in general may be threatened when such relationships become public; and former patients may be harmed if the relationships goes bad (Pipes, 1997).

A Strained Relationship

A psychologist borrowed several thousand dollars from a former patient to open a business. The business failed, prompting the former patient to request the return on his lost investment. When the psychologist balked at the request, the patient complained that the psychologist exploited the goodwill generated by their treatment relationship to induce him to invest in an ill-conceived enterprise.

The psychologist initially minimized the extent of his interpersonal influence over his former patient. However, upon receiving legal consultation, he was advised that a disciplinary board might view the situation differently. The psychologist managed to repay his former patient.

UNAVOIDABLE MULTIPLE RELATIONSHIPS

The 1992 Ethics Code (APA, 1992) prohibited multiple relationships except when they were accidental or incidental encounters. In contrast, the 2002 Ethics Code prohibits only multiple relationships that are likely to be harmful or exploitative.

Some multiple relationships are quite unpredictable. One psychologist left her office during a break in the day to go to the gym where she had maintained a membership for years. While she was taking her shower, she turned around and faced the patient who had just left her office an hour earlier. Another psychologist found herself competing with a patient in a dog show. Another psychologist came home one night to see a patient working on the plumbing in the addition to his new house. Apparently the contractor had subcontracted to a business that employed the patient. Still another psychologist sat with a patient for half an hour in the waiting room of a local physician. Another psychologist arrived at the office of her physician to see that a former patient of hers was the technician responsible for completing the mammogram.

Multiple relationships for psychologists in small towns or rural areas appear to be especially likely (Schank & Skovholt, 1997). As the size of the community shrinks, the likelihood of such encounters expands (Roberts, Battaglia, & Epstein, 1999). In frontier communities, psychologists may depend on their patients to sell them groceries or to repair their televisions. Often psychologists in rural areas must schedule patients so that neighbors do not encounter each other in the waiting room.

In addition, the family of the psychologist may encounter patients in any of the previously mentioned situations. The patient of one psychologist asked him how his wife liked her new car. He had sold her the car earlier that week, although the wife of the psychologist had no idea that the car dealer was a patient of her husband. Sandifer (1989) wrote that a psychologist and spouse found out on the first day of school that a former patient was the new fifth-grade teacher for their child.

Another psychologist responded to the doorbell only to see a young woman patient at the door. She appeared as surprised as the psychologist. She had a date with the adult son of the psychologist (the psychologist had a different surname than her son) and had no idea that the young man was the son of her therapist.

Although these small-world hazards are more common in rural areas, they are not restricted to rural areas. Unavoidable multiple relationships can also occur in smaller communities such as defined social groups that exist in urban areas. For example, professionals who are lesbian, gay, or bisexual commonly have relatively defined social circles even in urban areas and may encounter patients in that context. Encounters with patients through religious organizations are also common (Lamb, Catanzaro, & Moorman, 2004).

According to Standard 3.05b, Multiple Relationships,

> If a psychologist finds that, due to unforeseen factors, a potentially harmful multiple relationship has arisen, the psychologist takes reasonable steps to resolve it with due regard for the best interests of the affected person and maximal compliance with the Ethics Code.

Psychologists who anticipate random meetings with their patients can use the *you-first rule* by which patients retain control of whether or not they will recognize their psychologist in a nontherapeutic context (Knapp & VandeCreek, 2003b). According to this rule, patients decide whether or not to acknowledge the psychologist first, thus ensuring control over the social situation. They may or may not want to speak or acknowledge the psychologist, depending on the circumstances (e.g., their companions, the setting, degree of comfort).

Often psychologists feel surprise, uncertainty, or discomfort in these situations (Sharkin & Birky, 1992). Psychologists who anticipate encounters with a patient do well to address the issue proactively and revisit it as often as is needed. Barnett (1999) described how he handled an unavoidable multiple relationship. After agreeing to start therapy with a mother, he encountered her at a soccer practice involving their children. They discussed the likelihood of future encounters and preserved a working therapeutic relationship. Nonetheless, "we did revisit these issues several times during treatment to be sure there was no adverse impact on the patient or the treatment relationship" (p. 20). Barnett displayed the virtue of sensitivity in his handling of this situation.

An Unavoidable Multiple Relationship

A child psychologist had a policy of never treating children who went to the same school district as her children. One child patient, however, transferred into her son's school district during the middle of therapy. The patient was in the same classroom as her son.

The psychologist appropriately discussed the rules of confidentiality with the patient's parents as soon as she was aware of the situation. However, the child patient recognized the relationship and told the psychologist's son that he was a patient of her mother's. This revelation led to a frank discussion between mother and son about the role of a psychologist and the need to protect patient privacy.

SUBTLE BOUNDARY CROSSINGS

Boundary crossings can be overt, such as concurrent or consecutive business or social relationships with a patient. Boundary crossings can also be subtle in instances in which the boundaries are crossed by just-noticeable gradients of behavior. Common subtle boundary crossings are touching or hugging, gift giving (or receiving), therapist self-disclosure, selling products, bartering, intrusive advocacy, and psychological voyeurism (Knapp & VandeCreek, 2003b). Many psychologists are flexible in their boundaries, and depending on the needs of the patient and the context of therapy, may cross these boundaries and touch a patient, accept token gifts, disclose personal information, extend therapy beyond the scheduled time, or engage in social amenities such as the discussion of current events (Johnston & Farber, 1996).

Psychologists should be aware of the potential for harm from subtle boundary crossings. A psychologist could be disciplined for engaging in a pattern of subtle boundary crossings, which on the whole would give a reasonable person the impression that the psychologist was attempting to transform the relationship from a professional to a personal one. However, isolated, clinically reasonable, and nonexploitative boundary crossings on the part of psychologists should not be grounds for disciplinary actions (Knapp & VandeCreek, 2003b).

Even those crossings that do not move the treatment relationship into a social one could, nonetheless, reduce the quality of treatment. A subtle boundary crossing may cause harm if the patient misunderstands it, such as when a patient views the self-disclosure of the psychologist as an invitation to create a social relationship. Even small boundary crossings may establish precedents whereby patients expect more movement away from a professional role. Sensitive psychologists are alert to problems or feelings of discomfort created by boundary violations.

Although these subtle boundary crossings are usually harmless or even helpful, judicious psychologists think carefully about them. When evaluating the potential impact of subtle boundary crossings, it is helpful to consider the clinical purpose and likely outcome of the boundary crossing and the degree to which it creates the possibility of future entanglements.

Every intentional boundary crossing needs to have a therapeutic rationale. Decisions about boundaries should be informed by the needs of the patient and the likely outcome. Psychologists should not underestimate the ability of some patients to misconstrue seemingly innocuous events, such as being scheduled as the last appointment of the day. Patients have misconstrued clinically relevant telephone conversations between sessions as an attempt to move the relationship from a professional to a social one.

An Unexpected Outcome

A psychologist was treating a woman with a long history of disturbed interpersonal relationships. The psychologist brought a small cake to one session so that they could "celebrate" her birthday together. The psychologist used some moderate self-disclosure for therapeutic purposes.

She promised the patient that she would always be there for her and would never abandon her. As therapy progressed, it became clearer that the patient needed more intense services, perhaps a day hospital program, than the psychologist could provide. When the psychologist discussed the possibility of a transfer, the patient alleged that the psychologist had "groomed" her for a social relationship and was now abandoning her.

Our interpretation of this situation suggests that the psychologist had done nothing that would warrant a disciplinary action. However, in hindsight the psychologist had made some mistakes. The patient misinterpreted (or alleged to have misinterpreted) the birthday cake and the self-disclosure. The patient appeared to interpret the promise to "always be there" as a license for her to engage in numerous boundary challenges without any consequences to her.

Of course, psychologists who deliver services in the homes or residences of their patients need to be especially vigilant that their presence in the home does not activate a "guest schema" on the part of the patients. That is, in such situations the patients may be more likely to cross boundaries and provide refreshments, engage in social conversations, or otherwise treat the psychologist more as a social guest than a treating professional (Knapp & Slattery, 2004).

Keeping strict boundaries should not be seen as making the psychologist rigid, distant, or cold (Borys, 1994; Guthiel, 1994). Boundaries allow psychologists to be warm and supportive toward patients, and patients should not fear that their psychologists will turn the relationship to their own advantage. According to the professional acculturation model, integrated psychologists demonstrate a balance of personal compassion and professional boundaries (see chap. 4, this volume). They neither show the same degree of self-disclosure or emotional involvement as found in friendships (as would a professional in the separated stage) nor are they cold and distant (as might a professional in the assimilated stage). Finally, psychologists should be cautious about any boundary crossing that would result in mixing roles to the extent that the boundary crossing loses its clinical rationale or results in relationships whose outcome cannot be predicted.

Self-Disclosure

All psychologists disclose some information as soon as the patient enters the office. The clothing of psychologists and the decorum of the office all disclose something about them. Also, virtually all psychologists would agree that brief disclosures about the psychologists' areas of proficiency would be clinically appropriate. However, in this context, self-disclosure refers to other nonpublic (i.e., private) information about psychologists.

Psychologists differ on how they handle the self-disclosure of private information. Some psychologists, especially those trained in an analytic tradition, eschew all self-disclosure. Others, especially those trained in humanistic or existential traditions, believe that self-disclosure can be clinically indicated in certain situations (Barnett, 1998). Although individual feminist psychologists may vary in the extent to which they self-disclose, some share personal information such as sexual orientation, religious background, or political beliefs as part of the informed consent process or to equalize the relationship between the psychologist and patient (Mahalik, Van Ormer, & Simi, 2000).

However, it is desirable for psychologists to think through their feelings and clinical perspectives on self-disclosure. Often patients attempt to elicit self-disclosures for various reasons. Glickhauf-Hughes (1998) recommended that psychologists look for the motivations and clinical needs that prompt these questions and not just to respond (or fail to respond) to the surface meaning.

An Honest Question

A divorced psychologist was treating a couple with serious marital problems. In the middle of the first session the husband asked, "Are you married?" The psychologist did not respond to the manifest nature of the question, but to the implied concern of the patient. The psychologist said, "Perhaps you want to know if I have the ability to help you? Perhaps you are worried that you will have to invest a lot emotionally in this process, without any likelihood of saving your marriage. Let me address those issues. . ."

Part of the "culture of safety" involves anticipating problems ahead of time. This psychologist had anticipated such questions about her marital status, especially when she was conducting marital therapy, and she had thought through her responses.

This psychologist did not believe that self-disclosure at this time would serve a clinical purpose or achieve a desirable clinical outcome. She was also aware that if she answered one question she might be opening the door for greater entanglement by which the patient would ask more and more personal questions.

Peterson (2002) noted that the decision to self-disclose may be viewed from a consequentialist perspective or "one's evaluation of the potential results of that self-disclosure for the client" (p. 29). Barrett and Berman (2001) found that selective therapist self-disclosure (directed at patient welfare) led to reduced symptoms of patient distress and led patients to like their therapists more. Similarly, Bridges (2001) noted that "psychologically attuned and patient-centered, intentional disclosure opens up space for deep therapeutic engagement between therapist and patient" (p. 21). A balance needs to be drawn because too much self-disclosure may weaken the therapeutic alliance (Ackerman & Hilsenroth, 2001).

We make several recommendations concerning self-disclosure derived primarily from Barnett (1998), C. Hill and Knox (2001), and Peterson (2002). These suggestions include (a) disclose infrequently; (b) self-disclose to normalize, model, or strengthen the therapeutic alliance; (c) ensure that self-disclosures focus on the needs of the patient; (d) observe how patients respond to self-disclosures; (e) consider self-disclosures for patients who have trouble forming therapeutic relationships; and (f) document self-disclosures and the clinical rationale behind them.

Gift Giving or Receiving

The proper attitude to have about gifts, as with other boundary issues, is to focus on the welfare of the patient. Some psychologists reject all gifts and use the offer as an opportunity to discuss its implications for the psychotherapeutic relationship. Others accept small or token gifts. As with self-disclosure, we recommend that psychologists analyze their feelings and clinical rationales ahead of time so that they can respond thoughtfully.

Most gifts are tokens of nominal value and are appropriate for a special occasion such as when patients bring in Christmas cookies or a child patient brings in a hand-drawn picture. Although the theoretical orientation of the psychologist may dictate how such gifts are received, most psychologists would accept a nominal gift with the appropriate expression of appreciation and let it go at that. They are merely courteous social conventions.

Other gifts, however, raise concerns about the nature of the psychologist–patient relationship. We know of psychologists who have been offered a chair, an expensive pen and pencil set, a VCR, intimate and erotic sleep wear, erotic wood prints, wine, cocaine, pornographic magazines, and an all-expenses-paid vacation.

Ordinarily these gifts would have to be refused because they are emotion laden, intimate, or involve a substantial amount of money. In addition to refusing these gifts, a psychologist may need to inquire about how the patient perceives the therapeutic relationship. Gift giving may be a well-meaning but ill-advised effort to express appreciation, to level the power balance between the psychologist and patient, to set the groundwork for soliciting special favors, or to encourage the psychologist to step into committing an ethical transgression. Other patients may view such gifts as a form of bartering and expect to have the psychologist reciprocate with a reduced fee or other monetary considerations.

Psychologists who take such gifts risk exploiting the dependency of the patient during a period of vulnerability. Furthermore, the quality or objectivity of treatment could be impaired if the psychologist were to accept the gift and feel a need to reciprocate in some fashion.

An Inappropriate Offer

The husband of a prospective patient called a psychologist to arrange treatment for his wife. He said, "I am the director of a managed care network, and I will see to it that you get in the network." The psychologist turned down the referral immediately and told the husband that any such offer, however good the intention, could imply that the psychologist owed something to the husband, thus compromising his commitment to the welfare of the wife. He suggested that the wife call another psychologist herself or, if the husband called, to get a psychologist outside of the network, where there could be no implied obligation to the husband.

Touching and Hugging

Social attitudes vary about touching and hugging. Some people are "huggers" or "touchers" and feel little reluctance to put their hands on other people in the course of conversations. Others reserve hugging for romantic or special occasions and would never touch a nonrelative except under the most unusual circumstances. Patients with a history of involvement in Alcoholics Anonymous (AA) may expect hugs as part of the treatment because it is commonly done at the close of AA meetings. Attitudes toward touching and hugging also vary according to culture and according to the particular age or gender mix. Similarly, psychologists vary in their attitudes toward touching and hugging. Some never touch or hug; others do so with discretion.

Some patients may feel uncomfortable with touching and hugging especially when combined with the intense emotional affect that often occurs within psychotherapy. Consequently, psychologists should hug or touch patients with discretion. A gentle touch to a patient in grief can convey a thousand sympathetic words. However, a patient with a history of eroticizing relationships who insists on an intensive hug may be challenging appropriate boundaries and trying to foster a social relationship. Psychologists should consider their own motivations for wanting to touch patients and the way that attitudes toward touching may vary according to the gender or age of the psychologist and patient. Psychologists should consider the purpose of the touch (e.g., Is it to console the patient?), the likely outcome (e.g., Will it assist the patient's recovery?), and the possibility of future entanglements (e.g., Will it set a precedent for behavior that could be clinically contraindicated?).

Selling Products

It would be inappropriate for a psychologist to try to sell patients a product unrelated to their therapeutic needs. Psychologists may have a vested interest in the sale, but the product may or may not be needed or wanted by the patient. Patients may feel subtle pressure to purchase the items out of fear of offending the psychologist. The very nature of the professional relationship, as opposed to a business relationship, is that the professional needs to place the welfare of the patient first. That is not likely to occur if the psychologist sells products unrelated to treatment.

However, it is quite acceptable for psychologists to sell products directly related to treatment at cost. For example, a psychologist who relies on progressive muscle relaxation or bibliotherapy as part of treatment may sell a relevant relaxation tape or a book directly to the patient at cost. The purpose of selling those products would be to provide low-cost materials related to treatment to the patient. There is unlikely to be any negative outcome or future entanglements from those transactions.

Psychological Voyeurism

Psychological voyeurism occurs when psychologists elicit details of the patient's story for their own enjoyment. In psychological voyeurism the purpose of therapy becomes the entertainment of the psychologist and not the care of the patient. However, it may be more difficult to acknowledge psychological voyeurism if patients enjoy their role as entertainer. This is not to say that psychotherapy should not be gratifying for the psychologist. However, the gratification should come as a result of seeing patient growth (Sommers-Flanagan et al., 1998).

A Cautionary Tale

A psychologist was entertained by his new patient who told dramatic and lively stories. After several weeks, however, the patient began to deteriorate substantially and attempted suicide. In retrospect, the psychologist realized that he had been so engrossed in the interesting stories that he had neglected to attend to the psychosocial stressors and relationship problems that foreshadowed the deterioration.

Intrusive Advocacy

Intrusive advocacy refers to using therapy to enlist patients for social causes, no matter how worthy (Pope & Brown, 1996). For example, some psychotherapists have pressured survivors of childhood abuse to "detach" from their families or to confront or sue the alleged perpetrators. Some have argued that their patients have a social responsibility to punish all child abusers. However, the purpose of the treatment relationship is to benefit the patient, not to further a particular social cause.

Conversely, intrusive advocacy can also occur when psychologists pressure their patients to "forgive" an abuser. Forgiveness is a complex concept, and the way the psychologist uses the term may or may not benefit patients or be consistent with their values. The psychologist should not "push" forgiveness but help patients decide what forgiveness means to them and whether it is consistent with their therapeutic goals.

ROLE CONFLICTS IN TREATING INDIVIDUALS FROM THE SAME FAMILY OR SOCIAL NETWORK

Nothing is inherently wrong with treating members of the same family or social network at the same time. In fact, the reputation of the psychologist and background of information about the family may help facilitate trust and ensure a good treatment outcome, and often the psychologist can be placed in a unique position to provide special help to all parties.

However, problems may arise if the relatives or friends have incompatible treatment agendas. For example, a psychologist may see a couple for marital therapy and then decide that they both need individual therapy. It can be a role conflict if the psychologist treats the wife for assistance in how to get out of the marriage while seeing the husband for assistance in how to keep the marriage going. Similar role conflicts occur when a psychologist treats the mother whose goal is to become emotionally closer to her daughter while also treating the daughter whose goal is to set limits with her intrusive mother. Role conflicts can occur any time psychologists treat patients who are friends or who otherwise know each other. Finally, multiple patients do not have obligations of confidentiality with each other. Psychologists can do nothing to prevent patients from talking to each other.

FORENSIC MULTIPLE RELATIONSHIPS

Several types of multiple relationships can occur in forensic settings. Sometimes psychologists treat patients who have been ordered by the court to receive treatment, and the court requires some accountability for their services. This creates a dual role in that the psychologist is responsible for treating the patient and for providing information to the courts. Other psychologists may be treating patients who, in the course of therapy, become involved in litigation, and the information from therapy is relevant to the outcome of the court case.

Still other psychologists may work in small towns where no one else is available to evaluate patients for the courts, even though the psychologist may have previously had a treatment relationship with the individual who is to be evaluated. Issues related to forensic multiple relationships are covered in chapter 11 (Forensic Psychology).

MULTIPLE RELATIONSHIPS WITH SUPERVISEES, TRAINEES, OR STUDENTS

The relationship between psychologists and their supervisees, trainees, and students is not completely analogous to that between psychologists and patients. Nonetheless, abuses can occur, and discretion is needed in the personal relationships between faculty and students.

Multiple roles between faculty and students are inevitable. Faculty members may be instructors, supervisors, advisors, researchers, or mentors for students. Also, faculty members have dual allegiances when dealing with students. They have obligations not only to promote the welfare of their students but also to protect the public from incompetent practitioners. Furthermore, the relationship between faculty members and students is not stagnant. Students start as neophytes but mature to advanced students and then to colleagues (Biaggio, Paget, & Chenoweth, 1997).

Students often benefit from contact with faculty members outside the narrow constraints of the classroom. Faculty members can advise students on academic or career choices, provide emotional support, and offer advice on personal matters. In the ordinary give and take of personal relationships, small favors may be asked, such as giving a ride home. Friendships or small business relationships may develop (from babysitting to assisting in research). Faculty members need to be aware that students may not feel the option of saying no to even minor requests (e.g., Can you babysit Friday night? or Can you cover a class for me next week?).

An Overly Demanding Supervisor

A faculty member who did not yet have tenure "encouraged" his graduate assistant to help him write articles that would help prepare him for tenure. He prodded the graduate assistant to work far in excess of his required workload and often called him at home late at night to discuss details of article preparation.

Furthermore, faculty members need to ask themselves whether they give preferential treatment to students with whom they have multiple relationships or whether they are equally available to advise and mentor other students (Biaggio et al., 1997). Of course, sexual relationships with students over whom faculty members have evaluative authority are harmful and wrong (see section on sexual contact between supervisees and students later in this chapter).

SEXUAL RELATIONSHIPS

According to Standard 10.05, Sexual Intimacies With Current Therapy Clients/Patients, "Psychologists do not engage in sexual intimacies with current therapy clients/patients." This is one of the few absolute statements in the APA Ethics Code. There are no qualifiers or recommendations to use clinical judgment in deciding whether to engage in sexual relationships with patients.

Courts have traditionally viewed sexual relationships with patients as grounds for malpractice. According to *Roy v. Hartogs* (1975), "there is a public policy to protect a patient from the deliberate and malicious abuse of power and breach of trust by a psychiatrist" (p. 297). Subsequent courts have invariably adopted similar positions.

Despite isolated stories of happy marriages between psychologists and their patients, sexual contact usually harms patients, and sometimes the harm is severe (see also reviews by Lamb, Catanzaro, & Moorman, 2003; Pope, 1994). A number of studies with varying methodologies, samples, and definitions of sexual contact have found the frequency of lifetime sexual contact between mental health professionals and their patients to range between .02% and 3.0% for female psychotherapists and .09% and 12.1% for male psychotherapists (Pope, 1994). Sexual contact with former patients is more frequent than sexual contact with current patients. Although this generalization has many exceptions, the most common pattern is for an older male psychotherapist to have sexual relations with a younger female patient. In addition to the harm to individual patients, sexual contact between psychologists and patients harms the public image for psychologists in general and may deter some people from seeking help.

Data suggest that the frequency of patient–therapist sexual contact is decreasing in recent years (Lamb et al., 2003), although the reasons for its decline are unclear. It may be because several states have criminalized this behavior, the number of female psychologists (who have lower rates of exploitation) has increased, or the educational and preventative efforts by training institutions and psychological associations have been effective.

Sexual Relationships With Former Therapy Patients

According to Standard 10.08a, Sexual Intimacies With Former Therapy Clients/Patients, psychologists may not "engage in sexual intimacies with former clients/patients for at least two years after cessation or termination of therapy." In addition, psychologists may not engage in sexual intimacies with former patients even after 2 years except in highly unusual circumstances. According to Standard 10.08b, if they do have sexual intimacies with former patients, psychologists have the burden of demonstrating that

> there has been no exploitation, in light of all relevant factors, including (1) the amount of time that has passed since therapy terminated; (2) the nature, duration, and intensity of the therapy; (3) the circumstances of termination; (4) the client's/patient's personal history; (5) the client's/patient's current mental status; (6) the likelihood of adverse impact on the client/patient; and (7) any statements or actions made by the therapist during the course of therapy suggesting or inviting the possibility of a posttermination sexual or romantic relationship with the client/patient.

Thus, the 2002 APA Ethics Code almost always prohibits sexual relationships with former patients. This standard does not mean "two years and a green light." It means "two years and a flashing red light." "It is an 'almost never' standard" (Knapp & VandeCreek, 2003b, p. 156).

Former patients are vulnerable to exploitation. Although therapy may be over, a former psychologist still has influence and information that can be used to keep the relationship going. Even before the explicit prohibition against sexual relationships with former patients appeared in previous versions of the APA Ethics Code, APA commonly disciplined psychologists who terminated therapy to enter into a sexual relationship with a patient.

Sexual Relationships With Close Relatives or Friends of Patients

In addition to the problems that develop with sexual contact with patients, students, and former patients, psychologists can also cause harm by having romantic relationships with close relatives or friends of patients. For example, a psychologist who initiates a romantic relationship with the mother of a child patient is entering into a potentially harmful relationship with that child and betraying the primary fiduciary relationship to that child.

Sexual Relationships With Students and Supervisees

The APA Ethics Code prohibits sexual relationships with students and supervisees (Standard 7.07, Sexual Relationships With Students and Supervisees). Although educators or supervisors do not control the supervisee as much as the psychologist controls the patient, they still have substantial control. Teachers have control over students through grades, letters of recommendation, and for graduate assistants, the quality of their work life. Faculty and supervisors cannot be objective if they are having sexual relationships with students or supervisees (Sullivan & Ogloff, 1998). Although sexual relationships between supervisors or faculty and students are always forbidden, even nonsexual multiple relationships must be avoided if they impair objectivity or are exploitative (Standard 3.05, Multiple Relationships).

A majority of the relationships are between older male psychologists–educators and younger female students. Respondents to a survey on these sexual relationships tended to view them as exploitative and harmful (Hammel, Olkin, & Taube, 1996). Some data suggest that the frequency of these relationships is declining (Hammel et al., 1996).

The sexual exploitation of students or supervisees is not grounds for malpractice because no psychologist–patient relationship exists. However, it could be grounds for disciplinary action by a licensing board, ethics committee, or educational institution.

In addition to the harm that may come to the supervisee, some evidence suggests that supervisees who have had sexual relationships during training were more likely to have sexual relationships with patients later in their careers, although the data for this are mixed (Lamb et al., 2003).

The sexual exploitation of patients is probably multidetermined. Nonetheless, several factors have emerged in the study of psychotherapists who have engaged in sexual misconduct. On the basis of his experience in treating professionals accused of boundary violations, Schoener (2002) described great diversity among these offenders. For example, sometimes the exploiting psychologists have long-standing personality or sexual disorders (e.g., pedophilia, sexual sadism). Others are impaired either through the abuse of drugs or alcohol or from a serious mental illness. Often the offending psychologists are "lovesick" (i.e., believe themselves in to be love) and ignore or overlook their role as a psychologist. Some poorly trained psychologists have not learned to recognize or manage the feelings engendered by therapy or the boundary issues in psychotherapy. Schoener noted that there are other categories of offenders and many cases have multiple determinants.

Several surveys have produced results that are consistent with and expanded on Schoener's (2002) description. H. Jackson and Nuttall (2001) and Lamb et al. (2003) found that psychologists who had relationships with patients often did so during periods of personal distress. H. Jackson and Nuttall found that being sexually abused as a child was associated with sexual misconduct as a professional. Hamilton and Spruill (1999) concluded that psychology trainees who committed sexual boundary violations were often inexperienced or lonely.

It is very difficult to prevent sexual exploitation by psychologists with long-standing personality or sexual disorders. However, the profession can do more to prevent misconduct by psychotherapists who are undertrained or temporarily impaired.

Gabbard (1996) argued that it is inappropriate to view sexual misconduct from an "us versus them" perspective. It is true that some mental health professionals who engage in sexual misconduct have serious character flaws and should never have been admitted into the profession. However, many transgressions occur because of a confluence of clinical error, poor training, and personal vulnerabilities.

According to Gabbard (1996),

> The majority of those that I have seen over the years are more *similar* to the rest of us than different. Many have felt that they were in love with their patients, others have self-destructively surrendered to demands for demonstrations of caring, and still others have been desperately needy and situationally vulnerable because of impoverished personal lives or acute stressors like divorce or the death of a loved one. (p. 312)

Psychologists, like other humans, are sexual beings. Sexual feelings permeate our everyday lives, and sexual behaviors often reflect more pervasive personality traits. "The sexual arena is a distillation, a shorthand in which psychological motifs can often be seen more readily than they can in more complex social interactions" (Glenmullen, 1993, p. 245). In addition, the emotional intensity of the treatment relationship commonly activates sexual needs and fantasies on the part of both the psychologist and the patient. These sexual feelings can create discomfort, guilt, and anxiety on the part of the psychologist and distract the attention of the psychologist away from the needs of patients (Rodolfa et al., 1994).

From the standpoint of both the patient and psychologist, sometimes the intensity of feelings is fueled by unresolved issues and reflects a means to gain control, express appreciation, or solicit affection. Sometimes the seduction may be overt; at other times it is subtle or unconscious. Sexual attraction should be viewed as an occupational hazard for psychologists. The problem is not the presence of sexual feelings but the way those feelings are handled. As a profession we can do a better job of reducing sexual exploitation by appropriately addressing sexual feelings in psychotherapy.

Reframing the Sexual Exploitation Issue in Terms of Optimizing Treatments

Typically the issue of sex with patients is framed in terms of How do we stop sexual exploitation? However, a better way may be to frame the problem as How do we improve the overall quality of the therapeutic relationship? Specifically, how should psychologists handle sexual feelings that develop in therapy in a manner that fulfills the moral principles (i.e., beneficence, nonmaleficence, fidelity, justice, and respect for patient autonomy) that should guide treatment?

Reframing of the "sex-with-patients" issue becomes especially important from the standpoint of education and prevention. Efforts that focus only on stopping sexual exploitation may send a message that it is desirable to suppress or minimize sexual feelings. However, efforts that focus on acknowledging and understanding sexual feelings send a message that it is desirable for psychologists to be alert to sexual feelings so that they can have more productive treatment relationships with patients.

Few psychologists had specific learning experiences in their graduate training program that dealt with the responsible management of sexual feelings in the therapeutic relationship. The minority who reported that they did have such training felt better prepared to handle such sexual feelings (Paxton, Lovett, & Riggs, 2001).

Hamilton and Spruill (1999) urged graduate programs to teach students about transference, countertransference, and the inevitability of sexual attraction between psychologists and patients. They encouraged supervisors to discuss sexual feelings when it would improve the quality of patient care or the self-awareness of the supervisee. Because these feelings or situations are inevitable, Moursund (2001) encouraged students to anticipate sexual attraction and their reactions.

> You will handle such situations much better if you've thought in advance about what you might say and do with them. Moreover, thinking about these issues now gives you a chance to set your own internal radar screen, to be sensitive to your own feelings and to the out-of-awareness messages you may be sending to an attractive client. (p. 53)

This change in the culture of training may not occur easily. Sexual topics are very sensitive, and intense sexual feelings are typically not discussed except in the most intimate situations. However, psychologists who acknowledge and understand sexual feelings should be able to provide a higher level of service to all of their patients, rather than just abstaining from sexual relationships with them. The goal is not just to minimize the harm that can occur because of sexual exploitation. Although the prohibition against sexual misconduct should be emphasized throughout training, the goal is to understand why sexual feelings emerge and how they can be handled to ensure the best possible outcome for the patient.

Three ways to address this issue are through didactic training, supervision, and self-monitoring (i.e., self-care). Of course these are not mutually exclusive categories, as ideally, training will be congruent with the goals of supervision, supervision will encourage self-care, and self-care will involve further training or supervision. Although we discuss these strategies in terms of preventing sexual exploitation, they have implications for handling all boundary issues.

Didactic Training

Hamilton and Spruill (1999) noted that psychologists who were more likely to engage in a sexual boundary violation had a background of volunteering or working in a social service position before entering training in psychology. This fact raises the question of whether these psychologists' socialization into the profession was adequate. The ability to work within boundaries can be conceptualized according to the acculturation model presented in chapter 2 (Foundations of Ethical Behavior). That is, students may handle boundaries most appropriately if they have integrated professional ethics into a well-founded sense of personal ethics. Students who have poorly integrated their personal ethics into their professional ethics are at greater risk for boundary violations (see Table 6.1).

Students who have achieved integration have successfully combined good personal ethics with the spirit and rules surrounding professional boundaries. As such, they are more likely to have anticipated their reactions to boundary issues ahead of time and to have developed a response based on clinically relevant standards implemented within a caring personal style. Depending on their personal orientation, for example, they may or may not

TABLE 6.1
Boundaries Viewed From an Acculturation Model

| Personal ethics | Professional ethics | |
	High	Low
High	Follows professional rules, and personal values such as compassion guide behavior in gray areas	Personal values or intuitions guide behavior and trump professional rules
	Integrated	Overinvolved
	Likelihood of exploitation is very low	Likelihood of exploitation is low, but may be involved in "rescuing"
Low	Follows professional rules but lacks a well-developed personal moral code to guide behavior in gray areas	Does not respect professional rules and lacks a well-developed personal code to guide behavior
	Rigid	Dangerous
	Likelihood of exploitation is low, but may come across as distant	Likelihood of exploitation is high

self-disclose or accept small gifts from patients. But whatever they do is done from an understanding of professional roles and a genuine concern for the patient.

Students who are high on personal ethics but low on professional ethics (i.e., separated) may not understand the importance of keeping professional roles distinct from personal roles. They may be more willing to loan a patient money, give advice, self-disclose personal information, and give or receive gifts, as they might do with a personal friend. They may allow momentary feelings of compassion to trump professional ethics and become too involved and seek to rescue their patients. These students (or psychologists) are at low risk for sexual offenses, and when those offenses occur it is probably the result of a rescue fantasy.

Students who are low on personal ethics, but high on professional ethics (i.e., assimilated) may attend to the letter of the APA Ethics Code but fail to understand the meanings behind it. They only feel guided by the Ethics Code when it gives them a clear direction on a particular issue. As a result, they may be inclined to adopt a legalistic stance. For example, they may fail to reach out to touch the hand of a grieving patient, even though to do so would be compassionate and clearly clinically indicated. They are at a low risk for sexual offenses, but unfortunately, their relationships with patients may be less than optimal because they come across as too distant or uninvolved.

The most dangerous trainees are those who are low on both professional ethics and personal ethics. They are motivated primarily by self-interest and not by concern for their patients. Of the four groups, they present the highest risk for sexual exploitation of patients.

Fortunately, more graduate training programs are beginning to address these issues (Samuel & Gorton, 1998). One of the primary goals in the context of multiple relationships is to encourage future psychologists to seek consultation and possibly personal therapy whenever sexual feelings toward a patient appear to interfere with the quality of treatment. Surveys suggest that about 60% to 70% of psychologists who have experienced sexual attraction to patients sought consultation, supervision, or discussed these issues in their personal psychotherapy (Rodolfa et al., 1994; Stake & Oliver, 1991). However, that means that between 30% and 40% of psychologists did not. It is interesting to note that those who sought consultation were significantly less likely to believe that they would act on the sexual feelings (Rodolfa et al., 1994).

Other educational goals are to help students understand the relationship of sexual feelings to the overall outcome of treatment. Curricula have been developed, including training exercises and vignettes to sensitize students and practitioners (Bricklin, Knapp, & VandeCreek, 2001; Samuel & Gorton, 1998; Schoener, 1999). Samuel and Gorton recommended introducing the curricula on boundary violations early in the educational program and then having it developed, reinforced, and integrated throughout the training program. First-person accounts of individuals who have been sexually exploited can be especially useful in helping students to appreciate the harm that may occur. Training in how to handle sexual issues should involve not only sexual attraction in therapy but also basic information on human sexuality (Ford & Hendrick, 2003). Students who have the best understanding of the ethical issues involved in sexual feelings that arise in therapy are more likely to discuss patient attraction with their supervisors (Housman & Stake, 1999).

Schoener (1999) described a number of educational programs, videos, and exercises on boundaries in general but also on sexual feelings. One structured exercise is "How to Seduce a Client" in which the participants state what they would do to set up the emotional seduction of a patient, and the group leader lists them on chalkboard or chart. After the list is reviewed, the leader can ask participants to note which ones are inherently unethical. Few of these actions are inherently unethical. The mere process of listening to the intimate details of another person's life can create a sense of intimacy and intense feelings.

Another exercise asks students to create two lists, one for the characteristics of a friend and the other for the characteristics of a professional. The friend may, for example, loan money, exchange gifts, or engage in mutual self-disclosure. A psychologist, however, would do none of those. This exercise is important because it helps differentiate social and professional roles and social from professional ways of expressing care and moral behavior.

Supervision

Although almost all internship directors believe that education about boundaries should be included in their training programs, they greatly underestimate the extent to which their interns are likely to experience eroticized countertransference (Samuel & Gorton, 1998). Supervisors who openly discuss the reality of sexual attraction can help their trainees to acquire the objectivity needed to deal with these emotions constructively. However, this needs to be done tactfully. Because supervisors have a degree of control over the career paths of their supervisees, the trainees may be naturally reluctant to discuss these "forbidden feelings." "Those aspects of their thoughts, feelings, or actions that they would most like to keep secret from the supervisor are precisely the issues that should be openly discussed in supervision" (Gabbard, 1996, p. 317).

Supervisors can initiate the process by selectively self-disclosing their own sexual feelings and how they are handled. Again, according to Baur (1997),

> The supervisors who guide therapists need to be able to discuss their own, real experiences of powerful sexual attraction. If they cannot tell all, then the therapists coming to them will not trust them with their embarrassing secret feelings while there is still time to avoid an affair. (p. 7)

Care must be taken that these disclosures are done tactfully and discretely and that the interns understand that the disclosures are focused on their needs as trainees to help them better understand how to identify and handle sexual feelings in therapy. Supervisors may have to be explicit as to why the disclosure was made and how it relates to the training of the supervisees.

Self-Care

We have already discussed the need for self-care, which involves conscientiously monitoring one's feelings and embedding oneself in a protective social network that provides regular, honest, and caring feedback. However, the need for self-care is heightened by awareness that loneliness, personal distress, recent personal losses, and personal dissatisfaction are related to sexual misconduct. Rodolfa et al. (1994) reported that those psychologists who had engaged in sexual boundary violations with patients self-reported that the factors related to their misconduct were a breakup or absence of a primary romantic relationship, poor self-concept, or job stress.

Even psychologists who do not exploit patients sexually may have less than optimal outcomes if they feel distress. It is harder to be aware of personal feelings that emerge in a therapeutic relationship when those feelings are masked by a background of general dysphoria or anxiety. It is helpful to engage in ongoing self-examination of feelings toward patients.

7

INFORMED CONSENT OR
SHARED DECISION MAKING

Informed consent is a legal and ethical obligation to provide information to patients before they initiate assessment or treatment. Informed consent procedures reflect respect for patient autonomy. It is assumed that patients will be capable of making, or at least having the right to make, decisions in their best interests when they have been given relevant information. Psychologists should respect the autonomy of their patients except for very narrow circumstances, such as when patients are incapable of giving consent or the lives of individuals are at stake. We discuss these exceptions in more detail later in this chapter.

Optimally, the patient and psychologist collaborate to identify mutually agreed-on goals and intervention strategies. The phrase *shared decision making* probably better reflects the underlying goals, although the initial session may involve giving information concerning the treatment process.

The minimum standards of what constitutes informed consent can be found in the Ethics Code (American Psychological Association [APA], 2002a). In the Ethics Code, the key or foundational standard dealing with respect for patient autonomy states that psychologists "obtain the informed consent of the individual or individuals using language that is reasonably understandable to that person or persons" (Standard 3.10a, Informed Consent). Other ethical standards expand on the requirements of informed consent and delineate exceptions.

Also, malpractice courts have used the "reasonable person" standard to determine what information should be given to patients. That is, courts ask, What would a reasonable person want to know about the medical procedure before agreeing to it? ("Physicians' liability for nondisclosure is to be . . . approached from viewpoint of reasonableness of physician's divulgence in terms of what he knows or should know to be patient's informational needs" [*Canterbury v. Spence*, 1972, p. 774]). The standards of informed consent were developed primarily from physical medicine or surgery, and the degree to which they apply to mental health treatment is controversial. In addition, the informed consent process was altered in 2003 when the Health Insurance Portability and Accountability Act (HIPAA; U.S. Department of Health and Human Services [HHS], 2002) Privacy Rule went into effect and required covered entities to give privacy notices to patients (see chap. 8, this volume).

Informed consent procedures are also part of maintaining a "culture of safety." The content of the informed consent procedures is intended to anticipate questions that most reasonable patients would have and to prevent future misunderstandings and disappointments. If implemented properly, informed consent procedures promote open exchanges between psychologists and their patients.

In this chapter, we review basic information about informed consent and special issues that may arise in couples, family, or group therapy or in supervised services. We also cover the desirability of obtaining assent (i.e., agreement) or greater participation from individuals who are not legally capable of giving informed consent. In addition, we consider options when patients appear unable to participate in decisions about treatment. Informed consent is also covered in chapters 11 (Forensic Psychology), 12 (Assessment), 15 (Clinical Supervision), and 16 (Research and Scholarship).

ENSURING SHARED DECISION MAKING

The early references to informed consent in the legal literature concerned the nature and type of information that patients should receive before agreeing to undergo medical procedures such as surgery. The *medicolegal model* of informed consent had at least four salient characteristics that are in contrast to a *participatory model*.

First, it was a passive activity in that the patient had a "right to determine what shall be *done with* [italics added] his own body" (*Canterbury v. Spence*, 1972, p. 772). Although a receptive or passive attitude may be appropriate for surgery, it may not be the optimal attitude to have when involved in an interactive and participatory relationship such as psychotherapy. A medicolegal model of informed consent as applied to psychotherapy may be misleading because it could imply that the patient is passively consenting to something presented by the psychologist (Beahrs & Guthiel, 2001).

Second, according to the medicolegal model, informed consent was seen as a specific event, typically occurring before the start of treatment. In contrast, a participatory model that views consent as occurring throughout the entire course of treatment may be more appropriate for psychotherapy.

Third, the medicolegal model was dichotomous in outcome in that patients either did or did not give informed consent after receiving basic information. The ability to give consent was conceived as a fixed trait. In contrast, the participatory model views the ability of patients to participate fully in treatment as varying according to their emotional needs, interpersonal influences, and the content of the information given to them.

Finally, the medicolegal model was dichotomous in process in that patients either did or did not accept a fixed treatment. In contrast, the participatory model involves the patients in creating the form and nature of the treatment that occurs. The patient is involved in numerous decisions throughout the course of treatment, such as whether to involve other family members, to seek an evaluation for psychotropic medications, or to use complementary (alternative) medical treatments.

In this chapter, we elaborate on each of these characteristics of the medicolegal model. However, the shortcomings of the medicolegal model do not necessarily mean that it has no merit for our discussion here. The medicolegal model emphasizes the ability of the individual to give meaningful consent, requires sharing of some information, and requires that the information be given at an understandable level. Indeed, patients value accurate information about services, an understanding of the costs of treatment, and the opportunity to have questions answered (H. Johnson, Cournoyer, & Bond, 1995).

Nonetheless, because mental health treatment typically encourages independence and autonomy, we believe that the participatory model is most appropriate for psychotherapy. The very process by which psychologists engage patients in treatment is part of the treatment. The initial information sharing process is an opportunity to do more than inform patients about the therapeutic process. It is an opportunity to develop agreed-on goals and methods of treatment.

In an analogue study, Sullivan, Martin, and Handelsman (1993) found that "clients may be more favorably disposed to therapists who take the time and effort to provide [informed consent] information" (p. 162). Also, in their review of goal consensus and collaboration, Tryon and Winograd (2001) found evidence suggesting that agreement on goals is positively associated with better patient outcomes and greater satisfaction. They recommend that to maximize the possibility of achieving a positive treatment outcome, therapist and patient should be involved throughout therapy in a process of shared decision-making, where goals are frequently discussed and agreed upon. (p. 387)

Therapeutic contracting that involves patients in setting goals and treatment procedures may be especially effective in helping individuals with serious and pervasive mental disorders (Heinssen, Levendusky, & Hunter, 1995). By reframing problems in a goal-oriented framework, such contracts place maximum responsibility on patients and help patients to restore their personal effectiveness and perceptions of self-control.

WHO CAN PARTICIPATE IN THE DECISIONS?

Truly informed consent can only be given when the service recipients have the capacity to give consent. Generally speaking, any adult has the legal right to give consent. Also, many states have exceptions wherein minors may give legal consent for treatment under certain circumstances, such as during an emergency or if they are legally emancipated.

However, most minors are not legally allowed to consent to treatment. Also, some adults have had their guardianship or decision-making powers for health care granted to another individual, usually a family member, through a court order or other legally binding process. Even in those situations, psychologists should try to get patients' assent or agreement to treatment and to consider their preferences (Standard 3.10b, Informed Consent). The general goal is to maximize patients' control over treatment decisions and the treatment process as much as possible under the circumstances.

Some psychologists use a "sliding scale" or "shifting standard" with adolescent patients in which they vary the standard they use to obtain assent depending on the outcomes at stake (Howe, 2001a). If there are life-endangering qualities or if the welfare of the patient is seriously jeopardized, then these psychologists err on the side of insisting on treatment. That is, they temporarily allow beneficence (i.e., the need to protect the welfare of the patient) to trump respect for patient autonomy. Of course, they always attempt to get the assent of their adolescent patients, but they do not allow the lack of assent to stop treatment if necessary to prevent serious harm. However, they show greater deference to the wishes of the adolescent if the potential for harm is low.

A Sensitive Psychologist

A psychologist who commonly treated adolescent patients often established a "three strike" agreement with reluctant low-risk patients. That is, she told them they had to come in at least three times, and after that, she would respect their wishes concerning future treatment. The patients appreciated her efforts to consider their preferences and almost always preferred to continue in treatment after the three sessions were over.

Throughout her sessions, the psychologist continually involved the adolescents in all treatment decisions as much as was reasonable or clinically indicated. When treatment ended, she routinely asked her adolescent patients for constructive feedback. She stated, "I treat a lot of teenagers and it would be helpful for me to know what was helpful for you and what was not so helpful."

Sometimes psychologists encounter potential patients who have the legal authority to give consent but appear lacking in the cognitive abilities necessary to do so. Such patients may have a dementia or mental retardation. However, such patients are considered legally competent to give consent unless a court has held otherwise.

The issue is further complicated by the fact that the psychologist may not be able to ascertain the ability of the patient to understand the nature of the services being offered until the evaluation is well underway or even completed. A patient who initially presents as alert and intelligent may appear more and more demented as the evaluation continues. Or, the ability of the patient to give consent may vary over time. A patient may appear alert and competent one day but disoriented and confused the next. Psychologists who feel uncertain about the patient's ability to give informed consent should proceed with caution.

Nevertheless, even persons with serious limitations may be able to understand the process if sufficient time is given for the explanation or if they have time to ask questions or consult with others. Sometimes creative educational approaches can be helpful. For example, psychologists can arrange to have the patient talk to persons who have already had the treatment. Or they can ask family members to help explain concepts.

In addition, psychologists can sometimes *titrate* the information given to patients (Gottlieb, Handelsman, & Knapp, 2004). That is, they present the patient with a limited amount of information, determine how well the patient is able to understand and integrate that information, and then provide additional information as needed.

A Prudent Psychologist

A very distraught patient contacted a psychologist requesting couples therapy. It was not clear at the initial session whether couples therapy would be therapeutically indicated. The psychologist met with the patient several times to help her clarify her goals and assess the likelihood that couples therapy would reach her goals. In this case the psychologist accurately determined that the patient would not be able to make a clear decision about marital therapy until she was less emotional and could decide her future goals.

Furthermore, psychologists should not ignore the role of subtle factors that can influence the informed consent process.

An Experiential Process

The wife in an African American couple sought treatment from a European American psychologist. Although she wanted marital therapy, she wanted to get firsthand information as to whether the psychologist would be able to develop rapport with her husband.

As can be seen, the information that the wife wanted could not be reduced to a simple declarative sentence. Instead, the information came in the form of subjective feelings of comfort that could only be acquired through direct experience with the psychologist.

When it appears that the individual is not capable of giving meaningful consent, we urge psychologists to document carefully and honestly any explanation offered to the patient with regard to the procedure under consideration, and with the patient's permission, to consult with the patient's family or other surrogate decision makers. Even if the patient has not yet been adjudicated incompetent, informing the patient's relatives reduces misunderstandings and the likelihood that they will perceive the psychologist as having initiated an unnecessary health care procedure.

Consultation with colleagues or with other professionals treating the patient may sometimes be helpful. The psychologist can ask the consultant if additional ways can be used to assess the capacity of the patient to understand the procedures and the benefits or risks of participating in treatment.

WHAT INFORMATION SHOULD BE GIVEN AS PART OF DECISION MAKING?

It is necessary for patients to have basic information about the therapeutic process before they can give informed consent. The content of the specific communication should include legally mandated items, including what is required in the HIPAA privacy notice and the APA Ethics Code. A few states mandate specific ingredients in mandated informed consent forms, but regardless of these requirements, psychologists should give information that would generally be helpful to most patients. Of course, additional information may be given depending on the needs of the patient. The question is, What would the average patient want to know about treatment? Fortunately, researchers have asked patients that question (Braaten & Handelsman, 1997), and we present salient features from their findings in the following sections.

Information Required by the APA Ethics Code

Standard 3.10, Informed Consent, requires that psychologists get the consent of their service recipients using language that is reasonably understandable. Psychologists must also discuss the limits of confidentiality (Standards 4.02, Discussing the Limits of Confidentiality, and 6.02b, Maintenance, Dissemination, and Disposal of Confidential Records of Professional and Scientific Work), obtain consent for audio or video recording (Standard 4.03, Recording), and give information about fees (Standard 6.04, Fees and Financial Arrangements). Furthermore, as applied to psychotherapy, "psychologists inform clients/patients as early as is feasible in the therapeutic relationship about the nature and anticipated course of therapy, fees, involvement of third parties, and limits of confidentiality" (Standard 10.01a, Informed Consent to Therapy).

The APA Ethics Code amplifies on informed consent procedures when they involve new or experimental therapies (Standard 10.01b, Informed Consent to Therapy), when supervisees provide services (Standard 10.01c), when conducting family or couples therapy (Standard 10.02, Therapy Involving Couples or Families), and when conducting group therapy (Standard 10.03, Group Therapy).

Psychologists who provide new, experimental, or innovative therapies must inform prospective patients of the experimental nature of the treatment, the potential risks involved, other more standardized alternative treatments that may be available, and the voluntary nature of their participation. More information on new, experimental, or innovative therapies can be found in chapter 5 (Competence).

When treating couples or families, psychologists need to clarify their roles, their relationships with all parties, and the probable use of services and information provided. Two issues that commonly arise regarding the use of information concern the role of secrets in family or couples therapy and the rules for confidentiality with minors. More information on keeping secrets in family therapy and treatment of adolescents can be found in chapter 8 (Confidentiality, Privileged Communications, and Record Keeping).

Impact on Third Parties

A 30-year-old married woman called and requested treatment for depression and dissatisfaction with her marriage. In the first interview she revealed that she was a survivor of sexual trauma as an adolescent, and it appeared that the depression and some of the marital problems were linked to this trauma.

Here the informed consent process needs to address the possible impact of treatment on the spouse and the marriage. A common sequela of trauma is disrupted relationships with spouses or significant others, including emotional detachment, lack of intimacy, and impaired sexual relationships. In this case, the psychologist spoke candidly with the patient concerning the likely impact of the trauma and asked the patient to consider that some of her negative feelings about her current relationship might be influenced by the trauma itself and not any inherent incompatibilities between her and her spouse.

When psychologists provide group therapy, they need to "describe at the outset the roles and responsibilities of all parties and the limits of confidentiality" (Standard 10.03, Group Therapy). Psychologists need to ensure that patients in the group will understand their roles and respect the privacy of other group members. When the patients gather for the first meeting of the group, it is desirable to discuss the terms of participation, the purposes of the group therapy, and the kinds of sharing that will occur. Other information that should be discussed includes whether the group is time limited or ongoing. If ongoing, then the procedures for leaving the group should be discussed, although all patients have the right to leave at any time and for any reason. Although it is not a requirement of the APA Ethics Code, psychologists may reinforce these concepts by having all group members sign an agreement promising to hold in confidence all matters discussed in the group and agreeing to a policy regarding extragroup interactions.

Psychologists should also inform patients of how they will handle confidentiality if patients are being seen in both individual and group therapy. Conversely, psychologists avoid disclosing private or secret information about one patient to another patient in the group sessions. Disclosures should be limited to what the patient has chosen to reveal within the group sessions. Fortunately, Burlingame, Fuhriman, and Johnson (2001) reported that pregroup preparation and efforts to establish good group cohesion at the start of treatment tended to facilitate outcomes in group therapy. More information on confidentiality in group therapy can be found in chapter 8 (Confidentiality, Privileged Communications, and Record Keeping).

Patients have a right to know if they are receiving services from a supervisee (Standard 10.01c, Informed Consent to Therapy). Consent is especially important when the trainee is in the early stages of training because patients may elect not to receive the service under these conditions. Knowledge of the supervised status of the trainee may also protect the supervisor. It is preferable that the patient call the supervisor with a concern early in treatment rather than having the supervisor learn about the discontent of the patient through a formal complaint. Furthermore, the trainee or supervisee status may be relevant to insurance reimbursement issues. More information on informed consent with supervisees can be found in chapter 15 (Clinical Supervision).

Information Required by the Health Insurance Portability and Accountability Act Privacy Rule

The HIPAA Privacy Rule applies to all psychologists providing health care who transmit information electronically (except for those covered by the Federal Education Rights of Parents Act [FERPA]). The Privacy Rule applies to some employment evaluations, some forensic services, and has some limited applicability to services provided in some correctional facilities.

HIPAA is discussed in more detail in chapter 8 (Confidentiality, Privileged Communications, and Record Keeping).

The HIPAA Privacy Rule requires every covered entity to give every patient a *privacy notice*, which contains information such as the general exceptions to confidentiality, how to file a grievance, and rights to inspect records. It must be shared at the start of treatment, although reasonable delays may be permitted, such as in emergencies (HHS, 2002). Sample privacy notices can be purchased from APA, the American Psychological Association Insurance Trust (www.apait.org), and commercial entities.

Information That Reasonable Patients Want to Know

Several researchers have looked at patient interests in information (Braaten & Handelsman, 1997; Jensen, McNamara, & Gustafson, 1991). Some patients want information on the personal characteristics and competencies of the therapist, logistics (e.g., fees, how appointments are scheduled, payment procedures, emergency contact information), and information about the nature of therapy (e.g., therapy provides a supportive environment, discussing painful topics may make you feel worse at first, therapy helps with problems that you can't work out by yourself, certain techniques are inappropriate in therapy, patients have a right to a second opinion, patients have a right to know the procedure for terminating therapy). These studies also found that patients wanted general information about confidentiality and exceptions, the nature and anticipated course of therapy, therapists' characteristics, logistics (e.g., costs, meeting times, anticipated frequency), and an opportunity to ask questions and receive answers.

WHEN TO INITIATE THE DECISION-MAKING PROCESS

As discussed earlier in this chapter, the participatory model assumes that consent is ongoing throughout treatment. The information provided at the beginning of treatment may be insufficient as treatment progresses, treatment plans change, or new clinical issues may unfold. Ongoing discussions regarding treatment, therefore, may be warranted. This model encourages patient autonomy and recognizes that the nature of therapy and the goals of the patient may evolve over time. Psychologists may implement the process model through a combination of written agreements and discussions in which patients are given the opportunity to ask questions.

Contrasting Informed Consent Styles

A psychologist gave his patients an informed consent form to sign and did nothing to review or discuss it. When he charged one of his patients for a missed appointment, he explained, "It was all explained in the brochure I gave you which you agreed to read." The patient was offended by the bill and dropped out of treatment prematurely.

Another psychologist discussed essential features of informed consent with patients at the first meeting and then handed them a brochure and asked them to read it. In the next session he briefly went over the main features in the brochure and asked them if they had any questions. He seldom had misunderstandings with patients about the issues covered in the brochure.

The second psychologist understood that consent is a process that depends on open communication between psychologists and patients. He wanted patients to understand the issues ahead of time and to feel free to ask questions or express concerns. He did not view informed consent as a legal formality, and he did not want patients to commit prematurely to a process that they did not fully understand.

Written information or consent forms may help if they supplement the dialogue between psychologist and patient. The forms should not be used only to ensure compliance with a legal formality but should help the patient understand the process of therapy. Unfortunately, a review of consent forms used by mental health professionals in Colorado revealed a readability scale at the level of a college senior (Handelsman et al., 1995). This level of difficulty suggests that many patients are unable to benefit from the informed consent form.

Consent forms are more useful when they avoid legalese or intimidating language. Extensive discussions about the law surrounding the limits to confidentiality may have a chilling effect on patients and leave them confused and frustrated. Special emphasis on the exceptions to confidentiality necessitated by a child protective services law, for example, may be appropriate when first meeting with a family that presents with a background of excessive physical discipline. However, for most patients, such detailed information would distract them from their primary goals of therapy, and raise concerns about the judgment or priorities of the psychologist.

In the early 1990s, a number of mental health professionals, former mental health consumers, and relatives of mental health consumers organized a national movement to secure the passage of a "Mental Health Bill of Rights," which among other things, requires extensive informed consent procedures (National Association for Consumer Protection in Mental Health Practices, 1994). Advocates were primarily concerned about treatments that would create false memories of childhood sexual abuse. The informed consent procedure that was endorsed would

> include informing the patient of all known risks and hazards of the therapy, and of alternative treatments and procedures. All informed consent sessions shall be audio and/or video taped, and therapists must maintain such tapes and other therapy records for not less than ten years. (p. 5)

Among other things, the requirement to disclose "all known risks and hazards" is exceedingly burdensome and could require a substantial amount of time that could be better directed at addressing the patient's immediate needs. Furthermore, the requirement to tape the informed consent session represents an "event-oriented" approach to informed consent that is inappropriate for effective psychotherapy services (Hinnefeld & Newman, 1997).

One psychologist had an informed consent form that stated that the patient should not tolerate any sexual advances from him or other therapists. However, such an overinclusive statement inadvertently communicates that the psychologist has poor impulse control, might not be trustworthy, and needs the patient to exert external control (Gordon, 1993).

8

CONFIDENTIALITY, PRIVILEGED COMMUNICATIONS, AND RECORD KEEPING

The terms *confidentiality* and *privileged communications* refer to different, albeit overlapping, concepts. Confidentiality is a more general term, referring to the obligations of psychologists to protect the privacy of patient information. Privileged communications is a more specialized term, referring to the legal right of patients to withhold evidence from courts under certain circumstances.

Confidentiality rules can be found in the state licensing laws of psychologists and in other statutes or regulations. In addition, courts have found psychologists and other health care professionals culpable for malpractice, defamation, or other torts for the unauthorized release of patient information. Breaches of confidentiality have been the basis of complaints before licensing boards, malpractice courts, and the Ethics Committee of the American Psychological Association (APA; APA Ethics Committee, 2004). Furthermore, rules regarding the privacy of persons receiving health care are now included in federal law through the Privacy Rule under the Health Insurance Portability and Accountability Act (HIPAA; U.S. Department of Health and Human Services [HHS], 2002).

Confidentiality rules are based on the moral principles of beneficence, in that psychologists act to promote patient welfare; nonmaleficence, in that psychologists avoid actions that could harm patients; integrity (i.e., fidelity), in that psychologists keep their promises; and respect for patient autonomy, to the extent that patients have control over the release of the information generated from patient services. Confidentiality rules have a utilitarian aspect to them as well. It is assumed that patients will be more open in their communications if they have an assurance of confidentiality.

In this chapter, we review confidentiality (including the HIPAA Privacy Rule), privileged communications, record disposal, patient access to records, and common exceptions to confidentiality. Confidentiality with life-endangering patients is covered in chapter 9 (Life-Endangering Patients).

At first it would appear difficult to strive for moral excellence in the area of confidentiality. It would seem that the rules of confidentiality (e.g., to not release patient records without the consent of the patient unless done under one of the narrow circumstances set by law) are absolute and allow no room for moral excellence. However, it may be instructive to look at the goals that the rules of confidentiality are intended to support. Confidentiality rules function in a manner similar to the rules regarding psychotherapy boundaries; they are established to ensure that patients feel enough safety and trust to share information. When Cullari (2001) surveyed patients on what they expected and wanted most from therapy, two of the highest ratings went to "a feeling of safety and security" and "the chance to talk to someone in a safe environment and without fear of repercussion" (p. 104). The question for the psychologist then becomes, What can I do to facilitate that safe environment?

In part, psychologists can create that safe environment through the quality of the relationship and the sensitivity that they show to the revelations of the patient. Psychologists can earn that trust by being meticulous about keeping patient information confidential. Also, they can earn that trust by taking special care to inform patients of the limits of confidentiality before treatment begins and about the ways that information will be handled in gray areas where therapeutic discretion is required, such as when psychologists are treating families or adolescents.

THE HEALTH INSURANCE PORTABILITY AND ACCOUNTABILITY ACT PRIVACY RULE

As of April 14, 2003, all health care professionals, facilities, and insurers who transmit *protected health information* (PHI) electronically in connection with specified transactions such as submitting claims to third-party payers had to comply with the HIPAA Privacy Rule (HHS, 2002). The Privacy Rule does not apply to educational records, which are covered by the Federal

Education Rights of Parents Act. The rules applying to correctional facilities are complex, but a thumbnail description is that some HIPAA rules apply to services in correctional facilities. Some forensic services may be also covered by HIPAA (see chap. 12, this volume).

In this section we give only a brief overview of the most salient points of the HIPAA Privacy Rule. The Privacy Rule is difficult to understand because the interplay of state and federal laws regarding confidentiality can be complex and because the HHS (i.e., the federal agency responsible for the implementation of HIPAA) has not yet clarified some issues. Readers are urged to keep abreast of changes in the interpretation and applicability of HIPAA and to seek consultation on its more technical issues.

Even those health care psychologists who are not covered by HIPAA may want to consider complying with its standards. First, if a psychologist who is not required to be HIPAA compliant were to start billing electronically, then all of the practice must be in total compliance with HIPAA at that time. Second, over time the standards found in HIPAA may represent the standard of practice throughout the entire health care industry. It is conceivable that courts in the future could hold that psychologists who fail to provide the notices and other requirements of HIPAA are practicing below the minimum standards of their profession.

The HIPAA Privacy Rule mandates that covered entities have to meet certain minimal standards of patient privacy, including (a) giving a privacy notice to all patients, (b) following certain rules on what information can be disclosed to whom, (c) ensuring that certain types of information are included on all patient authorizations (i.e., *release of information forms* are required for certain disclosures), (d) having agreements with business associates to ensure they protect patient privacy, and (e) appointing a privacy officer for every covered practice. Further information and copies of the forms required for HIPAA compliance can be obtained from APA (www.apapractice.org) or from commercial vendors.

The HIPAA Privacy Rule is preempted by state laws when they are more protective of privacy from the standpoint of the patient. For example, HIPAA permits health care personnel to give information to police investigating crimes; but state laws typically permit no such exceptions for psychologists, so these state laws trump HIPAA. Because state laws regarding mental health generally have strong protections for patient privacy, most rules regarding the day-to-day handling of confidential patient information by psychologists have changed very little as a result of the HIPAA Privacy Rule.

Furthermore, the HIPAA Privacy Rule is *scalable*, which means that individuals or organizations may modify the requirements for compliance according to their size. For example, whereas a large hospital may have to develop a detailed and formal complaint process, psychologists in solo practices may use a simple form and meet with their patients themselves if a complaint arises. Whereas a large hospital may have to employ a full-time privacy officer, psychologists in solo practices can serve as their own privacy officers. Whereas a large hospital may need to have a full-time training director for all new employees, psychologists in solo practices may train their own employees.

The Privacy Notice

The privacy notice was discussed briefly in chapter 7 (Informed Consent or Shared Decision Making). Every covered health care provider must give patients a privacy statement that reviews the relevant limitations on privacy, information on disclosures and authorizations (i.e., release of information forms), and the patient's rights to review and copy records. Psychologists may provide the privacy notice at the same time they present an informed consent or service brochure to patients, although the two forms may not be combined. The privacy notice may be, but does not have to be, layered (i.e., have a brief summary on top followed by more detailed information).

Every covered entity must give all patients a privacy notice at their first encounter except in emergencies. Phone contacts to schedule appointments are not considered the first encounter. Providers who fail to get the patient signatures on the notice form are not penalized as long they made "good faith" efforts to do so. Psychologists should document good faith efforts to get the signature. In addition to giving the privacy notice to each patient, psychologists have to post it where patients or future patients can see it. Those health care professionals who have a Web site must have a copy of the privacy notice on that Web site (HHS, 2002).

Only one privacy notice is required for an organized entity delivering service. For example, each provider within the same mental health clinic would not have to give a patient a separate privacy notice.

Psychotherapy Notes

The HIPAA requirements (HHS, 2002) distinguish between *psychotherapy notes* and other PHI. This distinction is relevant for two reasons. First, HIPAA requires that patients have access to their health care information, but not to psychotherapy notes. However, as described in the section on patient access to records later in this chapter, state laws may preempt this and other portions of the HIPAA Privacy Rule if they are more protective of patient privacy from the standpoint of the patient or provide patients with greater access to records. Second, third-party payers may not condition payment on the basis of the receipt of psychotherapy notes.

Psychotherapy notes are defined as

notes recorded (in any medium) by a health care provider who is a mental health professional documenting or analyzing the contents of conversation during a private counseling session or a group, joint or family counseling session and that are separated from the rest of the individual's medical record. (HHS, 2002, 45 C.F.R. 164.501)

The definition of psychotherapy notes in the Privacy Rule specifically excludes

medication prescription and monitoring, counseling session start and stop times, the modalities and frequencies of treatment furnished, results of clinical tests, and any summary of the following items: Diagnosis, functional status, the treatment plan, symptoms, prognosis, and progress to date. (HHS, 2002, 45 C.F.R. 164.501)

Accounting of Disclosures of Protected Health Information

Finally, HIPAA requires psychologists to keep an accounting of releases of PHI, except when a patient has already signed an authorization or when information is given to business associates, oversight agencies, or for national security purposes. In reality, psychologists almost never disclose information without their patient's consent, so that accounting is rarely required.

CONFIDENTIALITY

Effective treatment requires an atmosphere of trust and openness. To a large extent, that trust is generated by an interpersonal style that is welcoming and reassuring. All of these efforts to engender trust can be shattered, however, if psychologists do not ensure the privacy of patient information. Prudent psychologists review their office procedures, their actions, and the actions of their staff members to ensure that confidentiality leaks do not occur.

Psychologists are responsible for training members of their office staff and professional supervisees in the rules of confidentiality. Most staff members accept their responsibilities conscientiously. They refrain from talking about patients in public places, protect patient charts, and take other steps to protect patient confidentiality. However, the most effective way to prevent breaches of confidentiality is to ensure a "culture of safety" in which confidentiality is viewed as everyone's responsibility. Secretaries should feel free to tell professional staff members when they see threats to patient confidentiality. The information should not flow on a one-way street.

For example, psychologists need to ensure that voices (or messages from the answering machine) do not carry from a treatment room into the reception area or waiting room. Clerical staff members can be crucial in informing psychologists about the effectiveness of soundproofing, carpeting, or music in reducing sound overflow.

An Effective Sound Control System

The clerical staff at a middle-size professional practice commonly kept the radio in the waiting room playing so that it would reduce the likelihood of their voices being heard while they phoned patients or insurance companies. Occasionally a patient would turn off the radio, thus subverting this measure. The clerical staff placed a sign on the radio that read "please do not turn off."

Other breaches of confidentiality occur as well. Consider the following example:

A Hurried Psychologist

A psychologist, who was in a rush, picked up the chart of the patient who was to see him for the first time that day. He looked at the name on the chart and said, "Well Mr. Hegel, how are you today." However, the psychologist had picked up the wrong chart and the name of the patient was Leibniz.

How could this have been avoided? Could the secretary have been more careful about the charts? Should the psychologist have been more alert to the possibility of errors when in a hurry? Careful psychologists try to determine how these slips can be avoided.

Special confidentiality issues may occur when psychologists locate their offices in their homes, where family members may inadvertently acquire identifying information on patients (Woody, 1997b, 1999). Family members may see patients entering the office portion of the house or see return addresses on mail addressed to the office. Cases have even occurred in which patients have wandered into the residential portion of the house or unruly children have intruded on therapy sessions. Psychologists who have offices in their homes need to take special measures to ensure that their families understand the importance of confidentiality.

Exceptions to Confidentiality

Except in emergencies or in response to a court order, psychologists should require a signed release (i.e., consent or authorization) from their patients before disclosing or sending out information. State and federal laws may specify the required contents of the form. Standard 4.06, Consultations, permits professional consultations as long as psychologists do not disclose identifying information and disclose only the information needed to achieve the purpose of the consultation.

At the beginning of psychotherapy, psychologists should inform their patients of the relevant exceptions to confidentiality (see especially chaps. 9, Life-Endangering Patients, and 10, Business Issues, this volume). In addition, family and group therapy and the treatment of adolescents or adults with serious and persistent mental illnesses have unique aspects.

Confidentiality in Family Therapy

The Ethics Code (APA, 2002a) requires psychologists to explain the rules of confidentiality at the outset of therapy (see Standards 4.02, Discussing the Limits of Confidentiality; 10.01, Informed Consent to Therapy; 10.02, Therapy Involving Couples or Families; and 10.03, Group Therapy). Before starting family therapy, psychologists should inform patients how they will handle information obtained through private conversations with individual family members.

Some of the information obtained from private conversations deals with other family members; other information deals only with the individual. A patient who speaks to her family therapist alone and says her spouse is having an affair is sharing information directly relevant to the family's functioning. A patient who speaks to her family therapist alone and says that she is having conflict with a coworker is sharing information that is less directly related (or perhaps irrelevant) to the family's functioning. Sometimes family members reveal information privately because they fear engendering anger or embarrassment with other family members but believe that the psychologist needs to know this information. At other times they want to develop a special alliance with the psychologist to increase their influence within therapy. Psychologists disagree on how to handle these kinds of situations. Some receive and use information from private conversations; others do not. The APA Ethics Code only requires psychologists to clarify their policy at the outset of therapy (Knapp & VandeCreek, 2003b).

Confidentiality in Group Psychotherapy

Psychologists have more difficulty protecting patient privacy in group therapy than individual therapy because a larger number of persons have access to the information shared in therapy. Nonetheless, psychologists can take precautions to reduce breaches. Corey, Williams, and Moline (1995) recommended addressing confidentiality through an open discussion with the group to help members become aware of the importance of protecting the confidentiality of others. Psychologists can inform patients at the outset of therapy of the need to respect the privacy of other patients and can promote a sense of responsibility by urging group members to see themselves as cotherapists to the other group members. They can also ask patients to sign statements promising that they will respect the privacy of the other members of the group, and they can make further participation in the group contingent on maintaining the confidentiality of the other group members.

Confidentiality With Adolescents

The general rule is that parents control the ability of their children to seek health care treatment. However, many states make exceptions and allow some children to seek psychotherapy without parental consent, depending on their age or other circumstances. For example, some states permit mental health professionals to treat a minor for a specified number of sessions or in an emergency without the knowledge of the parents.

Although it may not necessarily be stated explicitly in any state statute or regulation, the ability to authorize or consent to treatment implies the ability to control the release of information generated from that treatment. Consequently, if parental consent is needed to obtain treatment, it usually follows that the parents have a right to obtain the information generated from such treatment. However, a policy of sharing all information with the parents may dissuade the child from being candid in psychotherapy.

The best way for psychologists to handle the issue of confidentiality with adolescents is to discuss it openly with all parties at the start of psychotherapy (Koocher, 2003). In those states in which adolescents cannot legally control their confidentiality, psychologists can often establish private agreements wherein parents agree to withhold their requests for information to allow the adolescent a greater sense of privacy and thus encourage a stronger therapeutic alliance. Psychologists who discuss this issue with parents need to clarify that the adolescent may disclose sensitive information, such as the use of drugs or sexual activity. Most psychologists make an exception to confidentiality when the life or safety of the adolescent or a third party is imminently endangered and disclosure is necessary to protect a life (Knapp & VandeCreek, 2003b). Often psychologists add other narrow exceptions to confidentiality, such as information as to whether the child is using the time productively or whether the child has a problem that exceeds the competence of the psychologist.

Nonetheless, when parental consent to treatment is legally required, the parents have traditionally been able to insist on obtaining the information generated within therapy. However, the HIPAA Privacy Rule elevates the status of private agreements between parents, children, and psychotherapists. If the parents have signed a written agreement of confidentiality, it can be legally binding, and the parents might not have access to the confidential information about their children covered in the confidentiality agreement.

The determination of what threatens life or safety requires discretion on the part of the psychologist. Behaviors such as smoking cigarettes and sexual contact present varying degrees of danger. Many psychologists establish the standard to include imminent danger to self or others, to avoid the situation in which the parents expect a report on a wide range of activities in which the danger to self or others is remote. Nonetheless, psychologists may have to reflect or consult when the degree of danger is not clear.

For example, a 16-year-old in treatment revealed that she was having sexual relationships with a number of young men. They often, but not always, used condoms. The psychologist asked himself if the danger created from these unprotected sexual relationships rose to the level of danger to self that would require notification of the parents. Another psychologist treated a 15-year-old who drank alcohol to the point of passing out. Another treated a 17-year-old who often rode in cars with drunken drivers. Another psychologist treated a 14-year-old who associated with a gang known for their delinquent behavior and aggression.

No simple answer can be given to the psychologists in these cases. The response should depend on a comprehensive assessment that considers weighing the nature and frequency, intensity, and duration of the high-risk behavior, the likelihood that therapy will be successful in changing behavior (and reducing the threat of harm to the adolescent), and the harm to the relationship if parents are told without the consent of the child.

Psychologists often can be most effective when they refuse to dichotomize their options (e.g., either I tell the parents or I do not tell them). The process of discussing danger with the adolescent may reveal information about the family dynamics, or the concerns of the adolescent that will facilitate considerable growth and communication within the family. One conscientious psychologist said he almost never had to reveal dangerous behavior to a parent without the consent of the adolescent.

According to principle-based ethics (see chap. 2, this volume), psychologists generally adhere to moral principles, such as fidelity (i.e., keeping promises of confidentiality), respect for patient autonomy, and beneficence (i.e., working to protect the welfare of patients). However, when moral principles collide it may be necessary to override one moral principle. When the decision is made to override a moral principle, then efforts should be made to minimize the harm to the offended moral principle. Consequently, when psychologists decide to trump the autonomy of the child patient, they should nonetheless take reasonable steps to minimize harm to the offended moral principle. For example, they may allow the patient some control over the manner in which the disclosure to the parents is made.

Other confidentiality concerns may arise when treating children. Release of information forms must be signed by the person who is legally allowed to consent to treatment. Even when parents control the course of therapy, it sometimes may be clinically indicated to ask a mature minor to sign a release of information form also, although it would be legally meaningless.

The treatment of adolescents, like younger children, often requires coordination of services with schools, probation departments, or other agencies. Consequently, information may need to be released to a wider number of parties than would typically occur in the treatment of adults. Even if consent is not legally required from adolescents, it is often therapeutically wise to review with the adolescent the nature of the information that is to be shared.

A Psychologist With Foresight

A psychologist needed to send information to the probation officer of an adolescent patient. Although the patient was doing well, the psychologist was aware of the sensitivity of the issues that were being discussed. Consequently, the psychologist shared a near final draft of his letter to the probation officer with the adolescent patient. This action helped to ensure the trust of the patient and the accuracy of the information sent out.

Confidentiality With Adults With Serious and Persistent Mental Illnesses

Patients with serious and persistent mental illnesses present unique ethical challenges for psychologists. Although the patients may be adults, they often depend on their parents or other relatives for caretaker services. The effective treatment of these patients usually requires contact with a treating psychopharmacologist and the family members who are in a caretaker role.

The rules of confidentiality apply to these adults as they do to other patients, and it is advisable to get permission from the patients before talking to involved family members. Very often these family members already have been involved in therapy and would be a regular part of a psychotherapist–family dialogue anyway.

PRIVILEGED COMMUNICATIONS

Privileged communication is a legal term that allows patients to prevent information from being introduced into courtroom proceedings under certain circumstances. Although some privileges were developed through *common law* (i.e., the judge-made legal tradition that is part of our Anglo American legal heritage), most privileged communication laws are now based on state statutes (i.e., laws passed by state legislatures) or the federal privileged communication statute (passed by Congress). Privileged communication statutes run counter to the common-law tradition that courts need to have access to all relevant information to help them make accurate decisions. Consequently, most courts interpret privileged communication laws strictly because they are reluctant to exclude evidence relevant to the issues before them (Knapp & VandeCreek, 1987).

Most legal scholars justify privileged communication laws on utilitarian grounds. They may argue, for example, that in the long run society benefits when privacy is ensured in the psychologist–patient relationship because marriages are more likely to be saved, suicides are more likely to be prevented, and mental illnesses are more likely to be treated successfully. Although some information is lost to the courts when privilege laws are present, that loss is counterbalanced by the overall benefit to society (Knapp & VandeCreek, 1987).

All states have privileged communication statutes for attorney–client, husband–wife, clergy–communicant, and psychologist–patient relationships. Most states have a social worker–client privilege, and some states have privileged communication laws for family, sexual abuse, domestic abuse, and mental health counselors as well. Many states have physician–patient privileges, although these are often limited in scope.

Most of the legal cases in which psychologists become involved occur in state courts, in which the admission of evidence, including the rules for privileged communication, is governed by state law. Federal courts also are required to accept a psychologist–patient privilege (*Jaffee v. Redmond*, 1996).

Privileged communication statutes only apply to information acquired within a professional relationship. Casual conversations between acquaintances, business contacts, or friends are not privileged. The patient, not the psychologist, owns the privilege. That is, the patient or the patient's legal representative decides when to invoke or waive the privilege. Psychologists do not have the legal standing to invoke or waive the privilege against the wishes of their patients.

Patients or their representatives may waive their privilege whenever they choose. In addition, patients automatically waive the privilege if they enter their mental health as an issue in court, such as through a psychological malpractice claim, a personal injury case with claims for emotional damage, or an insanity plea. The privilege does not apply to court-ordered examinations (Knapp & VandeCreek, 1987).

Once the privilege is waived, it is waived completely. In malpractice suits against psychologists, for example, patients may not enter selected facts about their mental health that would help their cases but then try to withhold other facts that would hurt their cases. The privilege cannot be used as both a shield and a sword.

Subpoenas

A subpoena is a request for documents usually filled out and served by the attorney seeking the information. Sometimes attorneys use a record-copying service to secure those documents. Often subpoenas are expected. Psychologists may know that their patients are in litigation and have talked about the case (and their potential testimony) ahead of time. At other times, the subpoenas are unexpected. They may come from an attorney representing a party with interests adversarial to those of the patient. Or, the patient may have left therapy several years ago and the psychologist has no information about the lawsuit.

When a psychologist receives a subpoena, he or she needs to talk to the patient and the patient's attorney to learn how to proceed. If the patient wants to enter his or her records into court, then the psychologist needs to obtain a release from the patient before sending the records. Before obtaining that release, however, the psychologist needs to be frank about the general contents of the records or what he or she would say if called into court. It is better for the patient and the patient's attorney to know this information before the records are sent out. Perhaps the patient and the patient's attorney will determine that the information is harmful to the case and will withdraw the request for information, or they will modify their complaint so that the patient's mental health is no longer an issue entered into litigation.

A Stressful Encounter

A psychologist received a subpoena from an unknown attorney about a patient she had seen several years earlier. The psychologist called the attorney to say that she did not have an authorization from the patient and could not release the information. The attorney angrily responded that the subpoena was valid, the psychologist had an obligation to send the information, and that failure to do so could result in contempt of court charges.

Situations like this are not uncommon. However, the attorney was giving the psychologist inaccurate information. A subpoena from an attorney does not override the statutory rights of the patient to confidentiality. In these situations, psychologists may feel at a distinct disadvantage because they do not have the legal expertise of attorneys and may feel intimidated by the confrontational style of attorneys. Nonetheless, psychologists have the responsibility to understand their legal obligations. If the psychologist sent the records in response to the subpoenas without permission from the patient, the psychologist would have committed an ethical violation. In this case, the only obligation of the psychologist was to acknowledge the receipt of the subpoena and the reason for noncompliance.

At times, the records of the psychologist contain information that is potentially embarrassing to the patient or is irrelevant to the case before the court. In those situations, the patient's attorney can ask the judge to review the records *in camera* (i.e., in the judge's chamber, outside the view of the parties) and remove portions of the records that are not directly related to the question before the court. However, there is no guarantee that the judge will agree to that arrangement.

Court Orders

A court order differs from a subpoena in that it is signed by a judge. Psychologists must comply with a court order and turn over information or testify, depending on the request. However, if the psychologist believes that the court order violates a privileged communication law, then the psychologist may ask the judge to reconsider the order.

A Cautious Psychologist

A court ordered a psychologist to present information on his therapy sessions with a child under the protection of children and youth services. The psychologist wrote a polite letter to the judge noting that he would comply with the order of the court if necessary but asked the judge to reconsider the court order. He briefly gave reasons why the disclosure of this information would not be in the best interests of the child. The judge rescinded the court order because she believed that she could get the essential information from other sources.

Information on protecting copyrighted test information in response to a court order can be found in chapter 12 (Assessment).

RECORD KEEPING

The records of psychologists serve several purposes. They remind psychologists of what has happened in the past. Often the very process of writing notes helps psychologists to clarify their perceptions of a case. Records also justify the medical necessity of treatment to third-party payers (although the HIPAA Privacy Rule has placed substantial limits on the access of health insurers to psychotherapy notes). Furthermore, records provide useful information about treatment if the patient transfers to another health professional, are a source of data for archival research, and can protect the psychologist in the event of a charge of negligence. A common axiom in risk management is that if it is not written down, it did not occur. Courts tend to give great deference to psychotherapy records and will assume that whatever is recorded in them is accurate.

Patient Access to Records

Patient access to records is controlled by both the HIPAA Privacy Rule and state law. According to the Privacy Rule, patients generally have a right to access all of the information in their records except for psychotherapy notes (see definition on pp. 114–115). However, state laws that give the patient greater access to his or her records may preempt the Privacy Rule. Many states require psychologists to give patients access to their records, although some statutes make exceptions if the disclosure would harm the patient. Consequently, the state laws that require access to psychotherapy notes trump the Privacy Rule, although the psychologist may be able to withhold the notes if the state standard for "patient harm" is met.

Patients' requests to view their records often represent hidden clinical questions and concerns. The patient may wonder, What is wrong with me?

or What does my therapist think of me? For this reason, many information requests can be reframed to explore the motivation for the record request. If the records are written precisely and sensitively, it will usually be clinically acceptable or even desirable to show the patient the records. It may be an opportunity for the psychologist to engage patients more fully in the treatment process and focus patients on their treatment procedures and goals.

A Useful Decision

A patient requested that she receive a copy of her psychotherapy notes. The psychologist agreed to give her a copy of the notes but first read the note from the last session aloud to her, so she could get a general sense of what is typically contained in psychotherapy notes. They then engaged in a productive discussion of why the patient wanted to see the notes.

Under some circumstances, however, it may be contraindicated for patients to see their records. If these patients insist on seeing the records, then the psychologist may attempt to balance respect for patient autonomy with beneficence. For example, if the patient agrees, the psychologist may honor the request for information (without showing the patient harmful information) by writing a summary of the records, using lay terms. Usually, but not always, this will satisfy the patient.

If the decision is made to show the records to a patient, then it is desirable that the patient review the records with the psychologist present. Patients may misconstrue the technical terms found in the records unless the treating psychologist is there in person to interpret or translate the records.

Record Retention and Disposal

State licensure boards or state laws usually determine the length of time to keep records. After that time has expired, psychologists may legally destroy their records. However, psychologists may want to keep some records longer. Older records may be needed if the psychologist is the target of a malpractice suit or a complaint before a licensing board. Although the statute of limitations on a malpractice suit varies from state to state, it is typically 2 years or 2 years after the patient turns 18 years of age. Furthermore, some patients may have legitimate needs for old records. For example, a patient with a serious developmental disability may need old records to demonstrate the lifelong history of that disability.

Psychologists should take reasonable measures to protect their records in anticipation of retirement, disability, or death. Ideally, the retired psychologist stays in the same community and handles requests for records as they arise. In the event of death, the records can be given to a colleague who can handle those requests. Unfortunately, situations have occurred in which grieving spouses either have given out records without verifying the identity of the individual asking for the transfer or have refused to give out records even when the patient had signed a valid authorization.

For records that cannot be destroyed, the psychologist or the psychologist's executor can write a letter to the last known address of patients, informing them that the psychologist is retiring or has died and that they may request that the records be sent to another health care provider of their choice or that the records will be destroyed after a specified period of time, consistent with state law.

One of the best ways to manage the disposal of records upon the death or disability of a psychologist is for the psychologist to have specified in a will or other legal document what is to be done with records. This document can specify where records are kept, how long they should be kept, and who should maintain custody of them (S. Ragusea, 2002).

Content of Psychotherapy Records

Many state licensing laws and regulations establish minimum record-keeping standards, although they typically leave much discretion to the treating psychologist. In the absence of regulations from the state licensing board, the APA "Record-Keeping Guidelines" (APA, 1993b) should be followed. These standards provide the ethical floor for psychologists but give little direction on the content of the records.

A Challenging Patient

A patient agreed to enter therapy only if the psychologist agreed to take no notes. The patient explained that he was involved in litigation and was afraid that something he said eventually could be used against him. The psychologist refused and explained the legal requirements and benefits of keeping notes. The patient then asked the psychologist to promise that the notes would never be released. Again, the psychologist refused, noting the exceptions to confidentiality, which are rare but nonetheless do exist.

The psychologist acted appropriately in refusing not to take notes. In addition to being a legal requirement, properly kept notes promote the quality of care and protect the psychologist. The psychologist also acted appropriately in refusing to give a blanket guarantee of confidentiality. Although confidentiality protections are strong, they are not absolute, and the psychologist could not promise what kinds of situations (e.g., child abuse or duty to warn or protect) might occur in the future that could create an exception to confidentiality.

To a large extent the content of the psychotherapy records is determined by the theoretical orientation of the psychologist. Nonetheless, we suggest that good records are comprehensive, objective, consistent, retrievable, and kept in secure locations. Comprehensive records include the minimum required by APA record-keeping guidelines and state laws, such as the name of the patient; fee arrangements; dates and substance of each service event, including test results; results of formal consultations; correspondence; release of information (i.e., authorization) forms; copies of reports; notations of phone calls and other therapeutic contacts; and any documentation required by the HIPAA Privacy Rule (if applicable). Psychologists are advised to attempt to secure previous treatment records of patients. Good records include the patient's diagnosis (or presenting problem), the treatment plan, and how those determinations were made. Generally, psychologists who read past records better understand the nature of the presenting problem and prior treatment.

Comprehensive records also record the significant events in treatment. For example, it is important to document high-risk situations carefully, such as when the psychologist suspects child abuse, a patient threatens violence toward others, or serious boundary problems emerge during treatment. Prudent psychologists establish a standard procedure for assessing the clinical situation with life-endangering patients. When a patient threatens a third party, for example, it is desirable to record the assessment of the likelihood of the threat and to include reasons why the threat should or should not be considered imminent. More information on this topic can be found in chapter 9 (Life-Endangering Patients).

Good Intentions: Bad Outcomes

A psychologist acted on the presumption that the less written about a patient the better. She mistakenly believed that detailed records would compromise her patients' confidentiality and could be used against her in the event of a charge of negligence. Consequently, she kept skimpy records that primarily repeated a set of 10 or 15 stock phrases such as *patient feels better* and *talked about patient's concerns*.

This psychologist misunderstood the purpose of psychotherapy records. On the whole, the more details, the better, as long as these details promote the care of the patient and risk management system of the psychologist (Woody, 1997b).

Conscientious psychologists strive for objectivity in their records, although the psychotherapeutic process is in and of itself subjective. Psychologists should show sensitivity in what they place in patient records, exclude any gratuitous remarks, and use behavioral descriptions whenever possible. Although the records belong to the psychologists, patients may have a right to see them under the laws of some states. Consequently, psychologists should create records with the expectation that the patient will see them someday. Pejorative remarks, if seen by the patient, could provoke anger or a perception of the psychologist as uncaring or insensitive.

Good records should be internally consistent. The records should chronicle that the treatment plan is being implemented as intended. Of course, psychologists can change their treatment plan or diagnosis. However, this should be documented. Psychologists may comment on previous notes and include clarifications, but under no circumstances should they alter or destroy a previous note.

Finally, records should be retrievable, which means readable (at least to the writer). Although it is not unethical to be inefficient, a good filing system saves time. This means more than just placing charts in alphabetical order; it also means having a specific location in every chart (or a specific paper color) in the chart for intake forms, release of information forms (authorizations), psychotherapy notes, and other information.

Obtaining Past Records

Reviewing past records is often necessary to develop an accurate treatment plan. Psychologists should routinely ask patients to sign release forms and obtain past treatment records. However, some patients will present seemingly good reasons for refusing to allow the release of past records, such as past abuse on the part of the previous psychotherapist. At times, these reports by the patient may be accurate, but they also may represent falsehoods designed to hide an accurate report of the patient's past manipulative behaviors. Reports by patients of past misconduct by previous psychotherapists should not be a barrier to attempting to retrieve the records. Even if the patient's report of abuse is accurate, the records of previous psychotherapists may still contain some useful clinical information.

USE OF INFORMATION FOR DIDACTIC PURPOSES

Standard 4.07, Use of Confidential Information for Didactic or Other Purposes, permits psychologists to use information about patients for didactic purposes (e.g., professional writings or teaching) if the consent of the patient is obtained or if the identifiable information is removed. Although the letter of the APA Ethics Code can be met if the identity of the patient is disguised, psychologists need to be sensitive to the potential impact of the writing on the patient who may, for example, believe that his or her identity was not sufficiently disguised. It may be relatively easy to disguise very short vignettes, but it becomes harder to disguise detailed case studies. For that reason, some writers have created composite vignettes based on the experiences of many individuals. Also, patients may feel hurt or offended by the description contained in the writing.

A psychiatrist described his experience of writing about a patient with Asperger's syndrome (Brendel, 2003), although he had exaggerated the Asperger's qualities to emphasize certain features unique to that syndrome. The minimal ethical imperatives had been met (i.e., the patient gave consent and the identity of the patient was adequately disguised), but when the patient read the article written about him, he "reacted with horror and dismay" at the descriptions given of him (Carter, 2003, p. 97). Much to his credit, the psychiatrist worked closely with the patient to ameliorate the damage and the anger. He also used his experiences to write about what he had learned (Brendel, 2003) and the patient, writing under a pseudonym, also wrote about the experience from his standpoint (Carter, 2003).

9

LIFE-ENDANGERING PATIENTS

Virtually every professional psychologist encounters patients who threaten, attempt, or actually complete suicide. Psychologists also may encounter patients who threaten or actually harm identifiable third parties. Often patients harm their spouses or children. Some threaten the psychologists themselves. Pope and Tabachnick (1993) found that 97% of psychologists had, at least once in their career, feared that a patient would harm himself or herself or another person. Knapp and Keller (2004) found that in a 1-year period, 18% of the psychologists had a patient who assaulted a third party and 14% had a patient who committed suicide. These can be some of the most upsetting events in the careers of psychologists.

The moral principle of beneficence compels psychologists to act to protect patients who threaten themselves or identifiable third parties, under the assumption that assaulting others results in harm to the perpetrator as well as the victim. In addition, the moral principle of general beneficence compels psychologists to act to protect third parties from patients who threaten them. Because of the high stakes involved, these principles of beneficence and general beneficence may temporarily trump respect for patient autonomy.

Risk management principles become especially important when dealing with life-endangering patients. Patient suicides or the deaths by patient assaults are rare but high-impact events. Malpractice suits are often precipitated by the death of a patient or a third party. Consequently, it is highly recommended that psychologists pay close attention to virtue-based risk management principles. That is, they need to be competent (i.e., know how to treat patients with life-endangering features and how to document their interventions clearly), sensitive to the welfare of both the patient and the third party, knowledgeable (of the relevant laws in their state), and emotionally balanced (to avoid impulsive decisions). The last factor needs a special comment. Sometimes, to reduce the substantial distress experienced by dealing with dangerous patients, psychologists may temporarily reduce their anxiety by impulsively settling on the first "just-good-enough" solution that occurs to them. However, a just-good-enough solution may allow too much room for error in a life-endangering situation.

Self-care principles should not be ignored when dealing with life-endangering patients either. The death of a patient or a third party can create such turmoil in a psychologist that it can lead to anxiety, depression, or generally diminished professional effectiveness.

The Ethics Code (American Psychological Association [APA], 2002a) says little about life-endangering patients, except that it permits exceptions to confidentiality if necessary to protect others. Most of the guidance in this area comes from state statutes or malpractice court decisions. For example, whereas many states have statutes or precedent-setting court cases that require psychologists to warn or take protective action when a patient presents an imminent danger to harm an identifiable third party, a few states have statutes that expressly prohibit psychologists from warning others. Courts have established the criteria to be used when evaluating psychologists who were negligent in treating patients who later killed themselves. All states have statutes that require psychologists to report suspected child abuse. Many states have statutes that require or permit psychologists to report the abuse of older adults. A few states require psychologists to report impaired drivers. The Health Insurance Portability and Accountability Act (U.S. Department of Health and Human Services, 2002) privacy rule does not interfere with state laws that permit or require breaches of confidentiality to prevent harm to others.

We review the responsibilities of psychologists when dealing with patients who threaten third parties, are suicidal, and in other ways pose a threat to others. For each of these areas, we describe the applicable standards and recommend courses of action for psychologists. We use the five-step model for determining the optimal response (see chap. 4, this volume).

HARM TO OTHERS

The review of the ethical responsibilities of psychologists dealing with life-endangering patients begins with the 1976 *Tarasoff* ruling by the California Supreme Court (*Tarasoff v. Regents of the University of California et al.*, 1976). Subsequent court decisions have similarly considered the legal responsibilities of psychotherapists when their patients present an imminent danger to inflict serious physical harm on identifiable others. In an effort to clarify responsibilities of psychotherapists, numerous state legislatures have passed *duty-to-warn-or-protect* statutes that instruct psychotherapists what they must, must not, or may do when treating dangerous patients.

The Facts of the Tarasoff Case

More details on this tragic event can be found by reading the actual civil case or an account by Blum (1986), which includes some fictionalized dialogue but is otherwise accurate. Only the essential facts are presented here. Prosenjit Poddar, an exchange student from India, was attending the University of California at Berkeley when he met and fell in love with Tatiana Tarasoff. When she did not return his affections, Mr. Poddar deteriorated mentally. A friend strongly encouraged Mr. Poddar to seek treatment and even accompanied him to his first psychotherapy appointment with Dr. Lawrence Moore at the university counseling service. During a session in August 1969, Mr. Poddar confided to Dr. Moore his intent to kill Ms. Tarasoff when she returned from Brazil. The psychologist took the threats seriously and asked the campus police to involuntarily commit Mr. Poddar.

The campus police interviewed Mr. Poddar but did not commit him because he appeared rational and promised to avoid Ms. Tarasoff. Mr. Poddar discontinued therapy after the failed commitment attempt. Subsequently, Dr. Moore's supervising psychiatrist ordered him to destroy his psychotherapy notes and instructed him to make no further attempts to commit Mr. Poddar. That fall Ms. Tarasoff returned from Brazil unaware of the danger to her. On October 27, 1969, Mr. Poddar went to Ms. Tarasoff's house, shot and stabbed her repeatedly, and killed her.

The Tarasoff Decision

Ms. Tarasoff's parents initiated a wrongful-death suit against the Regents of the University of California, the treating psychologist, the supervising psychiatrists, and the police officers who were involved in the abortive commitment attempt. The defendants were not liable for the failure to commit Mr. Poddar. The court noted the California statute that exempts public employees from liabilities for injuries resulting from decisions to release mental patients. The defendants, however, were liable for their failure to warn Ms. Tarasoff of the danger to her.

Although the court noted that determining dangerousness is difficult and confidentiality needs to be given a very high priority, it held that the difficulty in predicting dangerousness does not remove the obligation to protect others when such a prediction is made. The court clarified that psychotherapists are not required to issue a warning every time a patient reveals an urge or fantasy to harm someone. Instead, the psychotherapist needs to establish the degree of dangerousness, using the standards of the profession to do so. In order for the duty to protect or warn to arise, the victim needs to be identifiable and the threatened harm needs to be substantial and imminent.

Although it has sometimes been phrased in terms of a "new" legal duty, the *Tarasoff* case actually applied old legal principles regarding tort liability and negligence to a new context. According to traditional Anglo American law, no person is required to assist another. There are exceptions for *public callings*, such as innkeepers, who have an affirmative duty to protect their guests, or public carriers, who have a duty to protect their passengers. The rule was later expanded to include other situations in which a "special relationship" exists.

The concept of special relationship also has been applied to psychiatric hospitals, which have a duty to use reasonable care to prevent the escape of dangerous patients. In addition, physicians are liable to third parties if they negligently fail to diagnose contagious diseases or if they diagnose the disease but negligently fail to warn foreseeable recipients of the infection. According to the *Tarasoff* case, the psychologist had a special relationship with Mr. Poddar, which created the obligation to act to protect an identifiable victim.

Legal and Ethical Requirements

The legal requirements under the *Tarasoff* case appear consistent with conclusions that could be reached through principle-based ethical decision making. Professional psychologists generally respect patient autonomy and acknowledge patient control over the direction and major events of psychotherapy. However, under rare circumstances, such as when a patient presents an imminent danger to harm others, psychologists may have to consider whether to temporarily invoke the principle of general beneficence (and, e.g., break confidentiality and notify an intended victim) to override the principle of respect for patient autonomy.

Using the process of balancing ethical principles described in chapter 2 (Foundations of Ethical Behavior), psychologists can ask themselves several questions before deciding to override a prima facie ethical principle. Applying those questions to a homicidal patient, psychologists would ask themselves, Is protecting the life of a third party more important than ensuring a patient's autonomy? Will breaking confidentiality have a realistic chance of protecting the life of the third party? Is there any other alternative to breaking confidentiality? Can I infringe on confidentiality as little as possible to ensure the safety of the patient? and Can I minimize the harm caused by the breach of confidentiality?

The psychologist can minimize the infringement of autonomy and maximize the involvement of patients when selecting interventions designed to reduce the likelihood of harm to others (VandeCreek & Knapp, 2001). For example, if the desired intervention requires notifying the intended victim, then the psychologist can ask the patient, How should we go about ensuring that you will not harm this intended victim? Would it be helpful if I cautioned him or her to stay away from you? and Do you want to be present when I share the information? When speaking to the intended victim directly, the psychologist should give only the minimal amount of information necessary to achieve the goal.

However, the desired intervention may include options other than breaching confidentiality. Depending on the circumstances, interventions could include a voluntary hospitalization, an increase in the frequency or duration of outpatient appointments, or the involvement of a family member who might be able to diffuse the situation. Of course, there may be individual cases in which the manner of proceeding is not clear. It is easy to imagine situations in which the clinical realities do not fit nicely with the general rules delineated in this section. The following section contains clinical recommendations that could help psychologists with practical issues that arise from the duty to warn or protect. Also, state law may require certain actions (e.g., warning an intended victim) to ensure immunity from tort liability. Such laws place a burden on psychologists to justify why they took an action that was not specifically identified in state law.

The Five-Step Model Applied to Aggressive Patients

The five-step model described in chapter 4 (Ethical Decision Making) can be helpful when determining the optimal response to aggressive patients. The five steps are (a) to identify or scrutinize the problem, (b) to develop alternatives or hypothesize solutions, (c) to evaluate or analyze options (i.e., to select the solution that incorporates the most advantages and the fewest disadvantages of the solutions generated in the second step), (d) to act or perform, and (e) to look back or evaluate the effectiveness of the solution. We later apply the same five-step model to other dangerous situations.

Identify or Scrutinize the Problem

In duty-to-warn-or-protect situations, the basic ethical conflict is between general beneficence and beneficence with respect for patient autonomy. That is, the psychologist has an obligation to protect the public (and the welfare of patients who are likely to engage in a self-defeating act) and to respect the autonomy of patients to make their own decisions.

From a practical standpoint, the clarification of the first step hinges on the determination of dangerousness by the psychologist. The assessment of dangerousness is an ongoing process, not a one-time event. From the first session that the patient gives indications of an intent to harm another person until the last session of therapy, psychologists should inquire about and keep alert for signs that violence may occur. Typically, the threat is against a specific person, usually a family member, former lover, or other acquaintance.

Although no formula can predict dangerousness with great accuracy, clinical information can guide psychologists in their decision making. For example, Swanson et al. (2002) found that past exposure to violence, violence in the surrounding environment, and substance abuse showed a cumulative association with violent behavior among persons with serious mental illness. When all three risk factors were present, the risk of violent behavior increased to 30%. When none of the three risk factors was present, the risk of violent behavior was less than .05%. One limitation of the study was that it focused on violence in general, not violence against any specific individual.

Various dangerousness prediction scales may have some utility, especially if combined with a detailed history and clinical interview. These scales typically rely on static (e.g., sex of patient, early childhood history) and dynamic (e.g., current psychopathology, violent fantasies) items. However, their application to populations other than those on whom they were standardized is uncertain. For example, the McArthur Violence Risk Assessment Scale, which was developed from a prospective study of violent behavior in persons discharged from psychiatric hospitals, may not generalize to other populations (Monahan et al., 2000). However, research on other dangerousness scales may be of value (see also the review by Borum, 2000).

Although the duty to warn or protect usually conjures up images of a patient threatening a nonfamily person, in reality most of the violent patients encountered by psychologists threaten current or former lovers or other family members. In that sense, the *Tarasoff* case is a good exemplar because it dealt with violence that occurred as a consequence of a failed romance. Partner abuse has a 1-year prevalence estimated between 9% and 17% (Riggs, Caulfied, & Street, 2000). In addition, abuse occurs in dating relationships and among homosexual couples. Consequently, psychologists should be alert to the presence of domestic abuse and routinely include questions of partner abuse in every intake interview.

In most domestic abuse situations that psychologists encounter, the spouse has already been assaulted or threatened directly. However, that spouse may not be aware of the severity of the danger and that women who leave their abusive partners are at an increased risk of being harmed (Riggs et al., 2000). Consequently, a psychologist may need to warn the intended victim of the increase in danger even if the victim has already been threatened directly. For example, in *Emerich v. Philadelphia Center for Human Development* (1998), a patient threatened to kill his girlfriend if she attempted to move her belongings out of their apartment. The psychotherapist warned the intended victim over the phone, but she ignored the warning and was subsequently killed. The allegation in the subsequent suit was that the warning was not adequate. The court, however, exonerated the psychotherapists from any liability.

A Thorough Psychologist

A psychologist accepted a couple in therapy, and according to his standard practice, he initially interviewed each partner separately. The wife initially denied any abuse. However, the psychologist followed up with specific questions about the manner in which they handled their disagreements. The questions gradually elicited more and more detail, such as the presence of pushing, threats, and thrown objects. The wife, who had grown up in a household with extreme violence, did not interpret pushing or throwing objects as "abuse" and emphasized that her husband never punched or choked her.

The psychologist understood that some abused individuals may deny the presence of abuse out of embarrassment, a desire to protect their partner, or an idiosyncratic definition of what constitutes abuse. If the psychologist had not followed up carefully, he might have missed an important aspect of their marital conflict.

Develop Alternatives or Hypothesize Solutions

The second step in the five-step model is to consider treatment options likely to reduce the danger. When danger to others is imminent, decisions about the treatment plan can focus on incapacitating the patient (e.g., through a hospitalization), hardening the target (e.g., through warning the intended victim), or intensifying treatment (Monahan, 1993). As much as possible, it is desirable to involve the patient in considering treatment options.

In some states, the options in this second step are limited by statutes or case law that do not permit warning the intended victim. In those states, the statutes limit the psychotherapists to either incapacitating the patient, such as through a hospitalization, or intensifying treatment.

Even in states that allow a full range of therapeutic interventions to diffuse the risk of harm, determining the optimal intervention can be difficult. Every situation contains unique contextual factors, and no one can give psychologists a precise decision tree to follow. Instead, psychologists are left to their clinical judgment, consistent with the standards of care or judgment of reasonable psychologists, as to the optimal intervention. Although warning the intended victim may make sense in some situations, in other situations the warning might be unnecessary or may even precipitate the violence that the psychologist is trying to prevent.

Although common sense may suggest that notifying the police is an acceptable way to discharge duties to third parties at risk of harm, Huber et al. (2000) found that many police departments do not have experience with *Tarasoff*-type warnings or do not even have policies in place if they were to receive such a warning. Consequently, notifying the police may not always be adequate to diffuse danger.

Evaluate or Analyze Options

The optimal treatment plan may be developed by theory knitting, or adopting the intervention that incorporates the most advantages and excludes the most disadvantages of the options generated in the second step.

A Skillful Intervention

A patient made a serious threat to kill the man who had an affair with his wife. The psychologist determined that the danger was not imminent and developed a treatment plan that focused on strengthening the spousal relationship. As the relationship improved, the homicidal thoughts decreased substantially.

In this situation, the psychologist was fortunate that the victim was temporarily safe (i.e., he was working out of town). The psychologist used the time wisely to focus on lifting the patient's depression and strengthening the marriage, thereby diffusing the risk of violence.

Act or Perform

The intervention must be implemented in a reasonable manner. Inadequately implemented interventions have led to tragedies. In the *Tarasoff* case, the murder occurred because the treating psychologist failed to implement the intervention as intended. The psychologist correctly predicted the danger and developed a treatment plan (i.e., an involuntary commitment) calculated to protect the identifiable victim. The murder occurred, however, after the attempted commitment failed. The police did not follow through with the commitment and the supervisor of the psychologist ordered him to take no further actions to protect Ms. Tarasoff.

Psychologists should attempt to involve the patient in the treatment plan as much as possible. For example, if possible, issue the warning with the consent of the patient or even with the patient present. Patients who participate in the decision to warn and who are informed of the need to protect an identifiable third party are more likely to continue in treatment (Binder & McNiel, 1996).

Most of the time, when a warning was made, the intended victims already suspected danger to themselves (Binder & McNiel, 1996). Typically the potential victims expressed appreciation and an intent to modify their behavior. Some, however, denied the danger. In such situations, psychologists may want to send the intended victim a certified letter reiterating the danger. The letter can help reinforce the verbal warning, and the paper trail documents the efforts of the psychologist to diffuse the danger.

It is best to attempt to involve the patients in all decisions, if possible. For example, if a hospitalization is considered, it may be possible to persuade (e.g., It is to your benefit to enter the hospital because . . .) or induce (e.g., If you enter the hospital voluntarily, you will retain the option of signing yourself out at any time . . .) the patient to agree to the treatment plan. Threats of involuntary hospitalizations should be avoided if possible.

If the patient is hospitalized, then the psychologist should clearly communicate the nature of the danger to the hospital and especially to the attending physician. A danger always exists that the information can be lost when multiple treatment providers (as in a hospital or nonhospital residential facility) are involved. For example, the emergency room personnel may not convey the severity of the dangerousness to the attending physician (VandeCreek & Knapp, 2001).

Look Back or Evaluate

The psychologist should continually look back or evaluate the impact of every intervention with life-endangering patients. The stages of decision making can overlap considerably. The assessment of dangerousness needs to be made periodically throughout the treatment process, and the treatment plan may have to be modified as the clinical realities and external circumstances of the patient change (e.g., the patient is noncompliant with the original treatment plan). A program of intensive outpatient treatment may be sufficient to fulfill the duty to protect at one point in time, but not later.

SUICIDAL PATIENTS

The five-step model can be useful for evaluating the responsibilities of psychologists in situations in which patients threaten to harm themselves.

Identify or Scrutinize the Problem

With suicidal patients, psychologists have obligations both to protect patients and to respect the autonomy of patients to make their own decisions. The clarification of the first step requires a determination of dangerousness by the psychologist. As with the assessment of dangerousness to others, the assessment of suicidality cannot be reduced to a box score or simple formula. Nonetheless, psychologists can estimate the risk by considering verbal threats to harm oneself, previous attempts, and the presence of a plan and availability of means to do so. Other relevant factors include the presence of depression or alcohol abuse, overall physical health, level of optimism, presence of a social support system or religious belief system, the degree of adherence and commitment to treatment, and the strength of the therapeutic alliance (Bongar, Maris, Berman, & Litman, 1992).

Documentation is always important, but especially for hospitalized patients because the record is a vehicle of communicating to other staff members. The documentation should be explicit about any decision to reduce a suicidal watch, allow leaves from the facility, or otherwise decrease surveillance. Discharged patients should be given follow-up appointments because suicide rates are especially high shortly after discharge.

A brief note that reads "the patient is suicidal" confuses more than it enlightens. It is not known if the patient threatened suicide or if the note reflects an unsubstantiated inference on the part of the writer. Instead, notes should be specific enough to guide other professionals in their treatment and patient management decisions.

Develop Alternatives or Hypothesize Solutions

The second step is to consider treatment options likely to reduce the danger. The decisions about the treatment plan should focus both on the long-term treatment of the mental illness and the short-term safety of the patient. As much as possible, it is desirable to involve the patient in considering treatment options.

The courts will not hold a psychologist liable only because a patient committed suicide. Instead, the plaintiff must prove that the psychologist was negligent in his or her assessment or treatment. Psychologists are responsible for developing treatment plans consistent with reasonable professional standards. Options can include outpatient psychotherapy, outpatient psychotherapy combined with medication, or psychiatric hospitalization. For outpatient treatment, some of the precautions are well established: If medication is prescribed, the amount of medication distributed should be nonlethal, and psychologists should offer emergency services, frequent therapeutic contacts, and evaluations of the need for hospitalization. Deviations from these norms should be documented and the reasons why indicated.

Consultations and quality documentation help demonstrate the adequacy of treatment. The importance of seeking consultation in difficult situations cannot be overstated. These consultations reflect an intention to ensure the highest possible service to the patients. They are especially needed if the patients are treatment resistant either because of their failure to respond to medications or because of deep-seated personality disorders. Difficult patients sometimes create countertransference reactions that can impair the objectivity and effectiveness of the psychologist.

The support and sensitive watchfulness of the family can be a strong factor in recovery. However, the decision to involve family members needs to be made carefully. At times, family involvement may be therapeutically indicated; at times, it may be contraindicated. Psychologists should defer to the wishes of adult patients about family notification unless the threat to harm is imminent and it appears that family involvement would be helpful. In those situations, beneficence may temporarily trump respect for patient autonomy.

Mental health professionals are permitted to breach patient privacy if, in their opinion, doing so is necessary to prevent imminent harm to a patient. However, breaching patient privacy could harm the psychologist–patient relationship, and in the long term, hinder the treatment process.

In one highly publicized case, the university counseling center at the Massachusetts Institute of Technology (MIT) had been treating a sophomore for depression. She declined their request that she voluntarily hospitalize herself and later killed herself through self-immolation. Her parents sued MIT for failing to notify them of the severity of her mental illness and her suicidal ideation. Her parents claimed that they had no knowledge that she was suicidal, even though she had been hospitalized a year earlier after a suicide attempt (Sharpe, 2002). Without detailed information about the case, it is impossible to know if the mental health professionals at MIT made an error in judgment. However, even if the failure to notify was an error, errors in judgment are not necessarily grounds for liability. The standard is whether reasonable mental health professionals knew or should have known that the danger of suicide was imminent and that involving the parents would have been therapeutically helpful.

Safety Agreements

Sometimes psychologists ask suicidal patients to sign a *no-suicide, no-harm,* or *safety* contract or agreement. The term *contract* is a misnomer; it is not a legal contract. We prefer the term *agreement* as it avoids legalistic connotations. The nature of these agreements varies, but generally the patients promise that they will not commit suicide and that they will contact the psychologist or take other safety precautions if the urge to commit suicide appears strong.

Data on the usefulness of these safety agreements are lacking; however, some patients have committed suicide in spite of having signed a safety agreement. Kroll (2000) found that 41% of the psychiatrists who used no-suicide contracts had patients who later committed suicide or made serious suicide attempts. Unfortunately, some psychotherapists misunderstand the purpose of safety agreements and use them inappropriately. Safety agreements can be clinically contraindicated if they are used primarily to reduce the anxiety of psychologists or if psychologists mistakenly believe that these agreements will somehow reduce their legal liability. A safety agreement is no substitute for a comprehensive evaluation and treatment plan. The mere fact that a patient has acquiesced to a safety contract provides little assurance that the patient will be safe (Weiss, 2001).

However, safety agreements can have value. How a safety agreement is implemented can be as important as whether it is implemented or what it says. Ideally a safety agreement reflects an ongoing process that encourages patient participation in the development and implementation of the treatment plan. The process should be consistent with the ethical principles of respect for patient autonomy, beneficence, and nonmaleficence.

A Helpful Agreement

It appeared that a patient with strong suicidal ideation could be safely treated as an outpatient; however, she feared that some unanticipated event would cause her to slip into a deep depression and cause her to harm herself impulsively. The psychologist suggested that it might be helpful for her to write down instructions to herself in the event that her hopeful attitude became threatened between now and the next appointment. The patient and her psychologist created a safety agreement that included the unique words and language that the patient used in her self-talk. The brief safety agreement read as follows:

"Sometimes when I feel depressed I forget about the hopeful attitude that I have now. When I start feeling real depressed, I need to read this reminder. If that does not work I will call Dr. S. . . ."

The psychologist made three copies (i.e., one for her office, one that the patient kept in her room, and one that the patient put in her book bag). The patient also purchased a "hope bracelet," which she wore to remind herself that her hopeful attitude was coming back.

Self-Mutilation

At times, patients mutilate themselves to reduce emotional distress or to draw attention to themselves. Although the various forms of self-mutilation are not always considered suicidal attempts, they may at times go too far and lead to an unexpected death. The treatment plan should not automatically require a hospitalization because it may, under certain circumstances, be clinically contraindicated. For some persons, hospitalization may represent a step toward regression and loss of personal responsibility. Instead, the psychologist can carefully consider clinical interventions designed to protect patient safety and reduce the psychological disorder and the cutting.

Evaluate or Analyze Options

As with patients who threaten others, the optimal treatment plan can be developed by theory knitting, or adopting the intervention that incorporates the most advantages and excludes the most disadvantages of the options generated in the second step. Again, the willingness of the patient to concur with the treatment plan is an important factor.

Current professional standards recognize that the treatment of suicidal patients may involve some degree of risk. Although in the long run it may be better to treat the patient in the community, there are short-term risks that the patient may attempt or succeed at suicide. Psychologists must balance the benefits of treatment against the risks of freedom. They can carefully assess the decision to reduce the supervision of suicidal patients, whether it involves a transfer to a less restrictive ward or a discharge out of the hospital. Of course, when the patient is imminently suicidal, hospitalization may be indicated.

Act or Perform

The best treatment plan means little unless it is implemented as intended. Courts have found hospitals liable when the ward personnel did not follow through with the directions given by the attending psychiatrist. For example, a hospital could be liable if its attendants or nurses did not keep a patient under 24-hour supervision as ordered by a physician. Conversely, physicians might be liable if they failed to consider the notes of nurses and other staff members regarding their observations of the patient.

Inpatient units can ensure a higher quality of care if they have written procedures for handling suicidal patients. Although the attending clinician usually makes the decision to place a patient on suicidal watch, the exact procedures for the suicidal watch should conform to hospital policy, including the presence of an order from a qualified professional, what objects may be permitted in the patient's room, how frequently monitoring is required, and how to record the observation.

Even for outpatients, the adherence to the treatment plans should be monitored carefully. Psychologists may need to reevaluate the treatment plan if the suicidal patient does not comply with it. Psychologists should continually update their documentation of the assessment of suicide and the extent to which the treatment plan is being implemented.

Look Back or Evaluate

As with life-endangering patients, psychologists should continually assess the degree of suicidality and the effectiveness of their interventions. If necessary, they should alter the frequency and nature of interventions as circumstances dictate.

PATIENTS WHO HAVE HIV OR OTHER INFECTIOUS DISEASES

State laws regarding reporting HIV/AIDS status or other infectious diseases such as the hepatitis C virus (HCV) differ considerably from those regarding patients who threaten to assault others. Psychotherapists in some states are prohibited from warning identifiable victims of persons who are HIV positive. In other states, the case law is just emerging. However, VandeCreek and Knapp (2001) were unable to find any cases in which mental health professionals were found negligent for failure to report HIV/AIDS infection.

Sometimes patients who are HIV positive present a concern because they may engage in behaviors that place others at risk for acquiring the infection. Consequently, there is an apparent conflict between general beneficence and beneficence with respect for patient autonomy.

Assessing the degree of risk requires an understanding of the serostatus of the patient as well detailed information on sexual behavior or use of drugs. At times the risk may be high and the victim easily identifiable, such as when an HIV-positive patient states that he or she is having unprotected sexual relations with a partner who is unaware of the infectious status. At other times, convincing evidence may be lacking. The risk may be extremely low or the evidence unclear, such as when a patient who is known to have frequented prostitutes is having sexual relations with a live-in partner but has not been tested for HIV/AIDS. Also, it is relevant to ask if the identifiable victim knows that he or she is at risk.

Although much attention has focused on HIV/AIDS, the transmission of HCV may pose just as much of a health risk. Some of the risk factors for HIV/AIDS, such as high risk sexual behaviors and drug use, also place individuals at risk to acquire HCV. If untreated, HCV can lead to cirrhosis, liver failure, and liver cancer.

An Anxious Psychologist

A psychologist learned that her HIV-positive patient had failed to inform her domestic partner of her serostatus. Disclosure of that fact precipitated great anxiety in the psychologist, who stammered that she needed to seek legal consultation before proceeding with therapy. The patient picked up on the high anxiety of the psychologist and also feared a compromise in her confidentiality. She never came back.

The psychologist was unaware that her state prohibited her from disclosing patient information in these circumstances without consent. Consequently, the psychologist lost the opportunity to work with the patient to address her presenting problem and to help the patient consider her relationship to her partner. If the psychologist had continued the interview, she would have learned that the patient tried to practice safer sex; justifiably feared an increase in abuse if she told her partner; and had a small child and feared that even if she was not assaulted, at the least she and her child would be made homeless.

Often the anxiety caused by treating a patient who is HIV positive may cause psychologists to focus so much on protecting third parties that they fail to focus adequately on the needs of the patient. As discussed in chapter 4 (Ethical Decision Making), psychologists who feel great anxiety may sometimes become fixated on warning or jump to the first just-good-enough solution without considering all of the possible options. Paradoxically, a psychologist who emphasizes the welfare of the patient and strives to build a good working relationship is likely to have greater success in promoting patient concern for third parties (Anderson & Barret, 2001).

Develop Alternatives or Hypothesize Solutions

The next step is to consider treatment options designed to diffuse the danger and to implement that plan. Psychologists who understand the psychological aspects of HIV/AIDS infection are best able to make interventions designed to address the danger. For example, Has the psychologist given adequate time to allow psychotherapy to work? Does the psychologist understand why the patient is reluctant to disclose? Patients may fear abandonment, social rejection (Kozlowski, Rupert, & Crawford, 1998), or abuse. Effective treatment needs to address these fears.

Psychologists who do not understand the psychological aspects of HIV/AIDS infection very well (or do not understand the same-sex or drug subcultures) may be more inclined to warn an identifiable third party. However, psychologists who understand HIV/AIDS and their patients better may be more inclined to consider other therapeutic options before even thinking about warning an identifiable third party. Recent research has shown how interventions have been successful in reducing high-risk behaviors with patients infected with HIV/AIDS, thus greatly reducing the need to warn (Kelly & Kalichman, 2002). These programs rely on a combination of communications training, social support, stimulus control, cognitive restructuring, and education. Follow-ups show that progress can be sustained, although relapses should be anticipated. Using these programs does not guarantee that behavior change will occur. Nonetheless, the outcomes are sufficiently promising that psychologists should implement these or similar behavior change programs rather than just assuming that warning a third party is the only way to diffuse the danger.

Even when permitted by law, warning an identifiable third party should be a last resort, used only when all reasonable efforts at a voluntary disclosure have failed. In typical duty-to-protect situations, a single gunshot has a high likelihood of being fatal. With HIV/AIDS and other STDs, the dangerousness of sexual contact is less imminent and varies according to many factors, such as use of barrier contraceptives, the nature of the sexual contact (i.e., anal penetration, oral sex, or vaginal sex), and the health status of the partners. Consequently, psychologists have time to give therapy a chance to work.

Evaluate or Analyze Options

Again, the optimal solution will combine the advantages of the different options considered in the second step and attempt to involve the patient in the decision making. We anticipate that most interventions will focus on treatment options. Warning an identifiable third party without the consent of the patient would be done rarely, even if permitted by state law. If the decision is made to warn an identifiable party, it is prudent, if feasible, to minimize harm to the offended principle of respect for patient autonomy by informing the patient that the contact is going to be made and trying to involve the patient in the notification process.

The psychologist can offer to make a phone call with the patient present or have the patient present when the psychologist discusses the situation with the sexual or needle-sharing partner in person. The openness of the psychologist helps reduce the suspicion about what might have been said and may reduce the harm to the psychotherapeutic relationship. If the patient is not willing to give voluntary consent for the disclosure, then the psychologist should disclose the minimal amount of information to effectuate the warning. Another option is for the psychologist to use *partner notification programs* in which trained state employees notify the partners at the request of the patient.

Act or Perform and Look Back or Evaluate

As with aggressive or suicidal patients, it is important to ensure that the treatment plans are being implemented as intended. It is also important to reconsider the effectiveness of the interventions and modify them as needed.

CHILD ABUSE

Psychologists encounter other difficult situations in which the life or welfare of patients is at risk. This may occur when treating older adults who are dangerous drivers (Knapp & VandeCreek, 2005) or when treating vulnerable adults or older adults who are being abused. Perhaps the most common situation that psychologists encounter, however, involves children who are suspected of being abused.

Every state has a child protective service law that requires professionals to report suspected child abuse. The five-step model does not apply neatly to child abuse reporting because the intervention (i.e., reporting suspected child abuse) is mandated by the child protective services law.

Psychologists should be aware of at least three important features of the child protective services law in their state: how their state defines child abuse, the conditions that activate the duty to report, and the definition of a perpetrator of child abuse. The definition of child abuse varies from state to state, but most include nonaccidental injuries, neglect, emotional abuse, and sexual abuse. The exact wording of these definitions may vary from state to state.

In some states the duty to report under the child protective services law only applies when the child victim comes before the psychologist in a professional capacity. In other words, professionals may not have a duty to report under the child protective services law if only the alleged perpetrator has come before them in therapy. Nevertheless, in situations in which the psychologist sees only the perpetrator, the psychologist may still have to act under a duty to protect if the perpetrator should reveal a credible intent to inflict serious harm to an identifiable child victim in the immediate future. Privileged communications or confidentiality laws do not exonerate professionals from their duty to report suspected abuse.

The threshold of certainty for making reports is low. Most states require that mandated reporters only need to suspect or believe that a child was abused. They need not have proof. The child welfare agency, not the psychologist, should have the responsibility to determine whether abuse actually occurred.

State laws vary in their definition of *perpetrator*. In every state, the guardians or parents of the child could qualify as perpetrators under the child protective services law. Other states include teachers, babysitters, paramours of parents, or live-in adults in the definition. However, sometimes children reveal that they were harmed or abused by neighbors or other persons who are not guardians, parents, or perpetrators under the state law. Unless state laws include these individuals in their definition of perpetrator, these crimes against children should be processed through the criminal justice system, not the child welfare system.

Despite the positive goals of child-abuse-reporting laws, they can create a barrier to effective therapy if parents view the psychologist primarily as a punitive agent who is required to report them. Psychologists can minimize the negative influence of these laws by informing patients of the confidentiality limitations before starting treatment. Of course, there may be nonlegal consequences to an unfounded report, such as the loss of confidence between the psychologist and patient that may prompt the patient to discontinue psychotherapy prematurely.

Psychologists can take other steps to minimize the harm to the therapeutic relationship. For example, if possible, it may be helpful to discuss with the family the necessity to file a child abuse report and to obtain their consent before filing the report. If at all possible, the family should call the child welfare agency, or the psychologist can call with the family present. The effort to clarify what was done and why it was done may minimize damage to the relationship. Although most states allow mandated reporters to file anonymous reports, families often can guess the identity of the reporter.

It may be helpful for the psychologist to explain that the reporting decision is mandated by law and that criminal penalties can follow from a failure to do so. Of course, psychologists should carefully document their treatment of families in which child abuse is suspected (VandeCreek & Knapp, 2001).

An Ill-Informed Psychologist

A highly motivated patient revealed that he had physically abused his son several years earlier. On hearing this, the psychologist immediately reported the patient to the child protective services. However, the psychologist was not aware that the standards for physical abuse in his state required that the abuse had to have occurred within the last 2 years. The report was unfounded, and the patient never returned for treatment.

Here the failure to know the law in his state caused the psychologist to report behavior that should never have been reported. Here, as in other situations, ignorance of the law can be costly.

10

BUSINESS ISSUES

Professional psychology has a business as well as a service aspect to it. Ethical standards apply to collecting fees, billing insurance, and advertising just as much as they do to other aspects of practice. In this chapter, we first cover financial issues concerning informed consent, setting fees, bartering, referral fees, handling debts, and relationships with insurers and managed care organizations (MCOs). We also consider risk management principles as well as ethical issues concerning advertisements and public representations.

FINANCIAL ISSUES

The rules governing fees and billing come from the Ethics Code (American Psychological Association [APA], 2002a), regulations of state licensure boards of psychology, and laws in individual states. Although only a small percentage of the disciplinary actions of the APA Ethics Committee are based on insurance or fee problems (APA Ethics Committee, 2004), billing disagreements are often the catalyst that prompts patients to file complaints for other reasons. Sometimes patients who are dissatisfied with services believe they are "leveling the playing field" by refusing to pay an outstanding bill.

The moral principles that are especially important in billing and collecting fees are respect for patient autonomy (i.e., psychologists need to inform patients ahead of time about the costs involved) and fidelity (i.e., psychologists follow through with promises and previous statements concerning their fees and billing practices). Psychologists who understand these moral principles will be better able to develop and implement fair and reasonable billing and fee collection policies.

Informed Consent on Financial Matters

Standard 6.04a, Fees and Financial Arrangements, states, "As early as is feasible in a professional or scientific relationship, psychologists and recipients of psychological services reach an agreement specifying compensation and billing arrangements." According to the principle of informed consent, patients should know the important elements of treatment, including the costs for services. Patients can then decide whether the anticipated benefits of treatment are worth the costs. Discussing these issues ahead of time helps reduce confusion and misunderstandings in the future.

Prudent psychologists inform patients of the relevant financial aspects of their practices, such as the cost per session, acceptance of credit cards, assistance with completing insurance forms, policy on billing for missed appointments, range of services covered (e.g., report writing, testing, phone calls), when the charge is made (e.g., the day the service is rendered or at the end of the month), when payment is due, or when an interest or service fee begins on delinquent accounts. It is wise to give patients a written statement, contract, or service brochure that contains information on fees, billings, and collections at the initial office visit. This brochure may be given to patients at the same time that they receive the privacy notice (see chap. 8, Confidentiality, Privileged Communications, and Record Keeping), but it must be a separate document.

Some patients assume that their insurance contract guarantees payment to the psychologist and that any disputes over fees are between the psychologist and the insurance company. However, this is true only if the psychologist has a special arrangement with the insurer or MCO. Of course, the psychologist or office staff may assist patients in completing insurance forms. The very act of assisting the patients, however, may lead them to believe that they have no responsibility for the cost of services. Nonetheless, the patient, not the insurance company, is responsible for paying the psychologist unless the psychologist has signed a contract with the insurer specifying otherwise. This expectation should be made clear to the patient at the outset of treatment.

Psychologists may charge any amount for any professional service as long as they have explained fees and billing procedures to the service recipients ahead of time. Absent a contract with an insurer that specifies otherwise, psychologists may charge for a missed appointment, additional time if a session runs over an hour, phone contacts, time in preparing reports, time in professional consultations or collateral contacts, or any other professional activity if patients have been informed ahead of time. However, psychologists should not assume that insurance companies will pay for them.

Unless it is clear that an insurance company will reimburse for missed appointments or a company has given advanced approval, psychologists should not bill an insurance company for missed appointments. Also, some insurance companies limit reimbursement to a single procedure code per day. That is, they may not be willing to reimburse for the extra half hour of a session even if the psychologist bills the patient. Finally, most insurance companies do not reimburse for phone calls.

Furthermore, some patients may forget the financial policies of the psychologist. Although psychologists may legally bill for a wide range of services (if it has been explained to patients ahead of time), sensitive psychologists show restraint and prudence. A patient who is charged for a 10-minute emergency phone call may feel that he is being "nickled and dimed" by the psychologist. He may even suspect that the psychologist prolonged the phone call to get more money. Although the option of billing for those services may have been stated in a service brochure, many patients will not remember all of the details in that brochure. Although it may be legal for a psychologist to charge for the emergency phone call, such a practice may reduce the trust and goodwill of the patient. Of course, for some patients who have a tendency to misuse the option of emergency phone calls, charging for the phone calls may be clinically indicated as well as being fair to the psychologist.

A Discerning Psychologist
The service brochure of one psychologist states that he bills for all phone calls exceeding 20 minutes. Nonetheless, he routinely tells them that he is making a one-time exception for the first long phone call. Such a policy engenders good will on the part of patients and alerts them to their responsibility for future phone calls.

Psychologists should anticipate that they will increase their fees to keep up with the cost of doing business. Sensitivity should be shown toward ongoing patients, however, so that they do not feel trapped by the fee increase and their financial investment in therapy. At the least, the psychologist should give long-term patients considerable advance notice about the increase in fees.

Standard 6.04d, Fees and Financial Arrangements, states, "If limitations to services can be anticipated because of limitations in financing, this is discussed with the recipient of services as early as is feasible." It would not be desirable for psychologists to skim the cream and then refer their patients elsewhere (i.e., "creaming and dumping").

A Thoughtful Action
A psychologist accepted a patient but after several sessions realized that she had minimized the extent of her problems in the initial session.

In reality, she had pervasive and chronic Axis I and II problems. Although she had enough insurance and financial resources to pay for 15 therapy sessions, the psychologist correctly recognized that she would need many months (perhaps years) of treatment. He immediately focused the next session on helping her to develop a long-term treatment plan and to identify an agency or service provider that could provide the long-term continuous treatment she needed.

Billing Accurately

Standard 6.06, Accuracy in Reports to Payors and Funding Sources, states that "psychologists take reasonable steps to ensure the accurate reporting of the nature of the service provided or research conducted, the fees, charges, or payments, and where applicable, the identity of the provider, the findings, and the diagnosis." Also, Standard 6.04c, Fees and Financial Arrangements, states, "Psychologists do not misrepresent their fees." The underlying principles in billing insurance companies are honesty and accuracy. Standard 6.06 establishes a realistic perspective on billing. Accordingly, a psychologist would not be subject to a disciplinary action only because a clerk made a simple billing error. Of course, psychologists should not willfully misrepresent their fees to third-party payers, and psychologists need to use reasonable diligence in monitoring their billing services.

In recent years, insurers, including Medicare and other government insurance programs, have been giving special scrutiny to insurance fraud and abuse. A clear, bright line distinguishes fraud from abuse. *Fraud* means a deliberate and systematic effort to obtain money through deceit (Kalb, 1999). Fraud investigators are not interested in rare billing errors or in legitimate ambiguities in the use of specific procedure codes. In contrast, *abuse* means an error in billing. Psychologists who submit thousands of bills in their career can be expected to make some mistakes. Although all psychologists should bill carefully, they should not be unduly worried that a rare honest mistake will lead to an allegation of fraud.

Diagnostic Accuracy

Some psychologists feel tempted to alter the diagnosis to ensure that a patient will be eligible for third-party reimbursement. For example, a patient may have a diagnosis of borderline personality disorder or attention-deficit/hyperactivity disorder, but the insurer may refuse to pay for services for patients with those diagnoses. Often these patients have coexisting disorders (e.g., major depression, conduct disorder), which are reimbursable. However, psychologists should determine the diagnosis only on the basis of the patient's symptoms, even if it means that the patient will lose the opportunity for third-party reimbursement.

In some cases, it may be appropriate to treat a patient's Axis I symptoms, such as depression, and not the more persistent personality disorder and bill the insurer for the treatment. In such instances, the psychologist should be candid with the patient about any limitation on treatment and reimbursement.

Few insurance policies cover problems-in-living, such as marital discord, career dissatisfaction, or parent–child problems. Most policies require the treatment to focus on a "medical" diagnosis. Nevertheless, it is not unusual for one or both spouses to have significant emotional turmoil as a result of marital discord (or have significant emotional problems that cause the marital discord), and psychologists may legitimately give them a diagnosis from the *Diagnostic and Statistical Manual of Mental Disorders* (4th ed.; American Psychiatric Association, 1994) and report it to the insurance company as such. Patients with "only" a problem in living that is the focus of treatment should be reported as such even if it means losing insurance reimbursement.

Billing for Clinical Supervision or Consultation

Clinical supervision needs to be distinguished from consultation. As we describe in chapter 15 (Clinical Supervision), supervised services are those in which the supervisee is legally an agent of the supervising psychologist. Consultation, however, is an arrangement between legal equals in which the consultant provides the service, such as an opinion on a particular case, but the professional receiving the consultation has the right to accept or reject the opinion of the consultant.

Whether insurers will reimburse for the services provided by psychologists-in-training or unlicensed employees depends on the contract and the policies of the insurance company. Some companies reimburse for the services provided by supervised psychological assistants, and some do not. The underlying rules are to check state laws and insurance company policies to avoid misrepresentation.

Bartering

Standard 6.05, Barter With Clients/Patients, states, "Barter is the acceptance of goods, services, or other nonmonetary remuneration from clients/patients in return for psychological services." Psychologists may barter only if it is not clinically contraindicated and not exploitative. Bartering can be either ethical or unethical depending on the circumstances.

A Fair Exchange

A patient owed a psychologist about $200 and appeared unable to pay it. However, he offered the psychologist a gift certificate worth $200 off an electronic appliance at his brother's electronics store. There were no apparent clinical contraindications to this arrangement and both the psychologist and patient were satisfied.

A Problematic Exchange

A psychologist hired a patient to do yard work in exchange for receiving psychological services. The yard work was sloppy, and the patient was inconsistent in showing up for work. The patient insisted that the psychologist knew that he had physical limitations and could not be expected to perform optimal services.

In the second case, the psychologist and patient disagreed about the extent to which the sloppy work was the result of his physical limitations. However, this vignette shows the risks that may arise when psychologists barter for services.

From a practical perspective, psychologists who barter for goods have a lower risk of exploiting or harming patients than those who barter for services. Psychologists may inspect goods ahead of time, and along with the patient, predetermine their economic value. Although the value of the goods (e.g., a television set) in the first example was predetermined, the value of the labor in the second example was open to debate. Even with the bartering of goods, Woody (1998) recommended having a written agreement that specifies the worth of the object being bartered.

Referral Fees

Referral fees, sometimes misnamed "fee-splitting," are accepted as reimbursement for referring a patient to another practitioner for professional services. Standard 6.07, Referrals and Fees, permits referral fees only if payment "is based on the services provided (e.g., clinical, consultative, administrative) and is not based on the referral itself." The prohibition against referral fees does not preclude employers from dividing fees with employees nor does it preclude payment for services rendered, such as rent, secretarial services, or professional consultation.

Handling Debts

Patients are responsible only for payment of services that they agreed to before treatment or evaluation began. The two broad rules for handling patient billing are to have explicit rules and to use fairness and tact. Cautious psychologists make certain that unpaid bills do not accumulate. A "pay-as-you-go" policy can resolve this issue. Psychologists who allow debts to occur should address these debts early in the treatment relationship before they accumulate to large levels.

Patients may develop unforeseen financial problems that limit their ability to pay for psychotherapy. It is not unethical, per se, to terminate a nonemergency patient who cannot or will not pay for services. Nevertheless, psychologists could be liable for charges of abandonment if they precipitously discharged patients who were in crisis or psychologically vulnerable at the time that services were terminated. In these cases, a psychologist may consider reducing the fee, extending the length of time between sessions (if clinically indicated), or providing pro bono services until the patient has established services from an agency or provider who will accept the lower fee. At the very least, the psychologist should be available for emergencies until the patient is seen elsewhere.

Psychologists are not obligated to treat nonemergency patients who willfully refuse to pay for services. If patients with adequate resources fail to pay for services, then the psychologist should inform them of the consequences of nonpayment. Some patients express their dissatisfaction with treatment through the nonpayment of a bill. Problems with paying bills need to be discussed with the patient in terms of the overall satisfaction with and perceived value of psychotherapy.

Standard 6.04e, Fees and Financial Arrangements, states that "if psychologists intend to use collection agencies or legal measures to collect fees, psychologists first inform the person that such measures will be taken and provide that person an opportunity to make prompt payment." Nonetheless, psychologists should be aware that legal opinions may differ from patient expectations. Psychologists may avoid misunderstandings and ill feelings if their patients understand the consequences of nonpayment ahead of time.

Many therapists use collection agencies routinely with no problems. Much depends on the specific agency used and its practices. Nevertheless, attempts to collect unpaid bills may precipitate a malpractice charge or licensing board complaint. Occasionally writing off an unpaid bill may be more expedient in the long run than facing allegations of misconduct, even if they are frivolous.

Psychologists should choose a bill collection agency carefully because unprofessional or abusive behavior on the part of the collection agency reflects badly on them and the profession. Psychologists using collection services should limit their disclosures to collection agencies to the minimum necessary to collect the debts.

Managed Care Issues

Managed care has greatly changed professional psychology. It is difficult to make definitive statements about a highly varied and continuously changing entity such as managed care. The purported goals of managed care are to coordinate treatment, reduce unnecessary expenses, and ensure the wisest use of limited health care dollars. Certainly purchasers of health care insurance need to have some evidence that their moneys are being spent wisely, especially when health care expenditures are increasingly rapidly. Nothing in the aims of managed care is inherently in conflict with the goals of good psychological practice.

Nonetheless, from the standpoint of patients, the quality of services offered has generally declined. From the standpoint of psychologists (and other health care professionals), paperwork has increased and patient welfare, income, and career satisfaction have generally decreased. According to

Boyle (1996), savings created from limiting care for some patients can be justified if they have been used to increase the availability of services in other areas. However, a disproportionate amount of the savings from MCOs appear to go to covering their high administrative costs.

Psychologists encounter numerous practical problems when dealing with MCOs. Some directly impact patient care. For example, a psychologist was having difficulty getting a teenager to open up in the first session. Finally, the teenager revealed that this was the third psychologist he had seen in the last 3 years. Every year his father's insurance company subcontracted with a new behavioral health provider that had a different list of providers. The teenager said, "Why should I open up? I won't be able to see you in a few months anyway."

Other problems deal with financial or billing inconveniences. They may occur so frequently and consume such a large amount of time that energies are diverted from patient care. Furthermore, patients are often left uncertain as to what services could or could not be reimbursed. For example, an MCO that required the preauthorization of services rejected the treatment plan because the psychologist did not use the proper form. The case manager informed the psychologist that the proper form would be sent. The form that was sent was the same form that the psychologist had originally submitted. In another situation, a psychologist called to receive a preauthorization of services, only to be told that she needed to call another number. When she called that number, she was referred to a third number, which referred her to a fourth number, which was the original number she called. The entire process took about 2 hours.

Fortunately, some insurers try to deliver high-quality care and be responsive to the needs of the consumers. For example, a patient in crisis sought treatment from a psychologist who was not on the insurer's provider panel. When the insurer was contacted, it automatically considered the psychologist "in panel" for this patient and paid all bills accordingly. In another situation, the medical director of a Medicare carrier learned that certain vaguely written regulations were being interpreted to deny needed mental health services, especially in underserved areas. She used the discretion given to her to reinterpret the regulations to ensure the availability of services.

Psychologists need to consider carefully whether to participate in managed care programs. No one response is appropriate for every psychologist, and no one response is appropriate for the same psychologists at different times in their careers. Some psychologists may decide that the MCOs in their geographical area are so harmful to patient welfare that it is best to avoid participating with MCOs altogether. Others with different MCOs or different expectations may believe that the public welfare is better served if they do participate in MCOs.

Those psychologists who do participate in managed care programs should encourage patients to become informed of the conditions and limitations of their benefits. Often psychologists have had experiences with specific insurers and can anticipate what these problems will be. Patients are often unaware of these limitations until they try to access their health care benefits. In this context it is not surprising that some patients feel dissatisfied or angry with the limitations of their plan. Incongruent expectations on the part of the patient may translate into anger against the treating psychologist (Acuff et al., 1999).

Psychologists will encounter some patients who continue to need treatment and have unused benefits but whose insurer claims that treatment can no longer be justified. Although it is the patient's decision to appeal, psychologists can assist their patients by maintaining comprehensive case notes about their decisions on patient care and clearly communicating with review panels.

An Effective Psychologist

An MCO denied the request of a parent (and her psychologist) for the hospitalization of a seriously suicidal youth. The parent took advantage of the emergency appeal process as mandated by state law. Backed by the detailed documentation of the psychologist, the state agency ordered that the MCO reimburse for the hospitalization of the youth.

Systematic Advocacy[1]

Do psychologists have a moral obligation to address the systematic abuses of insurance companies? It is desirable for psychologists to treat patients pro bono, contribute to public projects, and otherwise donate services to others. However, are these psychologists being shortsighted if they believe that these efforts compensate for the greater injustices caused by unfair insurance laws or abusive MCO practices? Does it constitute greater moral virtue to engage in systematic advocacy to address these abuses?

Many psychologists have a jaundiced view of government advocacy or politicians in general. However, careful consideration suggests that government advocacy is not nearly as pernicious as some would believe. Those of us who have close personal contacts with elected officials realize that the large majority of politicians are honest and sincerely want to promote the public welfare. Dirty tricks or bribes are rare (Knapp & DeWall, 2003).

Also, all citizens (including psychologists) have an obligation to support the process of democracy by voting and participating in other political activities. Despite their limitations, democracies tend to promote citizen welfare more than authoritarian governments. On the whole, citizens in de-

---

[1]This section is an adaptation of "Ethics of Government Advocacy," by S. Knapp and T. DeWall, 2003, *The Pennsylvania Psychologist*, 63, p. 4. Copyright 2003 by the Pennsylvania Psychological Association. Adapted with permission.

mocracies tend to live longer, report greater happiness, and show more tolerance for individual differences. According to Myers (1992), a history of stable democracy and national well-being are clearly linked. Citizens from nations with continuous democratic institutions tend to enjoy greater life satisfaction than citizens from nations that only recently adopted democratic forms of government.

Many psychologists who believe in the desirability of public access to psychological services participate in or support ongoing advocacy to ensure or increase public access to high-quality psychological services. They recognize that policymakers at the federal and state levels determine many of the rules by which psychologists, insurance companies, hospitals, and others must abide. These rules can either help or hinder people's access to necessary psychological services.

These psychologists participate in government advocacy by retaining membership in APA and their state psychological associations, contributing to psychology's political action committees (PACs; e.g., the Association for the Advancement of Psychology/Psychologists for Legislative Action Now) or the PAC of their state psychological association), voting, meeting with or writing to legislators, writing letters to newspaper editors, or other activities. Many of us believe that the current system of political giving is seriously flawed. However, the option of eschewing that system would mean, de facto, abdicating our ability to influence public policy.

Ideally, psychology will have a policy agenda that focuses on public welfare, recognizing that the public is a collection of individual constituencies such as consumers, employers, and government. Can individual psychologists as well as psychological organizations ensure that their advocacy efforts promote the overall public good rather than just themselves? Psychologists can be accurate and honest in gathering and representing facts and communicate with those groups who may disagree with their perspectives, at least to the extent that those groups are willing to engage in honest dialogue. Psychologists engaged in governmental advocacy need to recognize that by helping to ensure adequate access to psychological services, all of society is better off.

The topic of systemic advocacy appears in this chapter because sometimes the advocacy goals of psychologists involve both public interest and guild goals (e.g., promoting parity in insurance coverage for physical or mental illnesses). Nothing is wrong with promoting one's self-interest politically, as long as such promotion is also in the public interest and is done in accordance with ethical standards of political conduct. Nonetheless, the advocacy efforts of psychologists often involve goals that are less directly related to their financial interests (e.g., the humane treatment or diversion of persons with mental illness from prisons) or irrelevant to their financial interests (e.g., programs that prevent youth violence).

PUBLIC REPRESENTATIONS

Psychologists communicate to the public through advertising or other public statements. *Advertising* refers to the use of public representations intended to attract clients or patients. Many psychologists advertise through telephone yellow page ads, but some also advertise through other media such as Web sites.

The moral virtues of integrity and respect for patient autonomy require psychologists to be accurate in their advertising. This honesty helps to ensure public confidence in the individual psychologist and the profession as a whole. Properly informed patients can make better decisions about psychological services. Advertising is regulated primarily through the APA Ethics Code and state licensure board regulations as well as through state and federal laws.

Psychologists also communicate to the public through statements designed to disseminate information through talks to groups of laypersons; radio or television interviews; and articles in newspapers, magazines, and on Web sites. The moral virtues of integrity, nonmaleficence, and general beneficence require psychologists to be accurate in their public statements. Properly educated members of the public can make better decisions for themselves. Public statements are regulated primarily through the APA Ethics Code and the regulations of state licensure boards of psychology.

Advertising

Standard 5.06, In-Person Solicitation, prohibits psychologists from soliciting business from persons who are vulnerable to undue influence because of particular circumstances. This standard prohibits the psychological equivalent of ambulance chasing. This standard does not preclude collateral contacts with significant others to benefit a current therapy patient. In addition, this standard allows psychologists to participate in disaster relief services through the Red Cross or other agencies in which they may encourage individuals to receive mental health services. Psychologists may also participate in community outreach programs, such as those designed to assist street persons with serious or persistent mental illnesses (Knapp & VandeCreek, 2003b).

Psychologists have wide discretion in what they may include in their advertisements and how they advertise. Nothing prohibits advertising through television, radio, billboards, leaflets, the Internet, business cards, brochures, newsletters, or other media. Although most psychologists would not advertise on a billboard, it is not inherently unethical. Although gaudy or ostentatious advertisements are not unethical, prudent psychologists avoid such advertisements (Knapp & VandeCreek, 2003b).

A Perceptive Psychologist

A psychologist had a very successful practice in which he engaged in career assessment, academic assessment, and life coaching. He hired a professional consultant who suggested several marketing strategies, including the use of billboards and promotional matchbooks. Although none of these strategies were unethical, the psychologist rejected them as inconsistent with the image that he wished to convey.

Advertising may not include false, fraudulent or deceptive statements (Standard 5.01b, Avoidance of False or Deceptive Statements). The mandate for honesty in advertising applies to advertising of continuing education (CE) programs as well. Psychologists describe workshops and non-degree-granting educational programs accurately, including the audience for which the program is intended, the educational objectives, the presenters, and the fees involved (Standard 5.03, Descriptions of Workshops and Non-Degree-Granting Educational Programs).

Most of the problems with advertising occur because of inadvertent deceptions. Otherwise conscientious psychologists may fail to appreciate the implications of what they are putting in their public announcements. For example, some psychologists may refer to their practices with such words as *associates* or *international*. The words associates or international may lead the consumer to expect substantial resources on the part of the practice. Such representations are acceptable as long as the psychologists actually have other professionals working with them or they have ongoing business activities in other countries. An occasional workshop or consultation in a foreign country, however, does not qualify as an international operation.

Other psychologists use the term *specialist* inaccurately. The term *specialty* needs to be distinguished from the term *proficiency*. A specialist has training and expertise in a specific content area above and beyond that of the average psychologist and dedicates a large portion of practice in that domain. A psychologist with a proficiency has general competence in a particular domain of practice. For example, a psychologist who has advanced credentials and expertise in marital counseling and sees about 60% of her caseload in marital counseling has a specialty in that domain. However, a psychologist who is competent in marital counseling and sees about 20% of her caseload for marital counseling has a proficiency in that domain. A psychologist who lists several specialties is probably confusing the word with proficiency.

Woody (1997a) noted that the term *specialist* has a seductive appeal and may attract consumers who expect a higher level of care. However, those expectations could quickly turn to disappointment if the term were puffery rather than substance. Furthermore, in the event of a malpractice suit, a self-proclaimed specialist could be held accountable to standards of specialists, not general practitioner psychologists.

Standard 5.01c, Avoidance of False or Deceptive Statements, states that psychologists who provide mental health services may only represent academic degrees that were the basis for their licensure or that were earned from regionally accredited universities. Psychologists who are teaching, conducting research, or providing other services may represent degrees from unaccredited colleges and universities, although some employers may forbid such activities.

Vanity credentials are poorly regulated in professional psychology. A vanity credential is one that is awarded upon the payment of a fee without having been earned through a legitimate examination or peer review process. Individuals can obtain certifications of advanced proficiency in a wide range of areas from impressive sounding groups, even though these credentials have no merit. Psychologists only need to send a resume or claim that they have a certain amount of life or work experience to obtain these credentials. Unfortunately, these credentials deceive the unknowing public into thinking that practitioners have expertise which, in fact, they might not (Woody, 1997a).

Psychologists who engage others to create or place public statements that promote their professional practice, products, or activities retain professional responsibility for such statements. They do not compensate employees of communication media for publicity in a news item and clearly identify paid advertisements as such (Standard 5.02, Statements by Others).

The acronym ABD (i.e., all but dissertation) is used informally to apply to students who have completed all of their academic requirements except for the dissertation but have not yet earned their doctoral degree. However, this informal description is not a degree and may not be used in advertising one's services. Most laypersons would not understand what ABD means and could mistake it for an actual credential.

Other misrepresentations can occur when psychologists supervise psychologists-in-training or other professionals. By definition, a *supervising psychologist* assumes responsibility for the work product and public presentations of the supervisee. The supervising psychologist must ensure that supervisees disclose their credentials and supervised status accurately. This can be especially important for psychologists-in-training who have earned a doctoral degree. The term *doctor* may mislead some patients into assuming that the supervisee is already an independently practicing professional.

Presentations to the Public

Media psychologists may appear on radio or television talk shows; write for newspaper columns; or present information through informational Web sites, chat rooms, or other media (Standard 5.04, Media Presentations). When they do, they should avoid sensationalism. The information should be reasonably consistent with scientific or professional standards.

Psychologists do not suggest that a professional relationship exists with the advice seeker. When psychologists establish a professional relationship, they tailor the information to the needs of the patient. However, this is not possible with callers or writers when the real audience includes all of the listeners or readers. In these situations, psychologists need to restrict their comments to general information about the question raised.

Psychological Advice in an Inappropriate Context

A psychologist hosted a radio talk show that encouraged listeners to call in with their sexual problems. The total context, however, was one of entertainment and not education. The cohost told sexual jokes and belittled the callers when their calls ended. An impression was given that the callers who had the most shocking problems were selected to talk with the psychologist, whereas those with more routine problems were not.

Although the psychologist was proper in her own behavior, a question arose as to whether her participation in the show could be justified.

Many psychologists develop Web sites or Web pages to advertise their practices or products. The presence of Web sites has led to increased opportunities to educate the public about psychological issues. However, some Web sites are more appropriately called *advertorials* because they put advertisements in the context of an informational Web site. The APA Ethics Code has no specific standards for Web sites. Instead the standards applicable to advertising or public statements in general apply to Web sites as they apply to advertisements and public statements presented through other media. Care must be used to ensure that the advertisements are clearly labeled as such and that the information does not appeal to fears of vulnerable persons and are accurate. Psychologists with Web sites that include a number of links need to show special care. Although the content of the psychologist's own pages may be accurate, balanced, and current, the content in the links may not be so.

Palmiter and Renjilian (2003) surveyed psychologists and prospective consumers about the content of Web pages. A majority of consumers identified as essential information such as office address, degree, years of experience, telephone number, hours of availability, whether insurance was accepted, types of therapies offered, information about fees, list of problems treated, educational background, and e-mail addresses. A majority of consumers also preferred Web sites that included a resume, directions to the office, license number, office policies, emergency procedures, professional philosophy, pager and emergency numbers, memberships in professional groups, a picture of the clinician, frequently asked questions, general therapy information, links to support groups, symptom checklists, and online office forms. Some of these items favored by consumers could present problems, however. For example, many clinicians have privacy concerns and would discourage patients or prospective patients from sending them e-mails. Others may have concerns that symptom checklists, completed in the absence of a personal relationship, may be misunderstood or misconstrued by prospective patients.

11

FORENSIC PSYCHOLOGY

Forensic psychology refers to psychological work applied to legal issues. Psychologists may be hired as forensic experts by an attorney or a judge, appointed to treat an individual and report periodically back to the court, or be involved in the judicial system only because they are treating a patient who is involved in litigation. Forensic psychologists provide a valuable service by helping courts make accurate and fair decisions. Also, many psychologists who have routine practices may sometimes find themselves unintentionally, through unusual circumstances, working in the forensic area.

Psychologists working in forensic areas (especially in the area of child custody) have increased exposure to legal risks. The reasons for this are not hard to understand. The good feelings and positive relationships common in the psychotherapeutic relationship do not exist in the forensic setting. The report of the forensic psychologist, if not favorable to the client,[1] may engender ill feelings, a desire for revenge, or the filing of a lawsuit or disciplinary action to "neutralize" the report of the psychologist. In addition, because of the close scrutiny given to the work of forensic psychologists, their mistakes

---

[1]We are using the term *client* instead of *patient* because the recipient of forensic services may not be receiving health care services from the psychologist. Also, sometimes the clients of psychologists are attorneys or the courts.

are rarely invisible (Brown, 2000). It is not possible to estimate the number of ethics complaints or disciplinary actions that arise out of forensic work because the offenses are sometimes listed under other categories, such as incompetent evaluations or boundary violations.

Guidance for forensic psychologists comes from the Ethics Code (American Psychological Association [APA], 2002a) and the "Specialty Guidelines for Forensic Psychologists," which were published by APA's Division 41 (Law and Psychology; Committee on Ethical Guidelines for Forensic Psychologists, 1991). The "Guidelines for Child Custody Evaluations in Divorce Proceedings" (APA, 1994) are also helpful. In this chapter, we cover competence, boundaries, confidentiality, informed consent, and fees in forensic activities. In addition, we consider ways that psychologists can strive to maintain integrity while working within the judicial system.

THE NATURE OF THE JUDICIAL PROCESS

The adversarial process found in the Anglo American legal tradition requires two sides to confront each other with facts, questions, and evidence. The court then issues a verdict in which one side is found not guilty or guilty, or negligent or not negligent, depending on the nature of the case. The adversarial role differs considerably from the psychotherapeutic role, in which reconciliation, agreement, and cooperation are the norm. Psychologists perform best in this system when they understand the adversarial process.

Psychologists often participate in the legal system as expert witnesses. Although the standards vary from jurisdiction to jurisdiction, the general rule is that expert witnesses give information to the courts that is outside of the expertise of the average layperson. Judges admit psychologists as experts if their education, training, and experience qualify them to render expert opinions related to the questions before the court. Although the opposing counsel may object to the admission of the expert witness, the judge has the final decision on who is admitted as an expert.

The general rule is that expert witnesses cannot be sued for malpractice for the content of their testimony, although there are exceptions in some jurisdictions. Nevertheless, the content of the testimony can be the basis for a complaint before a licensing board or ethics committee. Other judicial rules vary from state to state. Furthermore, within each state, some rules are made by the local court, and every court has its own cultural milieu.

COMPETENCE

According to Standard 2.01f, Boundaries of Competence, "When assuming forensic roles, psychologists are or become reasonably familiar with the judicial or administrative rules governing their roles." Whenever psychologists are involved in forensic work, they need to ensure that they are competent to perform the roles expected of them. Psychologists who are competent as health care providers are not necessarily competent as forensic psychologists. For example, it should not be assumed that a psychologist who is competent in evaluating children is competent as a custody evaluator. In addition to the ability to write a good report, competency as a custody evaluator requires the ability to present one's findings in court and to justify them under cross-examination. Furthermore, even psychologists who are generally competent in child custody evaluations may decline a specific case that requires expertise beyond their own. Even when they do take a case, prudent psychologists reserve the option of seeking expert advice on issues outside of their competence. In addition, work as a forensic psychologist typically requires a higher degree of accuracy and thoroughness than work done in general clinical practice.

How do psychologists know when they have competence in forensic work? Psychologists should submit their work product for a detailed and routine evaluation by another mental health professional who is an expert in that field. In some areas it is possible for psychologists to obtain a proficiency credential, such as that awarded by the American Board of Forensic Psychology. In lieu of earning credentials, a supervisor or consultant can review tapes, copies of reports, or other work products of the psychologist to determine whether the desired level of competency has been reached.

"Psychologists base the opinions contained in their recommendations, reports, and diagnostic or evaluative statements, including forensic testimony, on information and techniques sufficient to substantiate their findings" (Standard 9.01a, Bases for Assessments). It is vital that expert witnesses present accurate and precise information to the court. For example, when testifying as experts, clinical psychologists should know the psychometric properties of the tests they used, why they used them, the degree of confidence they have in their interpretations, and the limitations of their interpretations (Rotgers & Barrett, 1996). Many issues before the court are complex, and no simple answers can be given. Psychologists should expect, as a routine matter, that a professional working for another party in the case will review their notes, tests, and reports.

Standard 9.01a, Bases for Assessments, requires psychologists to base their conclusions (whether expressed in a report or any other communication) on information sufficient to substantiate their findings. However, the 2002 APA Ethics Code permits psychologists to express opinions based on secondary sources under limited circumstances. First, if psychologists are unable to conduct a direct examination, they may nonetheless provide an opinion of the individual not directly evaluated if they "document the efforts they made and the result of those efforts, clarify the probable impact of their limited information on the reliability and validity of their opinions, and appropriately limit the nature and extent of their conclusions or recommendations" (Standard 9.01b). Second, when psychologists conduct a record review, consult, or supervise, they may develop opinions if a direct examination is not warranted or necessary and they "explain this and the sources of information on which they based their conclusions and recommendations" (Standard 9.01c). For example, they may be asked to review the records that led to an educational placement or a court decision (Fisher, 2003).

Psychologists may face demands to abandon a completely objective standard when issuing reports or opinions. Sometimes the demands may be overt; sometimes they may be subtle. The difficulty of being objective is compounded by the fact that psychologists often are asked to testify on matters in which the state of the art does not ensure precision or complete certainty. For example, although the predictions of violence have improved substantially in recent years, they are based on probabilities and contain some false positives. Similarly, many skilled practitioners have provided useful information to courts on child custody matters, although it is often difficult to justify those decisions on the basis of scientific data.

Sometimes attorneys suggest reasonable changes in the content or format of a report. They may have relevant background information on the client, ideas on how to better address the legal issues involved, or suggestions to help psychologists to improve the clarity of their reports. Psychologists can make these changes, improve the quality of the report, and still protect their integrity.

At other times attorneys may suggest unreasonable changes in the report. The recommendations of the attorney may compromise the accuracy of the information so that it is more consistent with the desired position of the attorney. Psychologists need to be aware of these efforts to shade their work. Although psychologists should listen to the input from attorneys carefully, they should not let these opinions override their professional opinions. The primary concerns of the psychologist should be for accuracy and thoroughness.

Shuman and Greenberg (2003) noted that some psychologists may perceive that they have to choose between being an advocate for a particular position and being accurate. However, they argued that "pitting integrity against advocacy is a false choice" (p. 219). Instead, psychologists are the most effective advocates when they are candid about the limitations of their data and balance all perspectives fairly. "The role of the expert is not to deliver favorable testimony as a matter of contract. The obligation is to render services at the relevant professional standard of care" (p. 223). They argued that such candor and balance will, in the long run, protect the integrity of psychologists and the credibility of their testimony. Of course, some attorneys prefer not to work with psychologists who fail to engage in blind and unrestrained advocacy for their position.

Even after a report has been written, psychologists can take steps to ensure their integrity. Brown (2000) believes expert witnesses can empower juries by sharing information and their thought processes carefully.

> A feminist expert does not hide behind the mask of professionalism, like *The Wizard of Oz* behind his smoke and mirrors, but she or he instead steps out from behind the curtain, revealing her or his information in a respectful form that educates and empowers jurors and makes them a part of a collaborative thought process with the psychologist. (p. 81)

At times, psychologists may have to report that they do not know the answer to a certain question.

Psychologists who have worked with divorcing couples have seen the very destructive process that divorce and custody cases can sometimes have. Many psychologists, attorneys, and judges believe that the very nature of the adversarial process impedes the ability of parents to reach agreements concerning child custody, exacerbates family tensions, and harms the children. The adversarial system often requires parents to emphasize the faults and shortcomings of the other parent. It is difficult for divorcing parents to testify concerning the many weaknesses of a spouse on one day and then try to work out transportation to Little League practice on the next.

A Frequent Occurrence

A stressful custody disagreement turned into a 5-year battle. The mother, who previously had an agreeable and gentle demeanor, became increasingly stressed, histrionic, and angry. The father's drinking became more problematic. The children started to do poorly in school. The son got into fights in school, whereas the daughter spent most of her time alone in her room. The court battles cost more than $40,000 and wiped out all of the savings planned for the children's education.

Some courts and attorneys have proposed alternative dispute resolution mechanisms to solve disagreements concerning child custody. For example, many courts prefer mediation. Although mediation has many positive qualities, it may not be appropriate for all couples, especially if the relationship is marred by domestic violence or intimidation. Other courts require parental counseling, parent education, or other interventions designed to improve the ability of the parents to raise their children and to cooperate with each other. The exact nature of these interventions may vary considerably. The name is less important than the actual functions that are being required. One court sometimes orders couples to participate in *family education*. Despite the name, which suggests a didactic presentation, the actual service desired by the court is more akin to family counseling. Psychologists need to clarify the expectations of different parties.

Finally, some attorneys have developed *collaborative law* projects. Collaborative law requires more than just a verbal agreement to try to cooperate and mediate disputes. According to collaborative law, attorneys and their clients work exclusively toward settlement, and the attorneys agree not to represent the clients if they decide to litigate (Tesler, 1999). Often collaborative law projects involve a team approach. They may, for example, draw on the expertise of a child specialist to consult with the parents and assist them in raising their children. Advocates of collaborative law claim that their process results in less hostility, costs less, and results in quicker settlements than adjudicated cases.

The claims for this promising approach need to be considered judiciously, as it is possible that the more cooperative families are those who are able to benefit from the intervention. Nonetheless, the collaborative approach attempts to avoid or minimize the iatrogenic qualities of the adversarial process.

MULTIPLE RELATIONSHIPS AND PROFESSIONAL BOUNDARIES

According to Standard 3.05c, Multiple Relationships,

> When psychologists are required by law, institutional policy, or extraordinary circumstances to serve in more than one role in judicial or administrative proceedings, at the outset they clarify role expectations and the extent of confidentiality and thereafter as changes occur.

Psychologists should avoid mixing treatment and forensic relationships. However, accommodations may be made in limited situations. For example, some psychologists treat patients who have been court ordered for treatment, and the court requires some accountability for their services. Other psychologists work in small communities where no one else is available to fulfill both roles. Psychologists may treat patients who, in the course of therapy, become involved in litigation and their information is relevant to the court proceeding.

The forensic role differs considerably from the treatment role. Whereas a therapist focuses on the welfare of the patient, forensic psychologists have their primary obligation to the attorneys or courts that hired them. Their relationships with the clients are courteous but not necessarily intended to promote their welfare. Differences in the informed consent process, nature of record keeping, and fees are discussed later in this chapter.

What Is My Role?

A psychologist was asked by his patient involved in a custody dispute to "just write a short letter" describing his progress in treatment and parenting skills. The patient was generally pleased with the letter but asked the psychologist to include information about how the well-being of his children would improve if they could have regular visits with him. The psychologist rewrote the letter according to the wishes of his client.

Without intending to do so, the psychologist lets himself be maneuvered into making a custody recommendation. Any time psychologists write letters recommending custody or visitation arrangements, they are making a custody recommendation. This letter shifted the psychologist from a treating role into a forensic role. Such recommendations should only be made on the basis of an evaluation of all of the parties in the family, not on the basis of a therapeutic relationship with one parent. Furthermore, as the father's therapist, this psychologist lacked the objectivity needed to make a custody recommendation.

Court-Ordered Treatment

Sometimes courts order patients into treatment and demand access to treatment information. The disposition of a case against a patient may depend, largely or in part, on the nature of the patient's participation in therapy. For example, a court may order parents into treatment before they are permitted to visit with their children. The court may expect the psychologist to provide both information relevant to the disposition of the children and meaningful treatment to the parent or child. This places the psychologist in a hybrid role of having loyalties to both the patient and the court.

The demands of the court for all relevant information may conflict with traditional standards of confidentiality. On the one hand, the court needs assurance that the treatment fulfilled its goals. On the other hand, the psychologist's ability to help the patient is limited if the psychologist does not have a trusting relationship with the patient.

The best solution is to establish a balanced policy of confidentiality that all parties understand ahead of time. The psychologist should try to protect patient privacy as much as possible while meeting the demands of the court. For example, the psychologist can communicate general information to the court but withhold more specific information not directly relevant to the issues before the court. However, psychologists cannot guarantee full confidentiality because the release signed by the patient ordinarily allows the court to have complete access to information about the patient.

The hybrid roles of forensic therapists contain the potential for misunderstandings and ill feelings (Greenberg & Gould, 2001). Often these roles occur in high-conflict divorce or custody cases in which clients actively seek the opportunity to file a complaint. The failure to provide clear delineation of roles may give those clients just that opportunity.

Greenberg, Gould, Gould-Saltman, and Stahl (2003) noted that psychologists treating children involved in custody disputes can be most effective if they are "forensically informed" or understand the competing factors that influence the course of treatment. Among other things, forensically informed psychologists are scrupulous in maintaining neutrality and appreciate that the information they receive may be distorted. Parents may present information only supportive of their perspective, omit relevant information unfavorable to them, and otherwise intentionally or unintentionally misrepresent information. Parents may seek to undercut or remove therapists who do not support their agendas. Many of these problems can be reduced if the courts and attorneys are highly specific about the structure (e.g., costs and expectations) of the therapy, the use of information, and the relationship to extratherapeutic third parties, ahead of time.

Other Hybrid Roles

In smaller communities and rural areas, psychologists may be called on by a court to both evaluate and treat an individual. When this situation arises, "Specialty Guidelines for Forensic Psychologists" states that "the forensic psychologist takes reasonable steps to minimize the potential negative effects of these circumstances on the rights of the party, confidentiality, and the process of treatment and evaluation" (Committee on Ethical Guidelines for Forensic Psychologists, 1991, p. 443, IV, D, 2). That is, the specialty guidelines recognize that the hybrid role may create problems and urge psychologists to minimize the negative effects of the multiple relationship.

Also, psychologists may initiate a forensic evaluation only to learn that the patient needs immediate mental health services and that a delay in obtaining those services is not feasible. In such cases, forensic psychologists "attempt to avoid providing further professional forensic services to that defendant unless that relationship is reasonably unavoidable" (Committee on Ethical Guidelines for Forensic Psychologists, 1991, p. 446, VI, D, 2).

A Child in Need

A psychologist conducting a custody evaluation immediately learned that one of the children was seriously suicidal. One parent appreciated the depth of the child's depression; the other did not. The evaluator arranged for the emergency hospitalization of the child and then submitted his resignation from the case, noting that the extent of his involvement in arranging treatment compromised any perception of neutrality.

Therapy With Patients Involved in Litigation

Some patients are involved in litigation when they enter therapy. They may have initiated a lawsuit involving an automobile accident, a child custody dispute, or some other issue. They may have started therapy with the assumption that they could count on the help of their treating psychologist in their court case. These expectations may be reinforced by friends or attorneys who assume that the treating psychologist is necessarily a legal ally.

Psychologists should take steps to identify these patients early. They can ask all patients at the start of treatment if they are currently involved in litigation. Also, they can ask all patients who have sustained recent physical injuries or who request help for their children to give more details about their life circumstances and the possibility of litigation.

Nothing is wrong, of course, with treating patients involved in litigation. However, psychologists need to decide whether they are competent and willing to provide therapy to patients under these circumstances. Psychologists who decide to treat these patients should give increased attention to the informed consent process. These patients need to know that the confidentiality of the sessions may be compromised if they enter their mental health into litigation. In addition, the process of litigation may exacerbate whatever illness the patient has, place subtle pressures to maintain a sick role, and slow recovery. Because of the stress of the litigation or other factors, patients and clients may have difficulty hearing a psychologist discuss the distinction between treatment and forensic services. Care must be taken to ensure that patients understand the implications of treatment under these circumstances.

Other patients present themselves for therapy with apparently nonlitigious problems, but soon after treatment begins they solicit the involvement of the therapist in a court case. Psychologists need to anticipate the complications that may occur in these situations, and as soon as possible, communicate clearly to the patient the potential nature of their involvement. If possible, it is preferable for the treating psychologist to maintain only that treatment role and to insist that another psychologist be hired to conduct the forensic evaluation.

An Unprepared Psychologist

A patient asked a psychologist to testify on his behalf in a civil suit arising out of a car accident. The psychologist was insulted that opposing counsel had access to his therapy notes and was offended by the aggressive nature of the cross examination on the witness stand. The patient was offended by some of the remarks made by the psychologist. The psychologist failed to specify the payment arrangements with the patient ahead of time but ended up spending several dozen hours in preparing reports, talking to attorneys, traveling, and testifying. Although the patient won the case, he failed to pay the psychologist and never returned to treatment after the case ended.

This psychologist was unprepared for a forensic role. He did not appreciate the degree of scrutiny that would be given to his work, the amount of time that would be involved, the need to discuss the general nature of his testimony with the patient ahead of time, and the need to clarify payment.

INFORMED CONSENT

Psychologists should ordinarily obtain the informed consent of forensic clients. However, psychologists are not required to get informed consent for testing patients when testing is mandated by law or government regulation. Nonetheless, "Psychologists inform persons with questionable capacity to consent or for whom testing is mandated by law or governmental regulations about the nature and purpose of the proposed assessment services, using language that is reasonably understandable to the person being assessed" (Standard 9.03b, Informed Consent in Assessments).

Even when a court orders the evaluation of a client, it is still important to attempt to get the assent of the client even though the client does not have the legal ability or status to give consent. Clients should be informed of the nature and purpose of forensic work, including limits on confidentiality and probable use of the data. In a forensic environment, the psychologist should explain how an evaluator differs from a psychotherapist. Just the fact that the psychologist treats the clients with some basic civility may incidentally reinforce a mistaken preconception that the psychologist is there as a therapist.

Informed consent also applies to informing the attorney who may be hiring the psychologist. The "Specialty Guidelines for Forensic Psychologists" state that the psychologist should inform the party "of factors that might reasonably affect the decision to contract with the forensic psychologist" (Committee on Ethical Guidelines for Forensic Psychologists, 1991, p. 443, IV, A). The factors that need to be discussed include the amount of the fee, who is to pay the psychologist, the legal issues that the attorney wants addressed, and the type of services that are being requested. That is, psychologists should determine whether they are being asked to interview a client, write a report, appear in court, or do all of these. Also, psychologists should insist ahead of time that the data to which they have access (or the time available with the client) be adequate for them to complete the tasks requested of them. In addition, psychologists should discuss any prior or current personal or professional activities that might produce a conflict of interest, the psychologists' areas of competence and limits to their areas of competence, and (if relevant) the scientific bases and limitations of the methods that they will use. Psychologists should also inform the attorney or client of the possibility that they may need to seek additional consultation from other mental health professionals. Hess (1998) stated that the problems that arise between psychologists and attorneys can often be traced to "the first telephone call between the consulting psychologist and the attorney or client. A seemingly inconsequential issue that could be handled easily and early in the relationship may grow into a major problem if left unattended" (p. 109).

CONFIDENTIALITY AND RECORD KEEPING IN FORENSIC SETTINGS

The extent to which forensic services are covered by the Health Insurance Portability and Accountability Act (HIPAA) Privacy Rule (U.S. Department of Health and Human Services [HHS], 2002) is unclear. Forensic services provided for an attorney are probably exempt from HIPAA (Harris, 2003), and court-ordered treatment provided by a covered entity probably falls under HIPAA. However, there are hybrid roles, such as court-appointed parent educator, parent mediator, and case manager, which could or could not be interpreted as health care, depending on the circumstances. We can only hope that HHS will provide greater clarity in the future.

Whether forensic services are covered by the HIPAA Privacy Rule could have practical implications for psychologists. If services are covered by the Privacy Rule, then patients will have various rights, including the right to a privacy notice, the right to access their health records (excluding psychotherapy notes, unless permitted by state law), and the right to request an amendment to their records.

In any event, forensic psychologists need to attend carefully to record keeping. The "Specialty Guidelines for Forensic Psychologists" (Committee on Ethical Guidelines for Forensics, 1991) state that the record keeping standard "is higher than the normative standard for general clinical practice" and it should be the "best documentation possible under the circumstances" (p. 445, VI, B). Every important decision should be justified within the record. Salient information that appears to support conclusions contrary to those of the psychologist should be presented. Psychologists should document why that information did not change the conclusions found in the report. The documentation should start with the first phone call the psychologist receives and include information on every meeting, phone call, contact, or cancellation received during the course of the case.

Forensic psychologists should expect the court or another professional to review their documentation, including all records, original notes, test data, and test materials. Information on when or whether to send raw test data or test materials is covered in chapter 12 (Assessment). However, whether the information goes to an expert directly or through an attorney, another health care professional will likely scrutinize the rationale and selection of tests, the scoring, and the interpretation (including errors in computation and interpretation).

Psychologists may use computer-generated test reports. However, these reports cannot replace the clinical judgment of the psychologist. It is unacceptable for a psychologist to repeat the conclusions of the report without being able to provide a professional rationale for them.

Privileged-communication laws permit patients to withhold information from the courts in limited circumstances, but they do not typically apply in court-ordered examinations or court orders that are explicit about to whom the information should be released. Nonetheless, psychologists should scrupulously obtain signed release-of-information forms or be certain that the court orders explicitly give them permission to release information. Clients need to be informed at the start of the evaluation of the use of the information generated by the evaluation that will go to their attorneys or the courts.

An Unclear Court Order

A psychologist was hired as a custody evaluator and had a court order that permitted him to release information to the courts and the attorneys and to testify in a hearing concerning custody. However, one of the attorneys asked the psychologist to testify in a contempt hearing against one of the parents who was not complying with the interim court order on custody. The psychologist refused unless the court amended its order to permit him to testify in this hearing as well.

At times, attorneys ask psychologists to examine patients for them and may, or may not, use the information in court. In those situations, the judges, following the precedents in their jurisdictions, ultimately decide whether or not the work product of the psychologists gets admitted into court.

FEES

Standard 6.04a, Fees and Financial Arrangements, states, "As early as feasible in a professional or scientific relationship, psychologists and recipients of psychological services reach an agreement specifying compensation and billing arrangements." Judicious psychologists inform clients or their attorneys of the cost for the services and other payment policies, including acceptance of payment with credit cards, the policy on billing for missed appointments, and the range of services covered (e.g., report writing, testing, phone calls, court testimony). It is legitimate for psychologists to charge for all of the time expended in the case, including travel time, preparation, and time spent in the courtroom. Written confirmation of the understanding is preferable.

Psychologists working on forensic cases should not be paid on a contingency basis (getting paid only if the client wins in court). Such arrangements can give the appearance that psychologists might taint their testimony for their own financial gain (see "Specialty Guidelines for Forensic Psychologists," Committee on Ethical Guidelines for Forensic Psychologists, 1991, p. 443, IV, B). In addition, the client may lose the case, or the award may be much less than expected. It may be desirable to obtain a promise-to-pay letter from the client's attorney, although this is not a guarantee of payment.

Prudent forensic psychologists insist on getting paid in advance for their work. Failure to do so may result in a situation in which the client or the client's attorney may stall or withhold payment for the services if the report from the psychologist does not contain the elements that they wanted. Such a fee dispute can tarnish the perceived objectivity of the expert witness or result in subtle bargaining for changes in the report.

Even psychologists who get involved in the court system by virtue of their treatment of litigants in a case need to be concerned about fees. Certainly it would be reasonable for psychologists to provide some services to patients, such as writing a brief letter or making collateral phone calls, without charge, just as part of doing business. However, special care needs to be taken with forensic cases that can escalate into dozens or even hundreds of hours.

12

ASSESSMENT

An assessment can have many purposes, including the development of an educational placement of children, selection of job applicants, development of forensic reports, identification of neuropsychological strengths or deficits, or planning for mental health services. For purposes of the Ethics Code (American Psychological Association [APA], 2002a), assessment data include diagnostic information derived from clinical interviews (Fisher, 2003). Assessment data also include scores on intellectual, neuropsychological, objective, or projective tests; responses to structured personality inventories; behavioral ratings; psychophysiological responses; and other samples of behavior gathered systematically. Unfortunately, many managed care companies are discouraging the use of psychological assessments, even though they are often helpful and sometimes essential in developing an effective treatment plan (Eisman et al., 2000; Meyer et al., 2001).

The major source for professional standards and guidelines for assessment is the APA Ethics Code (especially Section 9, Assessment). Guidelines also are explicated in *The Standards for Educational and Psychological Testing* (American Educational Research Association, American Psychological Association, & National Council on Measurement in Education, 1999), "APA's Guidelines for Test User Qualifications" (Turner, DeMers, Fox, & Reed, 2001), and *The Rights and Responsibilities of Test Takers: Guidelines and*

Expectations (Joint Committee on Testing Practices, 1998), which is directed to those who take tests but also contains useful information for those who administer tests.

Negligent assessment can be the basis for complaints to licensing boards and ethics committees and for malpractice suits, although the frequency of such complaints is unclear because the classification systems of complaints do not always indicate whether the alleged infraction occurred because of an assessment or another professional activity. Assessments done in the context of a child custody or another forensic examination create a higher risk of an allegation of misconduct.

In this chapter, we review ethical and risk management issues surrounding assessment, including issues of competence, informed consent, and test security. Assessment issues unique to forensic work were covered in chapter 11 (Forensic Psychology). Assessment issues with persons from diverse backgrounds were covered in more detail in chapter 5 (Competence).

COMPETENCE

Psychologists need to be competent in assessment, as they should be competent in other domains of practice. A survey of neuropsychologists found that concerns about levels of competence (including application of assessment instruments and interpretation of results) were the most common ethical issue identified (Brittain, Frances, & Barth, 1995).

Defining Areas of Competence

The practice of psychological testing can appear deceptively simple. However, assessment and testing are professional activities and not simply the application of technical skills. Psychologists use informed judgment in the choice of tests and their administration and adaptation, the use of instructions and procedures, and the interpretation of the data. Moreland, Eyde, Robertson, Primoff, and Most (1995) and Krishnamurthy et al. (2004) have identified the many competencies necessary for the minimally competent use of psychological tests. These competencies cannot be reduced to simple phrases or a simple algorithm that untrained persons can follow. Turner et al. (2001) noted that competency in assessment requires both core knowledge (i.e., knowledge about psychometrics in general) and specific knowledge (i.e., knowledge about the responsible use of a specific test in a specific context).

> Although psychological tests can assist clinicians with case formulation and treatment recommendations, they are only tools. Tests do not think for themselves, nor do they directly communicate with patients. Like a stethoscope, a blood pressure gauge, or an MRI scan, a psychological test

is a dumb tool, and the worth of the tool cannot be separated from the sophistication of the clinician who draws inferences from it. (Meyer et al. 2001, p. 153)

Competence in psychological testing requires careful attention to the basics of test administration such as accurate administration and scoring of tests. In addition, the tests selected should be appropriate to the referral question, the patient's reading level, and the language and culture of the patient. The interpretation of test results requires psychological knowledge and an ability to integrate findings in a meaningful manner.

Professional Judgment in Selecting and Using Tests

Conscientious psychologists may disagree on certain topics regarding assessments, such as the appropriate role for projective tests or behavioral ratings. Nonetheless, psychologists should have a rationale for selecting the tests they use. Psychologists should select the appropriate tests or adjust their interpretation to meet the unique needs of the individuals being assessed. Test manuals can assist psychologists in those determinations. Ideally, the test manuals describe the purpose of the test and the qualifications of those who use it, offer instructions on test administration, and include psychometric and other useful data. Psychologists are obligated to use testing instruments as they were originally designed but may adapt them on the basis of research or evidence indicating the usefulness of the adaptation.

The interpretation of the test results must be based on a reasonable degree of competence as well. Tests scores should not be used in isolation but must be integrated with other information on the patient. Psychologists need to recognize limits to the certainty with which diagnoses, judgments, or predictions can be made about individuals and indicate significant reservations or limitations about test interpretations.

The use of assessment instruments with diverse populations requires special considerations. Cultural, racial, and other factors may affect the interpretations of many standardized psychological tests; misinterpretations can occur if a test is used for a group for which no normative data have been obtained and the psychologist fails to account for these limitations in the test interpretations. For example, the ability of a test to measure a particular psychological construct with one population may not necessarily mean that the same test has the same ability to measure the same psychological construct in another population (Fisher, 2003).

However, psychologists may be asked to assess clients or patients who are from cultures in which no information is available on how to provide culturally meaningful assessments. The APA Ethics Code does not prohibit psychologists from assessing these individuals but only requires that psychologists use appropriate caution and discretion in interpreting the test results.

Generally, psychologists administer the test in the language that the patient prefers or in which the patient is most competent, unless the purpose of the assessment is to determine the patient's abilities in the use of a particular language. Assessment reports should always indicate when tests have been administered in other than the patient's preferred language.

Certainly it is desirable to use tests that have been translated into or have been constructed in the primary language of the patient. However, caution needs to be exercised when using translated tests because at times no word, concept, or idiom in the second language corresponds precisely to the English word, concept, or idiom.

The quality of the data collected may be improved if psychologists speak to patients in advance concerning the nature of the tests and some of the questions that will be asked (including questions on sensitive topics) and the reasons why it is necessary to ask them. This is especially true for persons who, because of their cultures or backgrounds, are not generally familiar with the nature or purpose of psychological tests.

Obsolete Tests

Standard 9.08b, Obsolete Tests and Outdated Test Results, states, "Psychologists do not base such decisions or recommendations on tests and measures that are obsolete and not useful for the current purpose." Although the general preference is to use the most current version of the test available, psychologists may have professional justifications for using an earlier version of a test. Much depends on the purpose of the testing. Using an older version of a test in a longitudinal study may be more useful than using a more current version because of the desirability of keeping the posttest and pretest measures the same. Also, an earlier version of a test may have been subjected to more research relevant to its current use, justifying its greater usefulness with certain populations than a newer version. However, a newer version of a test may be desirable when new norms suggest it is more appropriate for the populations of patients being tested or when the test's discriminating ability has been refined. New versions of tests also sometimes include new subtests that are helpful to one's work.

A Careful Decision
A psychologist used an old version of an intelligence test for a man who had experienced a severe head trauma. The psychologist knew that the man had taken the same test 10 years ago and believed that using the same test would be the most effective method to determine the extent of his injury.

Online Assessments

Online assessments have advantages and disadvantages. On the one hand, online assessments are easy to administer and may provide useful information to some persons who are considering therapy. On the other hand, there are obvious problems of confidentiality and test security. Also, the results obtained from online assessment may not be valid. The psychologist cannot standardize the testing environment, make adjustments for the cultural or linguistic background of the patient, or ensure that the norms obtained from standardized-testing conditions would necessarily be the same for testing done over the Internet (Buchanan, 2002). For these reasons, psychologists need to be cautious in the use or interpretation of online assessments.

Collecting Data Adequate to Substantiate Findings

Standard 9.01a, Bases for Assessments, states, "Psychologists base the opinions contained in their recommendations, reports, and diagnostic or evaluative statements, including forensic testimony, on information and techniques sufficient to substantiate their findings." Among other things, this standard requires psychologists to be careful about their biases and unchecked assumptions. They need to ask if their conclusions are based on the data provided or are influenced by previous diagnoses or reports. The diagnostic label *borderline personality disorder*, for example, evokes apprehension and caution among many psychologists. However, psychologists need to be certain that the use of that label by a previous diagnostician does not unduly influence their interpretation of current test data.

Standard 9.01b, Bases for Assessments, now permits psychologists to develop opinions based on secondhand information if a direct evaluation of the individual was not practical. Then the psychologist must document the efforts and the results of the efforts to conduct a direct evaluation, clarify the probable impact of the lack of a direct examination on the reliability and validity of the opinions, and limit the nature and extent of opinions accordingly.

In addition, Standard 9.01c, Bases for Assessments, permits psychologists to develop opinions based on a record review. If a direct examination is not warranted or necessary, this is explained in the report, and the source of the information on which the psychologist based his or her conclusions and information is explained in the report. This exception could occur, for example, when a psychologist conducts a psychological autopsy, responds to a hypothetical question on a forensic examination, or conducts a record review for another legitimate purpose.

Automated Tests

Standard 9.09b, Test Scoring and Interpretation Services, requires psychologists to select "scoring and interpretation services (including automated services) on the basis of evidence of the validity of the program and procedures as well as on other appropriate considerations." In addition, Standard 9.09c, states, "Psychologists retain responsibility for the appropriate application, interpretation, and use of assessment instruments, whether they score and interpret such tests themselves or use automated or other services."

Psychologists retain responsibility for the selection of the particular test and testing service and the wording of the final report. Psychologists may use computerized assessments, but they still assume full responsibility for the wording of the final report. The interpretations derived from computerized services are based on group norms and are not adjusted to take into account the life circumstances of the patient. Psychologists must develop personalized interpretations based on the entire clinical picture of the patient and should note the limitations of their interpretations (see Standard 9.06, Interpreting Assessment Results). Automated tests do not replace the clinical judgment of psychologists.

Use of Tests by Unqualified Persons

Standard 9.07, Assessment by Unqualified Persons, states that psychologists do not promote the use of psychological assessment techniques by individuals who are unqualified unless "such use is conducted for training purposes with appropriate supervision." To an untrained person, it may appear that all psychologists do is add together a few scores, look up the results in a textbook, or cut and paste excerpts from a computerized printout. In reality, the appropriate use of psychological tests is far more complicated. Much harm can be done by the inappropriate use of psychological tests. Consequently, psychologists have a responsibility to restrict the use of these tests to those who know how to select, administer, and interpret them appropriately.

These standards, of course, do not preclude the use of assistants, employees, or supervisees who administer or score psychological tests under supervision. The responsibilities given to these individuals vary according to their qualifications and the demands of the testing situation. Nonprofessional employees could, for example, have their roles limited to submitting computerized forms to an assessment company, whereas an advanced psychologist-in-training who has had substantial supervised experience could perform almost all of the functions of test administration and interpretation.

Test Construction

According to Standard 9.05, Test Construction, "Psychologists who develop tests and other assessment techniques use appropriate psychometric procedures and current scientific or professional knowledge for test design, standardization, validation, reduction or elimination of bias, and recommendations for use." The development of tests can take years before the psychometric data are sufficient to ensure their professional usefulness. Psychologists who develop these tests need to develop a test manual or equivalent documentation that describes the purposes of the test, its psychometric information, methods of administration, scoring procedures, and other relevant information. Tests and manuals need to be updated and revised as needed. *The Standards for Educational and Psychological Testing* (American Education Research Association et al., 1999) describes the types of information that should be included.

Unfortunately, some individuals have developed and used short checklists purporting to measure certain traits but have failed to use a normative sample, to establish reliability or validity (other than face validity) of the checklist, and to gather information on the psychometric qualities of the test.

An Inadequate Service

A psychologist developed a "relationship checklist" based on several common issues that he had found through his work with couples. He intended to place the test on his Web site along with a scoring system in which he arbitrarily assigned the ranges for *troubled, potentially problematic,* and *secure* relationships.

Fortunately this psychologist sought consultation before placing the "test" on his Web site. The consultant noted the limits of online assessments (see previous section on online assessments) and urged that the psychologist abandon the test format and instead write a brief article in which several test questions were reframed as thought questions for couples to consider about their relationship. In addition to the psychometric limitations, the consultant correctly noted that the results of Web-based tests precluded the necessity of direct counseling in the event that the results became upsetting to the test taker. It also raised questions concerning the adequacy with which the test taker was informed of the nature, purpose, and limitations of the test (Kier & Molinari, 2004).

Explaining Assessment Results

Psychologists typically are required to give feedback to participants on the testing results (Standard 9.10, Explaining Assessment Results). According to the Health Insurance Portability and Accountability Act (HIPAA) Privacy Rule (U.S. Department of Health and Human Services [HHS], 2002), patients generally have access to test reports. Consequently, psychologists need to select their words carefully to ensure both accuracy and tactfulness in the event that the patient were to read the report. The best solution is preventive. That is, psychologists should be meticulous about the wording of their reports.

Under some circumstances psychologists may not have to share test results with patients. Such a restriction might occur, for example, in an assessment done in reasonable anticipation of a civil, criminal, or administrative hearing. Some other possible exceptions are unclear in the Privacy Rule, and we await clarification by HHS (the federal agency charged with oversight of HIPAA) or the courts.

Malony (2000) reported on the unique issues that arise when evaluating prospective religious professionals. The APA Ethics Code permits psychologists to evaluate applicants for occupations without sharing the results of that evaluation, as long as the process has been explained to them ahead of time. Nonetheless, Malony argued that evaluators owe the candidates a responsibility equal to the one they owe the hiring institution. Therefore, he urged that evaluators arrange with the referring institution to share the results with the applicant.

A Troubled Candidate

At the request of a religious denomination, a psychologist tested a lay missionary who was interested in ordination as a minister. However, the candidate had extreme PTSD as a result of witnessing atrocities in the country where he had served as a lay missionary. The extreme PTSD was likely to impede his ability to perform as a minister. The psychologist helped the denominational committee (and the candidate) consider options such as psychological treatment before a final vocational decision was made.

Sometimes psychologists are asked to evaluate the tests and reports of other psychologists, such as in the case of a child custody evaluation. In reviewing these tests and reports, psychologists should be aware of the limits on what they can say about persons whom they have not directly evaluated. They may, however, comment on the relationship of the test data to the test interpretation. They could point out, for example, that the original psychologist made a computational or an interpretative error, failed to address important questions in the reports, or failed to identify the bases for interpretations.

INFORMED CONSENT (PATIENT PARTICIPATION) IN ASSESSMENTS

Psychologists conducting psychological assessments need to obtain the informed consent of participants. As we described in chapter 7 (Informed Consent or Shared Decision Making), it may be desirable to reframe the issue as one of ensuring maximum patient participation in the assessment decisions. However, Standard 9.03a, Informed Consent in Assessments, provides for three exceptions to the general informed consent requirement in assessments. Informed consent for assessments may be waived when (a) testing is mandated by law (e.g., in response to a court order) or government regulation; (b) consent is implied because it is conducted as part of a routine educational, institutional, or organizational activity; or (c) the purpose of testing is to determine whether an individual is competent to make decisions.

Many difficulties can be addressed if psychologists clarify expectations and roles ahead of time. Often employers or third parties requesting testing have not considered the advantages, limitations, or implications of psychological testing. Psychologists can help them clarify their goals and expectations.

Sometimes psychological assessment is used to gather information or to create reports with a diagnosis (or statement of the problem) and treatment recommendations. The individual who requests the testing also expects to receive treatment. At other times, the referral for testing may be made by a third party. In either situation, the psychologist generally identifies the referral question and then proceeds to select and administer the tests. After the completion of the tests, the psychologist shares the product, report, or information with the patient, and if appropriate, gets consent to begin treatment. Although psychologists may be conscientious about involving patients in the treatment process, they may be less conscientious about involving patients in the assessment process, other than providing a general description of the nature of the testing process and the desired goals.

However, Finn and Tonsager (1997) have conceived of psychological assessment as a process that maximizes patient participation from the beginning of the assessment process, including collaboration on problem definition, goals, and strategies. C. Fischer (2004) likewise noted the importance of collaborating with patients in interpreting test data and identifying their relevance to particular life situations and concerns. C. Fischer noted that the need for a separate feedback session is minimized, because the patient has been getting (and giving) feedback through every step of the assessment process.

Similarly, Brenner (2003) has used the term *consumer-focused assessments* to refer to assessments that actively involve patients in formulating the referral questions and assessment process. In consumer-focused assessments, psychologists individualize the tests given so that they can best address the patient's concerns even if it means eschewing standardized test batteries. The assessments are strength focused and should include a follow-up session in which results are given in the context of a relationship with the patient. To communicate more clearly with the patient, psychologists avoid jargon. The debriefing with the patient also allows an additional source of information by which errors in the report may be uncovered or differences in perceptions may be addressed.

Although consumer-focused assessment as conceived by Finn and Tonsager (1997), C. Fischer (2004), and Brenner (2003) has much merit to it, it may not be a practical strategy when conducting forensic or employment assessments in which the court or an employer (not the person being evaluated) is the actual purchaser and consumer of the assessment. Nonetheless, C. Fischer (2004) has used a collaborative approach in some child custody assessments with success. This suggests that even in forensic testing, psychologists sometimes can increase the degree of collaboration with the person being tested when they can find some congruence between the needs of the person being evaluated and the referral source.

TEST SECURITY

Perhaps the most controversial of any of the revisions to the APA Ethics Code involved Standard 9.04, Release of Test Data, dealing with the release of test data (i.e., test reports, summaries, client responses or products from the test, and psychologist's notes and observations during the test) and Standard 9.11, Maintaining Test Security, dealing with maintaining test security and the release of test materials (i.e., test manuals, instruments, protocols, and test questions or test stimuli).

The challenges to test security have increased with the passage of the HIPAA Privacy Rule and the increased use of tests in litigation. Requests for the release of test data and test materials are likely to occur in two situations. First, patients may request access to or possession of their records, including test data or test materials. Second, requests may come for test data or test materials in the context of a court proceeding. The use of psychological data in courts has been increasing in recent years. These include cases that involve recommendations regarding child custody, civil suits in which emotional harm is alleged, and criminal suits in which the mental state of one of the parties is an issue. The changes found in the 2002 APA Ethics Code also need to be read in light of the HIPAA Privacy Rule and copyright laws.

Changes to the APA Ethics Code

The 1992 Ethics Code (APA, 1992) included two standards relevant to test data and test materials. Standard 2.02b, Competence and Appropriate Use of Assessments and Intervention, of the 1992 Ethics Code stated,

> Psychologists refrain from misuse of assessment techniques, interventions, results, and interpretations and take reasonable steps to prevent others from misusing the information these techniques provide. This includes refraining from releasing raw test results or raw data to persons, other than to patients, or clients as appropriate, who are not qualified to use such information.

In addition, Standard 2.10, Maintaining Test Security, of the 1992 Ethics Code stated,

> Psychologists make reasonable efforts to maintain the integrity and security of tests and other assessment techniques consistent with law, contractual obligations, and in a manner that permits compliance with the requirements of this Ethics Code.

These two standards placed an affirmative obligation on the part of psychologists to take reasonable steps to prevent the misuse of test information, ensure that "raw test results or raw data" were sent only to "qualified" persons, and protect the security of tests.

However, the 1992 standards presented at least three important problems. First, they never defined *raw test results* or *raw data*. Second, they did not clarify who was a qualified person. Reasonable psychologists acting in good faith might disagree about who is a qualified professional, depending on the circumstances. The narrowest interpretation of qualified persons could mean those who have the use of the particular psychological test within the scope of their licenses and have personally acquired the competence necessary to administer, score, and interpret the test. In this case, it would be necessary for the psychologist to learn about the credentials of the person who is to receive the raw data. This standard places a high burden on psychologists because they would have to evaluate the training and competence of all persons (including psychologists) who want to see the test data and materials. Smith and Evans (2004) described an even narrower interpretation of *qualified* in which a psychologist refused to share the test data with another professional who did not share his or her theoretical orientation.

A broader definition could include persons who have psychological testing within the scope of their licenses. In that case, qualified persons might mean either psychologists or physicians whose broad scope of practice legally allows them to perform many tasks also performed by other health care professionals. For some tests, a qualified person might be a mental health counselor or social worker, depending on the particular test being used.

The broadest interpretation of *qualified persons* could refer to persons who can use the raw test data for limited purposes as required by their role. According to this broader interpretation, some attorneys could be considered qualified persons.

The third problem with the 1992 standards was that the passage of the HIPAA Privacy Rule made them obsolete in certain respects. The Privacy Rule established minimal rules on patient privacy and patient control over health care information. As noted in chapter 8 (Confidentiality, Privileged Communications, and Record Keeping), the restriction of access to psychotherapy notes under the Privacy Rule does not apply to assessments (more information on forensic tests can be found in chap. 11 [Forensic Psychology], this volume). Consequently, patients in covered entities have access to their assessment results. The Privacy Rule created an exception whereby psychologists may deny patients access to their protected health information if doing so would be reasonably likely to cause substantial harm or endanger the life or physical safety of the individual or a third person.[1] Even in those situations, patients have a right to have the denial reviewed by another health care professional.

In response to the criticisms of the 1992 APA Ethics Code, the standards regarding test data and test materials were changed in the 2002 Ethics Code. Standard 9.04, Release of Test Data, of the 2002 Ethics Code states,

> (a) The term *test data* refers to raw and scaled scores, client/patient responses to test questions or stimuli, and psychologists' notes and recordings concerning client/patient statements and behavior during an examination. Those portions of test materials that include client/patient responses are included in the definition of *test data*. Pursuant to a client/patient release, psychologists provide test data to the client/patient or other persons identified in the release. Psychologists may refrain from releasing test data to protect a client/patient or others from substantial harm or misuse or misrepresenation of the data or the test, recognizing that in many instances release of confidential information under these circumstances is regulated by law.
>
> (b) In the absence of a client/patient release, psychologists provide test data only as required by law or court order. (Italics in original)

Standard 9.11, Maintaining Test Security, of the 2002 APA Ethics Code states,

> The term *test materials* refers to manuals, instruments, protocols, and test questions or stimuli and does not include *test data* as defined in Standard 9.04, Release of Test Data. Psychologists make reasonable efforts to maintain the integrity and security of test materials and other assessment techniques consistent with law and contractual obligations, and in a manner that permits adherence to this Ethics Code. (Italics in original)

Thus, the 2002 APA Ethics Code contains three major changes from the 1992 Code: Test data and test materials are defined; the criterion of releasing only to qualified persons was removed; and the Ethics Code was modified to be more in accord with the HIPAA Privacy Rule and general trends in law

---

[1]"A covered entity may deny an individual access, provided that the individual is given a right to have such denials reviewed . . . in the following circumstances:

(i) A licensed health care professional has determined, in the exercise of professional judgment, that the access requested is reasonably likely to endanger the life or physical safety of the individual or another person;

(ii) The protected health information makes reference to another person (unless such other person is a health care provider) and a licensed health care professional has determined, in the exercise of professional judgment, that the access requested is reasonably likely to cause substantial harm to such other person; or

(iii) The request for access is made by the individual's personal representative and a licensed health care professional has determined, in the exercise of professional judgment, that the provision of access to such personal representative is reasonably likely to cause substantial harm to the individual or another person." (HHS, 2002, 45 CFR 164.524 (a) (3))

and ethics toward more patient autonomy. Each of these changes is discussed in the following sections.

Test Data and Test Materials

According to Standard 9.04, Release of Test Data, of the APA Ethics Code, *test data* include

> raw and scaled scores, client/patient responses to test questions or stimuli, and psychologists' notes and recordings concerning client/patient statements and behavior during an examination. Those portions of test materials that include client/patient responses are included in the definition of *test data*.

As previously noted, the 2002 APA Ethics Code distinguishes between test materials (Standard 9.11, Maintaining Test Security) and test data (Standard 9.04, Release of Test Data). Behnke (2003) expands on this distinction between test materials and test data by noting that any data from a test that derives from, indicates, or reveals something about a specific patient falls under the definition of test data.

> When materials that would otherwise be test materials under Standard 9.11 contain information unique to a particular client, those materials become test data and thus fall under Standard 9.04. As an example, if a psychologist records client responses on *WAIS–III* scoring sheets that contain test items, the scoring sheets are now under Standard 9.04's definition of test data. (Behnke, 2003, p. 70)

For purposes of defining *test data*, the term *notes* refers only to notes taken during an assessment involving testing and does not include notes taken in a private counseling or psychotherapy session (Fisher, 2003). It could be argued that notes taken by psychologists during an initial interview for therapy would fall under the definition of *psychotherapy notes* under HIPAA and would be outside of the purview of what was intended in the definition of *test data* in Standard 9.04, Release of Test Data.

Psychologists must have a client–patient release or court order before they release any information, including test data or test materials. In addition, psychologists have the discretion to refuse to release test data or test materials under certain circumstances that are described in the following sections.

Also, the APA Ethics Code could be interpreted as having an implicit predisposition to permit the release of information to clients or patients or their representatives. According to Behnke (2003),

> psychologists may thus think of the Ethics Code revision as a shift in figure-ground: In the 1992 Code, psychologists presumed that test data would be withheld, unless certain conditions were met. In the new Eth-

ics Code, the presumption favors release unless the specified exceptions are present. (p. 71)

As Fisher (2003) noted, this represents a "sea change" toward greater respect for patient autonomy. However, many psychologists are concerned that the expansion of patient autonomy may come at a cost to the patient and public welfare as a result of the loss of test security.

Potential to Harm Clients or Patients

How should psychologists respond when a patient requests test data? Psychologists need to consider the APA Ethics Code, the HIPAA Privacy Rule, and state law. According to the Ethics Code, psychologists have the option of withholding test data if sharing those data would cause substantial harm to the patient or misuse or misinterpretation of the test. However, the Privacy Rule establishes a higher threshold for withholding test data from patients. Under the Privacy Rule, psychologists have an obligation to release protected health information to patients (except psychotherapy notes) unless they can demonstrate a threat to the life or physical safety of the patient or a third party or another highly unusual circumstance specified in the regulations (HHS, 2002, 45 C.F. R. 164.524 (a) (3)). This standard suggests that psychologists need to show discretion in what they place in psychological reports, knowing that patients are more likely to see them sometime in the future. Other than withholding test results and test data from a third party if the restriction was explained in advance and done in reasonable anticipation of a criminal, civil, or administrative hearing, there is much ambiguity.

Potential to Harm the Public Through Compromise to Test Security

How should psychologists respond when they receive requests for test data or test materials for use in courts? The general rule is that psychologists can send test data in response to patient authorizations (i.e., release of information forms) or a court order. In part, this standard represents greater respect for patient autonomy in determining the use of their records. However, it also reflects practical realities. According to HIPAA, patients have great access to their testing records. If patients can get the records themselves, then they can easily send those records to their attorneys or to anyone else. Thus, any prohibition against sending the testing records to third parties on the basis of a patient release would become moot.

How should psychologists respond when they receive requests for test materials for use in a court or by an attorney? The general concern is to protect the security of the copyrighted test materials. For example, an attorney may retain copies of tests and use them to coach future clients.

If tests gradually get into the public domain, their usefulness is eventually degraded. For example, individuals can alter their responses and manipulate test outcomes, resulting in substantial public harm. A coached student may be misplaced in a class for gifted students; an impaired airplane pilot may be able to fly; a court decision may be based on inaccurate information.

An Inaccurate Placement

A highly motivated parent insisted that her child be placed in a class for gifted students. She surreptitiously obtained a copy of the *WISC–III* and coached her child on the answers. The child was misplaced into a gifted program where she became unhappy and struggled with the class work.

Despite copyright protections, information about test materials sometimes leak into the public domain. It is often possible for motivated persons to find copyrighted test materials in libraries, bookstores, or other sources. In addition, some secure information has been posted on the Internet, thus increasing the likelihood that copyrighted information is being disseminated. For example, Ruiz, Drake, Glass, Marcotte, and van Gorp (2002) found that one psychologist had posted on the Web the stimuli of many common neuropsychological instruments and that another Web site contained accurate facsimiles of the Rorschach inkblot cards.

As the usefulness of tests degrade, it will become necessary to invest in substantial research programs to develop replacement tests, and there will be substantial costs to individual psychologists who will need to purchase the new tests and become trained in them. In addition, it appears unfair to the developers of tests, who will lose a substantial amount of income and thus the incentives to stay in the business of developing new tests. Much of the increased costs could eventually get passed on to the consumers.

Options for Psychologists

At this time, we cannot offer definitive answers for all of the scenarios that might occur with test reports, test data, and test materials. Case law may eventually clarify the obligations of psychologists. However, we present some likely scenarios and responses.

Patients may request to see test reports or test data. Psychologists who are a covered entity under HIPAA must release the test report or test data to patients unless doing so would fall into the narrow exceptions found in the Privacy Rule (HHS, 2002, 45 C.F.R. 164.524; e.g., a threat to the life or physical safety of the patient or a third party).

Patients may request to see the test materials. If it appears that it would be helpful for patients to understand the test data, it may be appropriate for psychologists to show patients limited amounts of test materials in their office. Also, C. Fischer (2004) noted that a collaborative approach in which patients are involved closely in the development and conclusions of the assessment reduces their interest in seeing copies of test data or test materials.

However, giving patients possession of the actual test materials or allowing them to take extensive notes on the content of the testing stimuli may conflict with copyright laws. As of the writing of this volume, we do not know how courts will reconcile the apparent conflict between the HIPAA Privacy Rule and copyright laws. We concur with Harris (2003) that psychologists should err on the side of test security, although there can be no guarantee that sometime in the future a court may rule otherwise.

Another scenario is that an attorney (other than one who has hired the psychologist) may request to see or possess test data or test materials. It is generally appropriate to send out test data in response to a patient request or court order. However, questions arise concerning the appropriate response when an attorney requests copyrighted test materials. The most prudent response would be to ask the attorney to designate a mental health professional who is qualified to review the test materials. One option may be, at the time of testing, to record patient responses on a form separate from the form that contained the test items themselves (Fisher, 2003). Other psychologists may elect to err on the side of withholding the test materials and wait for a court order for those materials or ask for a protective order pursuant to the release.

A third scenario is that a court may request to see or possess test data or test materials pursuant to a court-ordered evaluation. A proactive stance may be to request that the original court order for testing specify that the copyrighted test materials be released only to qualified persons. Ideally, the court will be advised as to the qualifications of those who can see the data. For example, for many personality or intelligence tests, the qualified person may be a psychologist or certain appropriately trained psychiatrists. For vocational or other tests, the qualified persons may include rehabilitation counselors or other professionals.

Psychologists who withhold copyrighted test materials should convey their concerns tactfully to the court and emphasize the public interest issues in their requests. Psychologists may ask the court for a protective order to prevent the attorneys or others who receive this information from disclosing or using it for any other purpose. Or, the court order may stipulate that the test materials must be sent to a professional qualified to interpret them. A psychologist who sends out test materials in response to a court order is not in violation of the APA Ethics Code.

13

SPECIAL TOPICS IN THERAPY

Many of the topics related to the practice of psychotherapy have been discussed in other chapters dealing with competence, boundaries, informed consent, confidentiality, advertising, and financial information. In this chapter, we address other topics related to psychotherapy, including the obligations of psychologists when approached by those who are already being served by others, coordinating treatment with other professionals, the duty to consult or refer, rules regarding the termination of patients, and determining the proper course of action when confronted with unethical institutional policies or with psychologists who violate ethical principles.

PATIENTS WHO ARE RECEIVING SERVICES FROM OTHERS

Sometimes psychologists are approached by patients who are currently receiving services from another professional. This decision may reflect impulsivity, poor judgment, deception, or pathology on the part of the patient. In these situations, it may be best for the potential new therapist to instruct the patient to go back to the prior therapist and try to resolve whatever issues appear to be present.

At other times, the decision may reflect good judgment on the part of the patient. The patient may have good reason to feel dissatisfied with the current therapist and want information about what other treatment options are available. Or, the patient may want more specialized services that the current psychotherapist is not qualified to provide, such as neuropsychological testing. Or, the prior therapist could have been dropped from the provider panel because the company was bought out, and the patient believes that he or she cannot afford the cost of treatment from an out-of-network provider. Or, patients who are participating in one theoretical approach of therapy may have heard about another approach and believe that the new approach will be better for them.

Standard 10.04, Providing Therapy to Those Served by Others, does not establish an inflexible rule for these situations but instead encourages psychologists to proceed carefully "in order to minimize the risk of confusion and conflict . . . and . . . . with caution and sensitivity to the therapeutic issues." On the one hand, the Ethics Code (American Psychological Association [APA], 2002a) does not require psychologists to refuse to accept any patient currently working with someone else without exploring the circumstances. On the other hand, it does not permit the psychologist simply to accept the patient without asking pertinent questions. Proceeding with caution and sensitivity means that psychologists who receive inquiries from patients currently being served by others need to ask the reasons for the inquiry and consider the best interest of the patient. Often it will be appropriate to consult with the first therapist with the consent of the patient.

COORDINATING JOINT TREATMENTS

Many times psychologists treat patients who are concurrently receiving treatment from other health care professionals for the same or related problems. To maximize effectiveness, psychologists need to coordinate their treatment with the other health professionals. Literature from the patient safety perspective may be instructive for psychologists in these situations.

According to the Institute of Medicine (2000), between 44,000 and 98,000 patients die every year because of medical errors, the eighth leading cause of death in the United States. Although the Institute of Medicine report may have overestimated the number of deaths caused by medical errors, the general consensus is that medical errors are too frequent, often fatal, and usually could have been prevented.

A *medical error* is defined as any mistake that substantially harms or creates a realistic threat of harming a patient. Many medical errors involve prescribing or delivering the wrong medication or the wrong dose of medication. Other medical errors include laboratory mistakes (e.g., the wrong name is submitted with a blood vial), dietary errors (e.g., providing the wrong diet in the hospital), or practitioner errors (e.g., conducting surgery on the wrong body part, failing to adequately monitor a patient who is suicidal or homicidal).

Most medical errors are related to systematic communication failures. For example, a nurse or pharmacist may have misinterpreted the medication abbreviation used by the physician, a resident may have been afraid to express his or her doubts or concerns to the attending physician, or patients may not have been given the opportunity to describe their symptoms clearly to their caregivers.

These communication errors obviously apply to psychologists who work in hospitals or other institutions, but the principles are also relevant to outpatient psychologists. Whenever two or more health care professionals are providing treatment, it becomes essential that they communicate with each other and foster a "culture of safety" to protect patient welfare. This means striving for enhanced communications not only with the patient but also with others involved in the welfare of the patient (e.g., other health care providers, family members) and members of the office staff. It also means showing a willingness to listen to others as well as giving out information.

Of course, it is essential to develop a trusting relationship with patients (or when clinically indicated, the patients' families), who will share valuable information essential for their treatment. However, patient welfare also requires that psychologists work closely and share information with psychopharmacologists and other health care professionals treating the patient. For example, medical errors can occur if psychopharmacologists do not receive accurate information from psychologists about their mutual patients. Psychopharmacologists need to know how the patient is responding to medications or if the patient is taking other medications, over-the-counter drugs, or alternative herbal remedies that could compromise the effectiveness of his or her prescription drug or otherwise jeopardize health and safety. Unfortunately, patients may not tell their psychopharmacologists about their use of alternative medical remedies.

Conscientious psychopharmacologists want what is best for their patients and appreciate constructive feedback. A majority of psychotropic medications are being prescribed by nonpsychiatrists, mostly pediatricians, family practitioners, and general practitioners. They may especially appreciate the input of psychologists.

Professional psychologists need a basic understanding of psychopharmacology and a general sense about which medications are appropriate for their patient's condition. However, prescribing medication can be very complex and involve multiple factors about which a nonmedically trained psychologist might be unaware. Psychologists should be careful not to go beyond the scope of their competence or license to practice.

A Physician Was Too Receptive

A psychologist was treating a patient who was receiving medication that appeared inappropriate for her diagnosis. When the psychologist called the physician to talk about her diagnosis, the treatment plan, and the possibility of a different medication, the physician asked, "What medication should he be on?" "What dosage should I start him at?" and "When should I begin to increase the dosage?"

Although we commend the physician for being receptive to the opinions of the psychologist, it would be helpful if the physician were more aware of the psychopharmacological treatments available. In this case, the psychologist asserted that the decision of medication rested with the physician, but she did note that "many patients with this kind of disorder have responded well to . . ." Because of her limited knowledge of psychopharmacology, she declined to comment on the starting doses and titration procedures.

An Unreceptive Physician

A psychologist was treating a patient who was receiving medication that appeared inappropriate for her diagnosis. When the psychologist called the physician to talk about her diagnosis, the treatment plan, and the possibility of a different medication, the physician said, "I think I know what I am doing, young lady. You just stick to your talking stuff and let me worry about the medication."

Here the psychologist felt herself to be in a quandary. On the one hand, she acknowledged that the physician had greater knowledge and skills in psychopharmacology, recognized the possibility that her concerns might be unfounded, and did not want to undercut the physician–patient relationship. On the other hand, she knew that this medication was not commonly used for this patient's condition, and the patient was not benefiting from it.

Although psychologists defer to psychopharmacologists on coordination of medications, this does not mean that psychologists have to be completely mute when it comes to discussing medications. When developing the treatment plan for patients, psychologists can help patients understand the costs and benefits of the medication, monitor the overall state of the patient, and inform the psychopharmacologist of any changes in the patient's status. In addition, psychologists should share information with other health care providers when their patients are using herbal remedies or nonprescription drugs that may interact with the prescription medications. Furthermore, psychologists should inform the psychopharmacologist of any suspected medication errors. Although they do not happen often, medication errors can be fatal (Fitzgerald, 1999).

DUTY TO CONSULT OR REFER

Psychologists have a duty to consult or refer when they know or should know that the patient is not benefiting from treatment or is unlikely to benefit from treatment. This duty may become apparent in the first interview with the patient or it may not become apparent until after many sessions.

Sometimes psychologists treat patients with disorders for which psychopharmacology and behavioral interventions are both effective. At other times, medication or therapy alone is indicated for therapeutic benefit. When patients have disorders that may respond either to psychotherapy or medication (e.g., many depressions, panic disorders), psychologists need to be especially careful to inform patients of treatment options. Patients need to know, in general layperson's terms, the nature of each treatment, approximate costs (i.e., money, time, and effort), and probable benefits.

An Informed Patient and an Informed Psychologist

A well-educated patient came to the first session with a psychologist with a detailed article about the benefits of a new medication for anxiety disorders. The psychologist was aware of the medication and the recent publicity about it. The psychologist appropriately described the benefits of the medication but noted that the outcome study had a high dropout rate, failed to include long-term outcome results, and was expensive. The psychologist also described nonmedical treatments for anxiety. Nonetheless, the psychologist offered to make a referral to a competent psychopharmacologist if the patient so wished.

Nonmedical psychotherapists sometimes work with patients with serious and chronic mental disorders such as schizophrenia or manic-depressive disorders. Effective treatment of these patients usually requires the psychotherapist to work with a physician, preferably a psychiatrist, or prescribing psychologist. Depending on the circumstances, a nonprescribing psychologist may refer the entire treatment of the patient to the psychiatrist or prescribing psychologist or may continue to provide psychotherapy while the psychopharmacologist prescribes and monitors the medication.

The failure to refer patients with serious and persistent mental disorders for medication could be grounds for malpractice. For example, in *Osheroff v. Chestnut Lodge* (1985), a patient was diagnosed as having a personality disorder and received 7 months of intensive psychodynamic psychotherapy in a hospital. His family complained about the lack of improvement, and after the hospital refused to change the treatment plan, transferred him to another hospital, where he responded well to medications and was discharged within 3 months. A malpractice suit was later filed against the first hospital.

The court determined that the psychiatrists in the first hospital were negligent in their diagnosis and treatment of the patient. Expert witnesses opined that the treating psychiatrists should have modified the treatment plan when it became obvious that the patient was not responding to the intensive psychotherapy. The lesson is that psychologists need to reconsider their treatment plans, seek consultations, or make referrals if patients are not benefiting.

However, the *Osheroff* case should not be construed to discourage psychologists from working with individuals with serious and pervasive mental disorders. A variety of psychosocial treatments have been found effective in reducing symptoms and improving the lives of patients with serious and pervasive mental disorders, especially when working in conjunction with a psychopharmacologist. Generally, effective treatments involve an optimistic therapeutic approach that emphasizes skill learning, self-regulation, and the mobilization of family and other nonprofessional resources (Bedell, Hunter, & Corrigan, 1997).

Neither psychotherapy nor medications appear to help some treatment-resistant patients (Ananth, 1998). When patients do not appear to be making progress, psychologists may need to consider an underlying medical problem or to rethink the diagnosis and treatment plan. Consultation and good documentation are especially important in these situations. Some of the questions that should be asked are, Is the treatment preventing the patient from deteriorating further? Does the patient value the treatment? Is the patient participating sufficiently in the treatment? and Are there life-endangering features? If the consultation fails to resolve the impasse, then the psychologist should consider discussing the prognosis with the patient in a candid and tactful manner. It may be appropriate to consider termination.

TERMINATION

Except when institutional policies state otherwise, psychologists may refuse to treat potential patients for any reason, including their perceived ability to pay for services. Once treatment has started, however, they do not have an unqualified right to terminate unless the treatment is completed; the patient ends the relationship; or the psychologist recommends alternative services and provides termination counseling, unless precluded by the actions of the clients or third-party payers (Standard 10.10, Terminating Therapy).

There are limited exceptions to this general rule, however. According to Standard 10.10, Terminating Therapy, psychologists may terminate treatment, even without the consent of the patients, if they no longer need treatment, are not likely to benefit from treatment, may be harmed by the treatment, or are threatened by the patient. Psychologists are required to provide termination counseling to patients, except when precluded by actions of third-party payers or patients.

Typically the moral principles of beneficence and respect for patient autonomy are not in conflict. Usually psychologists who initiate a treatment relationship with patients continue to provide that treatment until it is no longer needed or the patient decides to discontinue services.

Sometimes, however, the moral principles of beneficence and nonmaleficence conflict with respect for patient autonomy. That is, the psychologist reaches a conclusion that therapy is no longer helping the patient or may be harmful despite the desires of the patient to continue in treatment.

For example, the patient may have problems outside of the psychologist's areas of expertise. Or the psychologist may be unable to handle the transference or countertransference productively. A managed care company may have interrupted the services to the patient, or the patient (or someone associated with the patient) may threaten the psychologist.

Abandonment

Abandonment means termination of a patient when the psychologist knows or should have known that more treatment was needed. Abandonment can result in an ethics or licensing board complaint or a malpractice suit. The four *D*s of malpractice suits are the presence of a duty, the deviation from the standards of the profession, damage to the patient, and the direct connection between the deviation from duty and the damage to the patient (see chap. 1, this volume). An essential question becomes whether the termination of the patient was consistent with acceptable professional standards of conduct.

Abandonment can be intentional or unintentional. *Intentional abandonment* occurs when psychologists know that further treatment is needed but nonetheless terminate or withhold services or a referral. A lower standard of proof is required when a verdict of intentional abandonment is sought. The fact of termination itself, when the client clearly needed continuing care, might be sufficient to establish liability. In that case, expert witnesses would not be needed. *Unintentional abandonment*, however, occurs when psychologists terminate treatment when they did not know but should have known that further treatment was needed, and as a consequence, the patient suffers harm or harms another. Expert witnesses would be needed to determine the standard of reasonable care.

De Facto Abandonment

Patients may feel abandoned any time the psychologist is not reasonably available. This may occur when the psychologist takes an extended vacation and provides inadequate backup. Or, it may occur if a treatment relationship ends abruptly, such as when a psychologist suddenly moves to another city or leaves an internship setting and no efforts are made to prepare the patient for the change.

Limited Backup
A psychologist with a part-time practice provided no backup services. She had no answering service and did not check phone messages between sessions. She informed all prospective patients of these facts when they started treatment and screened out patients who appeared to have severe problems that might require emergency or after-hours interventions.

Is this psychologist acting ethically or showing good risk management practices? It is impossible to give yes-or-no answers. To a large extent the answers depend on the clarity of her disclaimers and the skill with which she screens out the more severe patients. Nonetheless, her practice involves some risks. One of her patients may manifest a mental disorder that is more severe than what initially appeared, and that patient may need the availability of crisis contacts.

Although not specifically addressed in the APA Ethics Code, psychologists should also consider their responsibilities for coverage when they go on vacations or if they become ill and must take extended leave from work. At such times, patients should be informed of the coverage arrangements of the psychologist. For example, it is acceptable for psychologists in solo practice to cover for each other, and it is also acceptable for those psychologists to give each other background information on patients who may be likely to need crisis services. However, it is desirable to inform patients of the coverage arrangements to eliminate any perception that confidential information was disclosed unnecessarily without their consent.

When Treatment Will Not Benefit or May Harm the Patient

Under rare circumstances, some patients may want to continue treatment when it would be meaningless or even harmful to them. Some patients with pervasive personality disorders may insist on more treatment by making threats designed primarily to engender reactions from others. Psychologists need to consider these threats seriously. Even patients who engage in manipulative gestures can seriously harm or even kill themselves. Nonetheless, it is possible for psychologists to conclude that continuing treatment would, in the long term, be harmful. Psychologists would not be acting competently if they allowed or encouraged this pattern of self-defeating behaviors. Consequently, psychologists may restrict or refuse appointments with patients if it is clinically indicated to do so (Guthiel, 1985). These decisions should be documented carefully.

A Difficult Patient

A patient with a serious and pervasive personality disorder was not benefiting from treatment or cooperating with the treatment program. She refused to seek consultation with a psychopharmacologist for medication and often missed appointments, only to call during the week for consultations under the false pretext that it was an emergency. When she did attend appointments, she idled away most of the hour resisting efforts on the part of the psychologist to focus on clinical issues, only to raise serious issues minutes before the sessions were to end.

The psychologist told her she could only remain in treatment if she (a) sought consultation for medication and took medication if clinically indicated,

(b) used therapy productively, and (c) discontinued calling between sessions unless it was an emergency.

The patient responded by making vague threats of suicide and refused to leave the office of the psychologist during the next appointment (unless she got a promise that the psychologist would always be there to treat her). She cajoled another health professional to call the psychologist and urge her to "quit being so mean" to her. The psychologist acted appropriately in insisting that treatment could only proceed if the patient engaged in behaviors likely to permit a favorable outcome. The response of the patient justified the wisdom of the psychologist's decision.

These situations may reflect a conflict between the ethical principles of respect for patient autonomy and beneficence and nonmaleficence. That is, ordinarily psychologists respect the wishes of the patient to continue to provide treatment. However, psychologists should not continue to treat if they believe that continued treatment would not benefit or would harm the patient.

Before making these decisions, psychologists need to ask themselves several questions such as, If it is necessary to terminate the patient, have I sought consultation on this issue? Have options been discussed with the patient? and Have attempts been made to reach a consensus with the patient on treatment goals? From a risk management perspective, it is advisable to document such decisions in detail.

If, after doing all of these things, the psychologist is still unable to help the patient, then consideration should be given to discussing the prognosis candidly with the patient. This situation requires great clinical acumen. Of course, it is possible that the treatment may be preventing the patient from deteriorating further or that the patient otherwise places great value on the treatment. When patients show life-endangering features, psychologists need to balance long-term benefits (the patient may eventually become cooperative with treatment—even if it is with another provider—and make progress) with short-term risks (the patient may actually attempt suicide). All factors being equal, psychologists should err on the side of continued treatment if the possibility of harm is realistic. Sometimes, not all of the factors are equal, and patients are better off with a psychologist who terminates an iatrogenic treatment.

CONFRONTING UNETHICAL INSTITUTIONAL POLICIES

Psychologists working in institutions, such as hospitals, schools, prisons, or public agencies may be asked to do things that are contrary to professional standards (Jacob-Timm, 1999; W. B. Johnson & Wilson, 1993; Weinberger & Sreenivasan, 1994). Sometimes supervisors or employers develop policies based on good intentions but with ignorance of clinical realities or the standards in the APA Ethics Code.

For example, psychologists in the military may have to turn over patient records in response to a military directive, even though the patient may refuse to grant permission for the release. A psychologist in a correctional facility may be asked to comment on the discharge of a prisoner, even though the prisoner was never informed that her psychologist would be asked to comment on her discharge. A psychologist in a state hospital might be ordered to prepare a patient for release to the community, even though the psychologist believes that the patient still poses a serious danger to public safety.

The standard for psychologists when faced with conflicts between the APA Ethics Code and organizational demands is to attempt to resolve the issues in a manner that permits adherence to the Ethics Code (Standard 1.03, Conflicts Between Ethics and Organizational Demands). Psychologists are not automatically subject to disciplinary sanctions because they followed the demands of their institutions, but they must try to correct the problems that give rise to possible ethical conflicts. That is, psychologists may not simply ignore the conflict and cooperate with the institutional policy without trying to change it.

W. B. Johnson and Wilson (1993) noted that a few military psychologists simply followed military regulations (the *military-manual approach*); a few passively thwarted directives that they believed were unjust by withholding information, deleting reports, or lying to protect patients (the *stealth approach*); but most tried to balance the needs of the patients with the needs of the military (the *best-interest approach*). The best-interest approach allows psychologists to vary their responses, depending on the circumstances. Often it is desirable for psychologists to take an educational approach and work quietly with institutional authorities to rectify the problem, or better yet, to anticipate conflicts ahead of time. Institutional leaders may have an important social goal that they are trying to meet. For example, a corrections administrator has the goal of providing as safe and humane a living environment as possible considering the inherent unpleasantness of a prison. Psychologists can often help them think of other ways to meet those goals while still adhering to the APA Ethics Code. The ethical-decision-making process described in chapter 4 (Ethical Decision Making) may help psychologists generate some useful solutions.

A Prison Disciplinary Board

A corrections administrator asked a psychologist to participate on a disciplinary board. The psychologist had a concern that such participation might cause him to lose credibility among his inmate patients. On speaking with the corrections administrator, the psychologist learned that the administrator was concerned about the wide differences and acrimony among members of the disciplinary board and some apparently capricious decisions. The psychologist offered to meet with the board to discuss ways to improve their internal decision-making process.

Unfortunately, sometimes psychologists fail to alter unethical institutional policies and have to decide whether the good they do by staying in the institution outweighs the harm created by institutional policies. In these situations, it can be helpful to look at both the proximal and distal causes of the conflicts.

The Long Perspective

A young psychologist was very frustrated by the increasingly high case loads in the community mental health center where he worked. Initially he blamed the supervisor for the problems, but on reflection he saw that the continual budget reductions (based on decisions by the state legislature) were responsible for most of the problem.

The psychologist joined his state psychological association and participated in advocacy efforts to increase funding for these public mental health centers.

IDENTIFYING ETHICAL MISCONDUCT

Psychologists occasionally learn from their psychotherapy patients about the ethical misconduct of a colleague. How should psychologists respond to this information? If the patient is intent on seeking redress for serious misconduct, the psychologist can direct the patient to the APA Ethics Committee, licensing board, or a malpractice attorney. If the patient is concerned about a relatively minor error, the psychologist may, with the consent of the patient, speak to the offending therapist directly and resolve the problem informally.

However, some patients do not wish to file a complaint when serious misconduct has occurred (e.g., sexual exploitation) and other patients may be at risk. Psychologists need to know what state laws govern their responsibilities in these situations. Unless state laws require otherwise, we encourage psychologists to follow the APA Ethics Code and to honor the patient autonomy and confidentiality rights. The Ethics Code balances general beneficence (or the obligation to protect the public in general) with respect for patient autonomy and confidentiality. Standards 1.04, Informal Resolution of Ethical Violations, and 1.05, Reporting Ethical Violations, require psychologists to report only if the conduct jeopardizes patient safety, cannot be resolved informally, and confidentiality rights are respected. Finally, it does not apply when a psychologist has been asked to review the work of another psychologist.

Few injured patients follow through with formal complaints. Often patients feel positively toward the offending psychologist, fail to see the behavior as exploitative, or assume responsibility for what happened. Psychologists who focus too much on the past ethical violation or the desirability of filing a complaint may be perceived by patients as pressuring them (see chap. 6, this volume, for discussion on intrusive advocacy).

Nonetheless, even if patients initially refuse to file a report, psychologists can educate them about proper professional behavior. For example, when therapeutically appropriate, the psychologist can explain to patients how sexual contact between patients and therapist violates the standards of the profession and harms patients. In addition, the psychologist should inform (but not pressure) the patient of the general nature of the disciplinary options available, including the time limits for filing complaints. These discussions with patients require therapeutic timing and sensitivity to the patient's preferences.

Psychologists should not adopt a dichotomous attitude in these situations (e.g., either the patient files a complaint or does nothing). Patients may be willing to take other positive actions other than filing a complaint.

A Careful Decision

A patient had sexual contact with a previous psychologist. Although she did not want the stress of filing a formal complaint or malpractice suit, she did write a letter to the psychologist informing him that she believed he had violated professional ethics and noted that she was considering filing a complaint. The patient asked her new psychologist to review the letter, which was subsequently sent. The patient believed that the offending psychologist would think twice about future misconduct after receiving such a letter.

14

PSYCHOLOGISTS AS TEACHERS

Although the teaching activities of psychologists are governed by the same disciplinary bodies as other psychologists, state boards of psychology provide little control over teaching psychologists except to the extent that the Ethics Code (American Psychological Association [APA], 2002a) is embodied in the regulations of the licensing board. Courts have had little involvement in the conduct of teaching psychologists. The teacher–student relationship is not a fiduciary relationship, and therefore no malpractice could occur. Institutional employers (i.e., colleges and universities) often provide the most meaningful oversight over psychologists who are teachers.

Even though the number of ethics complaints against teaching psychologists is low, they still face many important ethical issues. The behavior of psychologists as teachers should be guided by virtues and ethical principles as should the behavior of psychologists in other venues. Teaching psychologists should promote the welfare of their students by teaching competently (i.e., beneficence), avoiding harming them (i.e., nonmaleficence), respecting their autonomy,[1] and treating them fairly (i.e., justice). Teaching psychologists have some obligations to society at large in that their grades should

---

[1]In this chapter, we modify the principle "respect for patient autonomy" to read "respect for student autonomy."

accurately represent the work of their students, their institutions should only graduate qualified students, and their letters of reference should accurately represent the qualities of the applicants (i.e., general beneficence).

Of course, teachers should be competent in the courses they teach (Standard 2.01a, Boundaries of Competence), present information accurately (Standard 7.03b, Accuracy in Teaching), present students with the course requirements at the beginning of the course, and if changes are made in the course requirements, ensure that students still have the opportunity to meet these requirements (Standard 7.03a). Sexual relationships with students are unethical (Standard 7.07, Sexual Relationships With Students and Supervisees).

Tabachnik, Keith-Spiegel, and Pope (1991) reported that academic psychologists acknowledged a number of ethical issues beyond those noted in the APA Ethics Code, including the need for sensitivity (e.g., avoiding gossiping or betraying student confidences), integrity (e.g., acknowledging one's errors), and competence (e.g., being adequately prepared when teaching a course). Keith-Spiegel, Tabachnick, and Allen (1993) found that students valued fairness (e.g., faculty who do not ignore cheating or who use a fair grading system) and respect (e.g., professors who are courteous to students), and consideration (e.g., professors who refrain from telling students about their sexual attraction to them).

Competence

Psychologists must be competent in those areas in which they teach (Standard 2.01a, Boundaries of Competence), or they must undertake steps to gain that competence (Standard 2.01c). Psychologists must ensure that teaching assistants can perform their assigned duties (Standard 2.05, Delegation of Work to Others).

Competence means having not only a mastery of the subject matter but also an effective teaching style. The two are related. Those who have mastery over the content are better able to focus on the dynamics of the classroom and have more examples to draw on or personal research to cite when illustrating concepts in class.

Of course, sometimes unanticipated departmental vacancies occur, and psychologists have to teach courses in which they do not have adequate time to prepare or the optimal academic background. At other times, the quality of instruction is compromised by the physical facilities, class size, or other factors outside of the control of the instructor. It could hardly be considered an ethical violation if the department had to cut back on resources and teaching positions because of budgetary reasons. In those circumstances, psychologists should take steps to make the educational experience as rewarding as possible for the students.

Effective teachers have interpersonal as well as technical skills. The best teachers build a rapport with their students, know their names, learn something about them, and take an interest in their welfare. They are approachable and create opportunities for students to talk with them, such as by arriving early and staying late for classes, keeping office hours, or giving students their e-mail addresses. Effective teachers also listen carefully to students and respond thoughtfully to their questions or challenges. Their facial expressions and tone of voice indicate respect for the opinions of students.

When responding to comments from students, Howe (2001b) recommended that instructors "gear how they respond in large groups according to the most sensitive student they can imagine being in the class" (p. 104). Even when students give partial or incorrect answers in class, it is often desirable to find something in the student's response that contributed to the class discussion.

Individual attention is harder to give when classes are large. However, even in large classes, teachers can establish some personal contact by disclosing something about their professional background and interests, using collaborative or cooperative learning exercises, or being proactive about inviting students to visit during office hours (Whitley, Perkins, Balogh, Keith-Spiegel, & Wittig, 2001).

Psychologists can take steps to ensure a higher level of teaching. Student ratings are one source of feedback, although these ratings have their limitations (see, e.g., Greenwald, 1997). In addition, faculty members can share their syllabi, attend continuing education programs in teaching, keep abreast of changes in the content areas in which they teach, participate in a teachers' electronic mailing list, solicit and share feedback from colleagues on teaching style, and keep up-to-date on developments in teaching methodologies, such as the use of the Internet or AV equipment and cooperative or collaborative learning.

A Conscientious Teacher

One teaching psychologist followed the recommendations of Cerbin (2001) and developed a portfolio for every course he taught in which he recorded his reflection on the course goals, design, and outcomes. He included syllabi from other instructors, articles relevant to the course, and student evaluations from previous courses. He used the portfolio to guide future courses.

Fairness

Fairness is related to the ethical principle of justice in that students are treated impartially and equally. Not only is fairness intrinsically desirable but the perception of fairness can have an impact on the teacher–student relationship. Even minor acts, such as a delay in getting tests back to students or adding additional course work halfway through the term, can lead to a perception of arbitrariness and lack of concern.

An Instructor Tried to Be Fair

Halfway through a graduate class, the instructor assigned a recently published and lengthy book chapter that shed light on important concepts being covered in the class. Nonetheless, the instructor explained in detail why the change in course requirements was being made, gave appropriate attention to the book chapter in his lectures, and dropped a future assignment to ensure that the overall effort required in the course would not be substantially changed.

Instructors who try to be fair communicate objectives of the course and select methods of instruction that are appropriate to the goals of the course. They prohibit cheating and do not show favoritism. Of course, it is only natural that teachers like some students more than others. However, at a certain point, the overt expressions of attention may lead to a perception of favoritism, especially if other students feel that their needs are being ignored.

The course content should approximate what is described in the college catalogue. For example, survey courses cover a range of topics rather than just topics of personal interest. The syllabus is an informed consent document that tells students before, or at least at the start of, the course about its content and requirements. Tests should reflect the content covered in class and be appropriate for the difficulty level of the class. Grading criteria and procedures should be described to students in the syllabus.

Presenting Information Accurately

Standard 7.03b, Accuracy in Teaching, requires psychologists to present information accurately. At times psychologists may find it difficult to present information fairly and accurately. Some topics studied by psychologists are likely to engender controversy and elicit strong emotions in students. For example, should abstinence-only approaches be taught in HIV-prevention programs to adolescents? Does an abortion predispose some persons to develop later mental disorders?

At times these subjects may be more than just academic issues for the students. Some students may be infected with HIV/AIDS or know someone who is, may be struggling with the issues of sexual abstinence, or may have had an abortion. The difficulty of teaching these topics may be increased if students disclose personal information inappropriately or if they show intolerance of those who share other points of view.

Instructors can reduce problems by anticipating problems. They can set ground rules for treating others with respect during discussions. They can model that respect themselves by showing consideration for the feelings of others and presenting information fairly. "Students learn from the form as well as from the content of classroom instruction. Instructors' methods teach students not only about course content but more generally about the process of learning and making critical judgments" (Friedrich & Douglas, 1998, p. 555).

Furthermore, teaching about controversial topics has to be done within the context of course objectives.

Framing an Important Issue

At the first day of class, the instructor asked students to discuss the following question: "Are all men rapists?" The few men in the class felt offended that the question was even raised and were defensive. The classroom was quickly polarized.

It is important to ask about the goal of this discussion. Was it to discuss sexual assaults, gender issues, or some other issue? If so, could the goals of the discussion have been met without causing the men to feel defensive? If the goal was to discuss sexual assaults, could the question have been framed differently, such as "What can be done to stop sexual assaults?" or even framed positively, such as "What can be done to improve respect and understanding between men and women?"

Showing Consideration for Personal Beliefs

A psychologist taught at a religious college that encouraged sexual abstinence. When discussing HIV-prevention programs, the instructor accurately noted that abstinence-focused HIV-prevention programs typically have not resulted in significant reductions in high-risk sexual behaviors, pregnancies, or STDs. However, the instructor did not challenge abstinence as a goal because that reflected a value of many of her students. Also, she appropriately noted the methodological features of these programs that influenced the outcomes.

Here the instructor both presented accurate information and respected the religious values held by most of the students (and the college). She helped students appreciate that many "easy-solution" or "just-say-no" abstinence-focused programs were ineffective. Those who believed in abstinence as a goal had a better appreciation of what needed to be done to give abstinence-focused programs a more realistic chance of success.

Sensitivity to Diversity

Sometimes instructors encounter students who show prejudices or lack cultural sensitivity. These qualities can be especially problematic for students who are preparing to enter professions in which they will deal with culturally diverse groups. It would seem that psychologists, who have an ethical responsibility to refrain from unfair discrimination (Standard 3.01, Unfair Discrimination), should similarly encourage others to refrain from unfair discrimination. However, the principle of respect for student autonomy suggests that professors should avoid using their power and status to influence personal opinions. Consequently, academic psychologists need to balance the moral values of promoting a just society with the value of respecting student autonomy.

Several considerations can guide psychologists in addressing these challenges. First, culture is relevant to the science of psychology. A section on developmental psychology could not, for example, adequately cover Kohlberg's levels of moral reasoning without pointing out that other cultures define moral behavior differently. In that sense, an understanding of culture is essential for students to accurately understand the discipline of psychology.

Second, all members of the college or university community have a responsibility to ensure that the educational environment is free from intimidation and harassment. Comments or actions that demean students or other individuals because of race, sex, national origin, or other factors should be addressed.

Finally, it becomes difficult to draw the line between consensus values (i.e., opposition to overt racism, sexism, or homophobia) and particular policies or opinions that are more controversial (e.g., taking a position for or against affirmative action or a position for or against certain political candidates). No fixed set of rules can guide psychologists for every contingency in teaching controversial topics. Nonetheless, effective education generally builds on strengths, appeals to ego-syntonic ideals, confronts individuals in a supportive and respectful manner, and encourages nonjudgmental self-exploration. Efforts should be made to present the materials without stereotyping or blaming others (L. Jackson, 1999).

Handling a Delicate Topic

A psychologist teaching a developmental psychology course presented information concerning the differences in IQ performance among different ethnic groups. The psychologist strongly believed that such differences are due to environmental and not biological factors. She believed that it would be important for students to hear both sides of the debate, although she thought she had adequately countered the points raised by the nativist theorists. Nonetheless, the classroom was dead silent during her presentation, and the three African American students in the class appeared uncomfortable. After class she asked the African American students if they were offended by anything in the lecture or could give feedback on how the issue could have been presented better. The students gave little feedback but appeared to appreciate the effort to recognize their feelings.

Multiple Relationships and Professional Boundaries

Relationships between psychology teachers and students have a different quality than relationships between psychotherapists and patients. The APA Ethics Code prohibits any multiple relationships between psychotherapists and patients that are exploitative or clinically contraindicated. In addition, risk management principles suggest that such relationships between patients and psychotherapists should generally be avoided. However, at a college or university setting, certain types of out-of-classroom contacts between faculty members and students are viewed as positive. Part of the overall college experience is to get to know the faculty members and interact with them through Psi Chi (i.e., the National Honor Society in Psychology), departmental social events, or other venues. The challenge is to encourage relationships that are productive but not exploitative.

Of course, some actions are clearly harmful. According to the APA Ethics Code, sexual harassment is always wrong (Standard 3.02, Sexual Harassment), and sexual relationships with students in teachers' departments or over whom they have evaluative authority are prohibited (Standard 7.07, Sexual Relationships With Students and Superivsees). *Evaluative authority* could even refer to former students who may rely on the professor for a letter of reference.

Some may argue that a prohibition against sexual relationships restricts the autonomy of students to date whom they want. However, dating between faculty members and students creates a greater potential harm for the students. Faculty members have control over students' grades, letters of evaluation, academic advancement, and careers. For these reasons, many colleges and universities have instituted policies that prohibit dating between faculty and students.

Ei and Bowen (2002) found that students generally viewed sexual relationships between faculty members and students as inappropriate. However, engaging in other activities alone with instructors (e.g., going to lunch together) was given midrange ratings, and engaging in group activities with instructors (e.g., going to lunch with a group of students) was generally viewed as acceptable.

A Sensitive Professor

A young faculty member generally got along well with his students. He asked a student to babysit for him and his wife. The student had taken a course from him the prior semester but was no longer enrolled in his class or likely to be in future classes. He framed the offer in such a manner that she could feel free to decline.

This instructor was aware that sometimes students may not feel that they have the opportunity to decline these "offers." He was careful to ask a student who was not in his current class so that there could be no implication that her grade was in any way influenced by her decision.

However, the relationship between students and faculty should be governed by more rules than just avoiding exploitation. The broader issue becomes how faculty members can structure relationships with students to promote their well-being (i.e., beneficence), respect their autonomy, and treat them fairly.

One way may be to try to create a sense of community among students and faculty. According to Appleby (2000), this sense of community "is neither random nor accidental. It is something that certain UPDs [undergraduate psychology departments] consciously recognize as valuable, actively create strategies to produce and work hard to maintain" (p. 39). Some of these activities include supporting student organizations, involving students in research, having departmental celebrations and rituals, and sponsoring activities that bring people together to achieve a goal. These activities are intended to create emotional bonds between students and between students and faculty. However, they also can be viewed from an ethical perspective in that they promote student welfare (e.g., by getting them involved in research projects and learning from faculty members through informal settings) and student autonomy (e.g., by ensuring greater student control over their organizations, participation in department activities, and service on departmental committees).

Creating a sense of community can also involve a conscious attempt to discuss the atmosphere and goals of the entire department or curriculum. The ideal program also challenges students to strive to reach their highest potential, to talk openly about their ideals and conflicts, and to contribute to the atmosphere of their training programs.

Good departments facilitate these goals by talking explicitly about the values that motivate their behavior and by attempting to integrate ethics into all of their classes. A model might be drawn from some undergraduate colleges that have adopted an "ethics-across-the-curriculum" model. Although the nature of these curricula may vary, they often require students to take a certain number of classes in which mastery of ethics constitutes a substantial portion of the class grade. Furthermore, they openly articulate the goal of teaching ethics as primary to the education of the students. Finally, extracurricular activities are developed for the purpose of promoting certain values.

A Conscientious Effort to Promote Student Welfare

The six members of the psychology department of a small college developed a set of goals for their majors. The goals included traditional academic topics (e.g., basic research design and history of the discipline) but also topics that were more difficult to quantify, such as critical thinking skills and ethics (including ethical issues within the discipline and ethical conduct as a student). Relevant ethical issues were covered in every psychology course the students took.

General Beneficence

Psychology instructors also have responsibilities to society in general. They are obligated to give grades that accurately reflect the work of their students, take precautions to prevent cheating and plagiarism, discipline students who engage in those activities, and write accurate letters of reference.

Cheating has several harmful effects. If cheating were permitted, it would reward students who made an inadequate effort to master the material, demoralize those students who were honest, and undercut efforts to improve the moral character of all students.

Some professors address cheating proactively. They try to make it harder for students to cheat by forbidding students from wearing caps during examinations, requiring students to sit two seats apart from each other, or increasing classroom monitoring during tests. Other instructors emphasize the moral reasons why cheating cannot be permitted and attempt to get students to "buy into" the concept of academic integrity. Some colleges and universities develop honor codes in which the students participate in determining the definition and consequences for cheating. Ideally these codes clearly define cheating. Is it acceptable, for example, for students to study from tests given in previous terms? Is it acceptable for students to collaborate on presentations or research papers?

Letters of reference should be written accurately. Unfortunately, letters of reference often inflate the qualities of the students. Certainly students want to have strong letters of reference, but if a faculty member cannot write a positive letter of reference for a student, then it is desirable for that faculty member to be candid with the student or to share a draft of the letter with the student and then let the student decide if the letter should be sent.

One way to address the twin obligations of faculty is to consider the communitarian reformulation of the Golden Rule by Amatai Etzioni: "Respect and uphold society's moral order as you would have society respect and uphold your autonomy" (1996, p. xviii). That is, the best way to promote the welfare of the students may be to get them to focus on goals that promote the welfare of society. From this perspective, students should not only be taught not to cheat or plagiarize but also be taught why cheating and plagiarizing are harmful to society in general. Students should not only be treated with respect but encouraged to treat others with respect. Students should be encouraged to adhere to standards of academic integrity because, among other reasons, such standards are necessary to have the public assured that the grades accurately reflect the degree to which the course content was mastered.

Other Ethical Issues

Academic psychologists make decisions that have ethical implications every day. They need to decide classroom policies on makeup tests, missed classes, and extra credit. They need to create a course that has the appropriate difficulty level for the students. Courses that are too hard or too easy are unfair to students. They need to balance the price of textbooks against the benefit that students will receive from purchasing them.

Teachers decide what kinds of relationships they will have with other faculty members. Do faculty members have obligations to intervene if they hear a student complain about another? Certainly they have an obligation if the complaint involves physical or serious emotional harm to another student or the clear violation of a university rule. However, should the faculty member intervene if the allegation involves lectures that are not interesting or course material that is not perceived as relevant to the department's goals or students' needs?

These questions do not have easy answers. At times, conscientious psychologists may disagree as to the optimal answer. For example, Keith-Spiegel, Whitely, Balogh, Perkins, and Wittig (2002) described the case of a student who brought to the attention of the instructor that her test had been graded incorrectly and she should have received three fewer points. Keith-Spiegel et al. recommended that the student's grade be reduced by the three points. However, I (Knapp) have adopted a policy that I do not penalize students who inform me when errors were made in their favor (but I do alter grades when my error lowered their grades). My reasoning is that I do not want to penalize honest students who identify these errors when less honest students with similar errors are not penalized. Nonetheless, Keith-Spiegel et al. and I agree that these errors can usually be avoided by double-checking hand-scored tests.

SPECIAL CONSIDERATIONS IN PSYCHOLOGY TRAINING PROGRAMS

Some standards of the APA Ethics Code appear applicable primarily to psychologists involved in programs that train future psychologists. Such training programs have the twin responsibilities of trying to empower students and facilitate their development while protecting the public from incompetent psychologists (Kitchener, 2000b).

Competence

Faculty not only must be competent to teach subjects assigned to them but must ensure that their students will be competent professionals. Throughout the program faculty need to ensure that the students are acquiring the factual information, problem-solving skills, technical skills, and judgment to assume a professional role. Vacha-Haase, Davenport, and Kerewsky (2004) found that over half of the clinical programs surveyed had terminated at least one student during a 3-year period. Inadequate clinical skills was the most commonly identified reason for termination, although ethical misconduct and impairment were also common reasons.

The Wrong Approach
A number of years ago the faculty in a department evaluated students every year but never gave them results of the evaluations (unless it re-

sulted in dismissal) and gave them no input into the evaluation process. The periodic disappearance of a student increased anxiety and distrust among the students.

The faculty learned from their error and changed the evaluation process so that students were informed of the criteria used in the evaluation, were permitted to have input into the process of their evaluation, and always received feedback on their progress toward meeting departmental standards. The feedback informed students on how they could improve before problems reached the level at which a dismissal was considered. Current criteria for accreditation of doctoral programs by the APA include the requirement that students receive written feedback at least on an annual basis "on the extent to which they are meeting the program's requirements and performance expectations" (APA, 2002b, Domain E).

The assessment of the factual knowledge of students is relatively straightforward. However, assessment of technical skills and emotional competence is more difficult. Students may be strong academically but fail to show the compassion, sensitivity, or common sense needed for them to do well as practitioners.

A Marginal Student

A psychology department was perplexed with how to deal with a second-year doctoral student who did well in his course work but had a distant and detached interpersonal style. He often seemed to miss social cues and engaged in role-plays and other clinical skill activities in a mechanical fashion. The faculty seemed unsure of his ability to do well in a practicum, let alone to do well as a professional. However, they had no documentation to rely on to deny him a practicum placement.

The marginal potential of the student raises the question as to whether the department failed in its obligation to the public and the student. Perhaps they could have screened applicants more thoroughly for interpersonal skills and informed applicants that clinical skills would be evaluated throughout their program. The departmental catalogue could have emphasized the importance of demonstrating competence in clinical skills as a requirement for practicum placement. The department could have provided yearly evaluations to students on professional demeanor and competence in clinical skills or could have made competence in clinical skills an essential requirement of their clinical classes.

Informed Consent

Informed consent takes on special importance for those who work in psychology graduate training programs. Psychologists responsible for educational programs must take reasonable steps to ensure that they provide the experiences necessary for students to obtain the credentials advertised by the program (Standard 7.01, Design of Education and Training Programs). The descriptions of programs (Standard 7.02, Descriptions of Education and Training Programs) and individual classes (Standard 7.03, Accuracy in Teaching) should be accurate and should inform students ahead of time of any requirement for mandatory therapy (Standard 7.05a, Mandatory Individual or Group Therapy).

Programs may not require students to disclose sensitive personal information unless the requirements for such disclosures are clearly identified in advance or it is necessary to evaluate a student who appears to be impaired (Standard 7.04, Student Disclosures of Personal Information). Faculty may not provide mandatory group or individual therapy to students whom they also may be required to evaluate (Standard 7.05b, Mandatory Individual or Group Therapy). Psychologists who are supervisors inform students and supervisees of the procedures for evaluation at the outset of their work together (Standard 7.06a, Assessing Student and Supervisee Performance).

An essential part of the education of psychologists, especially for professional psychologists, is to ensure that students can demonstrate the emotional competence and technical skills necessary to be effective professionals. Part of emotional competence may include self-understanding, including the cultural traditions and family dynamics that influence behavior, values, or perceptions of events. Some of the technical skills include the ability to communicate empathically. Often these are demonstrated by classroom assignments that require a certain amount of self-disclosure. Graduate programs vary to the extent that they require these self-disclosures. The APA Ethics Code does not prohibit such self-disclosures as part of the graduate program; it only requires that graduate schools inform students of these requirements before they apply to the program.

Multiple Relationships and Professional Boundaries

Sexual relationships with students are prohibited by the APA Ethics Code. Hammel, Olkin, and Taube (1996) found that 15% of female respondents reported having a sexual relationship with an educator. The modal relationship was between a 40-year-old male married faculty member and a 30-year-old single female student. In retrospect, 84% of the students viewed the relationship as coercive and harmful to their working relationship. It appears, however, that the frequency of such contact has declined over the years.

Of course, relationships with students should be guided by more than just the axiom, "don't have sex with students." Multiple roles as mentor, instructor, supervisor, coauthor, and research supervisor allow the opportunity for enriched educational experiences if handled properly. Some encounters are desirable, such as talking to students at colloquia, receptions, and other special events (Biaggio, Paget, & Cenoweth, 1997). Other actions are often benign, such as going to dinner with a group of students or sharing rides with students going to conferences.

The obligation to remain objective in evaluating students may be compromised if a coexisting social or business relationship also exists (Sullivan & Ogloff, 1998). Students may fear adverse consequences if they refuse the offers. Whereas undergraduates can usually just drop out of courses, graduate students have fewer options when a disagreement or friction occurs between them and a faculty member.

Indeed, mentoring is viewed as an essential component of graduate education. In a mentoring relationship, a mature psychologist takes an interest in and promotes the career of a younger apprentice, going beyond the more routine advising role. However, astute mentors are concerned that these encounters could be construed as favoritism or could influence the evaluation process. Other students may ask if one of their peers is getting preferential treatment or if they are being denied equal access to a faculty member because of the attention given to one of their classmates.

Unethical Conduct by Students

Faculty members have an obligation to protect the public and need to be alert to cases of unethical conduct on the part of students. Fly, van Bark, Weinman, Kitchener, and Lang (1997) used a critical-incident-technique survey with the training directors of programs of clinical and counseling psychology. Their survey generated 89 incidents, of which 25% were concerned with breaches of confidentiality, 20% with professional boundaries, 15% with plagiarism or falsification of data, 10% with welfare, 10% with a procedural breach with ethical implications (e.g., taking a patient chart home against facility regulations), 9% with competency, 8% with integrity or dishonesty, and 3% with misrepresentation of credentials. More than half of the students had already completed a course in ethics. More than one fourth of these cases were resolved with a student leaving the program.

Ethical infractions of students are usually considered on a case-by-case basis. More serious consequences can occur for violations that risk harm to patients, reflect defects in character, or violate clear rules. However, often an educational approach is desirable. The infraction may have occurred because the student used poor judgment during a period of stress, or failed to think through or consult when faced with an ethical dilemma.

Creating a Positive Environment

The goal of training competent psychologists can be furthered when programs take deliberate steps to create an ethical milieu in the graduate program. Currently ethics typically is taught both formally through a compartmentalized course and informally or through an "implicit" or "underground" curriculum, which refers to the institutional atmosphere within the program. Students quickly learn about the milieu within their institutions (Branstetter & Handelsman, 2000) and what they need to do to survive or thrive within this environment. The stories, jokes, and anecdotes of the program function as part of the oral tradition that may either reinforce or undercut moral behavior. This "underground curriculum" may teach students more about ethics than the ethics course they take.

Any effort to provide a comprehensive education must address the "hidden curriculum" or the broader milieu in which training occurs. Students notice whether the faculty members are courteous, promote student welfare, and model collegiality, integrity, and hard work. Every faculty member and student should ask whether the messages being taught informally are congruent with the messages being taught through formal instruction.

Krumboltz (2002) described how he proactively improved the quality of student research projects in a doctoral program by focusing on team cooperation in research and combining a playful spirit with a serious work attitude. Although Krumboltz did not express these ingredients in terms of moral principles, they nonetheless focused on promoting student well-being while at the same time ensuring a high level of education.

In the ideal training program, faculty members model ethical behavior through their sensitivity to students and their willingness to talk openly about their ethical ideals and conflicts. The goal is to create a pattern of ethical awareness that students retain throughout their careers. The ideal training program also challenges students to uplift others and to talk openly about their ethical ideals and conflicts. Students are not only passive recipients of the atmosphere of their training program but also responsible participants who can improve the program by the nature of their attitudes and their conduct.

The "Three Sisters"

Three mature graduate students formed an informal study group. They did very well academically, asked good questions, showed respect for other students, and became popular with the faculty (one of whom affectionately dubbed them the "three sisters"). Before they left for their internship year, the department chair thanked each of them individually for their contribution to the program. She asked herself "How can we attract more students like this?" and "How can we influence other students in this direction?"

15

CLINICAL SUPERVISION

Clinical supervision is an ongoing relationship between a senior member and an apprentice or junior member of the profession in which the supervisor monitors the quality of the treatment given by the apprentice or junior member, enhances professional functioning, and may also be used to ensure the qualifications of the junior member to become an independently practicing professional (Watkins, 1997).

Clinical supervision differs from *administrative supervision*, in which psychologists are involved with nonclinical aspects of management, such as promotion, scheduling, salaries, or other general record keeping. Clinical supervision also differs from consultation in which psychologists provide expertise to other professionals who retain control over their final work product. Sometimes psychologists mistakenly use the term *peer supervision* to refer to *peer consultation*. However, unless individuals have surrendered their professional autonomy to a supervisor, discussion of cases with peers is more accurately called consultation.

Supervising psychologists retain authority over and responsibility for the services delivered. The supervisory relationship has an immediate impact on the patients of the supervisee because they are actually the patients of the supervising psychologist. The supervisor maintains the responsibility

217

of ensuring the quality of the services provided. The supervisees are the "arms and legs" or service extenders of the supervisor.

The supervisory relationship can have a long-term impact on the life of supervisees. Many supervisees recall encountering difficult patients and determining how to respond to these cases by recalling the words ("hearing the voice") of their supervisors. Supervisors are often the role models for their supervisees and are crucial in forming their professional identity. The senior psychotherapists interviewed by Rønnestad and Skovholt (2001) reported that their supervisors had left an internalized influence on them. These senior psychotherapists reported "powerful, passionate, and appreciative descriptions of professional elders" (p. 184).

Several sets of rules govern the supervisory relationship. The entire Ethics Code (American Psychological Association [APA], 2002a) applies to all areas of professional practice, including supervision, and it has several standards specific to supervision. Also, state psychology licensure boards develop regulations that specify the conditions required for supervising psychologists-in-training and other supervisees. Finally, malpractice courts require supervisees and their supervisors to adhere to minimal standards of professional competence.

Although they may not necessarily physically see the patients of supervisees on a regular basis, supervising psychologists still have fiduciary responsibilities for them. In their relationships with the patients of supervisees, supervising psychologists are guided by the principles of beneficence (i.e., ensuring that the quality of treatment is good), nonmaleficence (i.e., ensuring that the patients are not harmed), respect for patient autonomy (i.e., ensuring that the patients of their supervisees are informed about the salient features of supervision), and the other ethical responsibilities that exist between psychologists and their patients.

In their relationship with their supervisees, psychologists are guided by the principles of beneficence (i.e., promoting the welfare and competency of the supervisee), nonmaleficence (e.g., avoiding harmful multiple relationships with supervisees), fidelity (i.e., being explicit about the nature and standards for supervision ahead of time and providing accurate and timely feedback), and general beneficence (i.e., fulfilling obligations to society in general). General beneficence is especially relevant when psychologists are supervising individuals who are preparing to become independently practicing psychologists. The supervisors have an obligation to the public in general to ensure that these trainees have the necessary skills to practice competently.

At times supervisors' obligations to supervisees and patients may appear to be in conflict. On the one hand, supervisors want to enhance the welfare of their supervisees. On the other hand, they have to protect the welfare of the patients. If the supervisee is an apprentice intending to become a licensed professional, the supervisor also has a responsibility to future patients of that supervisee. Usually, but not always, these goals are congruent. Although their primary responsibility is for patient welfare, supervisors generally try to be supportive of their supervisees.

In this chapter, we review the general nature of supervision and applicable ethics codes and legal standards and make risk management suggestions for psychologists. We describe the need for supervisors to be competent as supervisors and to ensure competence on the part of supervisees. We also address the need for informed consent procedures for the supervisee as well as the patients being seen by the supervisee. Finally, we review multiple relationship issues in the supervisory relationship. References to supervisory responsibilities also have been made throughout this book in chapters 5 (Competence), 6 (Multiple Relationships and Professional Boundaries), 14 (Psychologists as Teachers), and 16 (Research and Scholarship).

COMPETENCE

The concept of competence can refer both to the competence of the psychologist as a supervisor and to the competence of the supervisee. We review the concept of competence as a supervisor first.

Competence as Supervisors

Psychologists need to be competent in all of the professional tasks that they undertake, including supervision (Standard 2.01, Boundaries of Competence). The competent supervisor is able to perform the services required of the supervisee and has the skills unique to those of an effective supervisor. All competent psychotherapists have some of the skills essential for success as a supervisor, such as the ability to listen, conceptualize cases, and communicate empathy. However, competence as a psychotherapist does not ensure competence as a supervisor.

Many psychologists get thrust into the role of a supervisor, with no training or experience other than having been supervised themselves at one time. No proficiency credential or sequence of courses or continuing education programs exist to ensure competence as a supervisor. Although the literature on supervision has many gaps, much is known about supervision, and beginning supervisors can benefit from knowing that literature. Fortunately, many doctoral programs now include course work in supervision. Of course, psychologists should become familiar with the requirements for supervision as specified in their licensing laws and regulations.

The competent supervisor clarifies the goals of supervision and the means for reaching those goals by including input from the supervisee as much as is consistent with promoting patient welfare. Competence as a supervisor requires consideration of the ethical principles underlying the supervisory relationship, the theoretical orientation used both in the treatment of patients and in the development of clinical skills in the supervisee, the means of assessment (e.g., process notes, videotapes, audiotapes, live treatment together), and the criteria for feedback.

Supervision models vary considerably. No one supervisor is highly effective for every supervisee, and supervisors may vary their style according to the personality and skill level of the supervisee. One supervisory style requires self-disclosure about family patterns and personal factors that could be triggers for countertransference issues. Such supervisors review problems in therapy by looking at "repetition of behaviors within the supervisee's life" (Pitta, 1996, p. 16). Other supervisory styles are more detached or didactic.

Lowery (2001) found that supervisees considered their most effective supervisors to have both technical skills (i.e., good clinical skills and a broad knowledge base as well as providing helpful feedback) and interpersonal skills (e.g., self-confidence, acceptance of the trainee, and a warm and supportive demeanor), leading to a perception that they were invested in the supervisory process. In contrast, their worst supervisors lacked both technical skills (e.g., poor clinical skills, unhelpful feedback) and interpersonal skills (e.g., poor communication skills, unreliable or unavailable) and gave the perception that they lacked an investment in the supervisory experience. These findings were highly similar to the traits of good and poor supervisors identified by graduate students (Martino, 2001). Similarity of theoretical orientation also appears to enhance the perceived quality of the supervision (McCarthy, Kulakowski, & Kenfield, 1994).

Informal comments from supervisors revealed that they liked supervisees who were highly motivated to learn, balanced their scientific training and their direct experience, and were self-reflective. They disliked supervisees who acted like they knew it all, could not reflect honestly on their relationships with patients, or tried too hard to create an impression of competence. One supervisor noted that the actions of the successful supervisee were counterintuitive for good students. Whereas students writing papers or giving class presentations are instructed to put their best foot forward, student supervisees need to put their conflicts and uncertainties forward.

A Good Supervisor

The internship supervisor at a university counseling center expected his students to know the outcome literature and treatment techniques. However, he always asked his supervisees "How does it feel?" or "What does your gut tell you?" His favorite phrase was "This isn't a math problem, you know."

Informal comments from supervisees showed that they liked supervisors who took supervision seriously, had a sense of humor, and focused on their strengths. Good supervisors had a good grasp of patient problems and could suggest alternative ways of approaching clinical problems when necessary. They seemed to appreciate the developmental nature of the supervisory process. One supervisee stated, "He believed in me even at times when I didn't believe in myself." Another said, "She taught me the overwhelming importance of kindness."

To achieve their fullest potential as supervisors, psychologists can read, consult, and take continuing education workshops on supervision. They can also form peer consultation groups about their supervisory activities or participate in a supervision electronic mailing list. The environment should provide a feedback loop whereby the outcomes and procedures are consistently being reviewed and modified. The various forms of external feedback include, but are not limited to, consultation, supervision of their supervision, and gathering systematic data on outcomes or patient satisfaction.

Competence of Supervisees

Psychologists only delegate to supervisees work that they are competent to perform, and they avoid delegating responsibilities to supervisees when a multiple relationship with a patient risks exploitation or the loss of objectivity (Standard 2.05, Delegation of Work to Others). Competence means emotional competence, technical skills, an understanding of the unique cultural issues in the population receiving services, and socialization into the roles of a professional.

Regardless of their work setting, psychologists can be held responsible for the actions of their supervisees under the doctrine of *vicarious liability*. This doctrine was originally applied to medical settings in which physicians were assumed to be the "captains of the ship" and responsible for all the actions of persons working under them. Just as captains are ultimately responsible for the actions of every crew member, surgeons are responsible for the actions of every member of their surgical teams, and supervising psychologists are responsible for the actions of their supervisees.

A Zealous Prosecutor

An employee at a large agency was accused of very serious ethical violations. The investigators for the licensing board could not prosecute the employee because she was not licensed, but they did file a complaint against the only psychologist who worked at the agency, alleging that she was the supervisor and responsible for the behavior of the employee. However, the director of the agency sent a letter noting that the psychologist was not the supervisor of this employee, had no control over her work product, had not hired or evaluated her, and had only spoken to her a few times during her entire employment at the agency. The case was dropped.

Unfortunately, some individuals interpret the word *supervisor* loosely. Although the psychologist had more training and had given some advice to the employee when asked, she never had line authority over this individual and never had the responsibility to monitor the supervisee's behavior.

Under limited circumstances, supervisors following reasonable standards of practice may be unaware of supervisees' actions that were done counter to instructions or behind their supervisors' backs. Under those circumstances a supervisor may be exonerated from any wrongdoing. Nevertheless, these exceptions are limited, and most aggrieved patients will assume that the supervisor knew or should have known of the negligent actions of the supervisee.

Psychologists can ensure competence by screening prospective supervisees carefully. In addition to information on academic credentials and work experience, it is important to know if their present skill level is consistent with the expectations of the supervisor.

Psychologists evaluate supervisees on the basis of their actual performance (Standard 7.06b, Assessing Student and Supervisee Performance). Oral feedback should be given frequently. Written feedback should be given periodically for all supervisees and more frequently with supervisees who are experiencing difficulty.

Standard 2.05, Delegation of Work to Others, requires psychologists to ensure that their supervisees follow all ethical rules, such as those requiring the informed consent of patients. Supervisors should take whatever actions are necessary to ensure the quality of services delivered to the patient. The extent of the monitoring will depend on several factors, including the skill level of the supervisee and the type of services being performed.

Because supervisors are responsible for the treatment of the patients, it appears essential that they regularly review the records of all of their supervisees. They should teach what they expect to find in the patient record, including what information should and should not be included in the notes and how certain information should be phrased. Prudent psychologists document all of their supervisory sessions. The documentation can include some information on each patient but also should include information on the training goals of the supervisee, whether he or she is meeting the goals, and if not, what needs to be done to meet those goals.

Psychologist have the same obligations to ensure the quality of services provided by all employees whether or not they are seeking licensure or another credential. It is advisable for psychologists, employers, and supervisors to have in place appropriate office policies, training programs, staff meetings, and a system for monitoring the quality of services.

Salient Professional Events and Stressors

Special attention should be given to prepare trainees for salient professional stressors and life events. Some of the common professional stressors for psychologists include dealing with difficult and draining patients, managing multiple responsibilities with little time, and dealing with institutional policies (see chap. 5, this volume). Some of the common professional stressful events for psychologists include treating patients who assault or threaten to assault them or who threaten to harm others or themselves. Successful patient suicides are especially stressful. Psychotherapists who have a patient commit suicide often respond with extreme distress that can substantially affect the quality of their professional and personal lives.

Consequently, attention should be given to training students to work with patients who are suicidal or homicidal. One survey suggests that between 14% and 17% of psychology interns had a patient who committed suicide (Jobes & Berman, 1993). Despite this high percentage of suicides, many training programs reportedly do not have clear administrative procedures to follow when the patient of an intern commits suicide (Ellis & Dickey, 1998). Nor do all programs always emphasize interventions with suicidal persons in their training or provide adequate emotional support to trainees when a suicide does occur.

Jobes and Berman (1993) recommended that agencies adopt specific policies in regard to suicidal patients. These include knowing the relevant laws and ethics, maintaining a written policy and procedure statement, assuring clinical competence, providing adequate documentation, and having adequate resources for consultations. Ensuring clinical competence means that interns will have basic information about risk assessment and intervention with suicidal patients. This includes understanding critical risk factors and the fact that suicidality may wax and wane throughout the course of treatment.

Having adequate resources, as applied to interns, means providing adequate supervision when faced with difficult patients, including the possibility of using outside consultants when appropriate. They note that special problems can occur with some difficult patients.

> Consultation with regard to suicidal patients is especially useful in that these patients (particularly those with borderline pathology) often assume demanding–dependent postures in the therapeutic relationship, thus presenting frequent and intense crises. (Jobes & Berman, 1993, p. 95)

The frequent crises may distract the psychologist intern from the long-term treatment goals. In addition, countertransference feelings, unless processed carefully, may sabotage the treatment relationship. Similar policies should be developed on other potentially critical events, such as homicidal or aggressive patients.

A Painful Decision

An intern entered her supervisor's office and announced in an almost mechanical manner that she was leaving her internship and intended to leave the field of psychology entirely. A patient had committed suicide several months earlier, and she had never been able to regain confidence in her therapeutic skills. She reported that she was frequently anxious, had trouble sleeping, and had to force herself to come to work.

The supervisor was shocked by her announcement because he had no idea of the depth of her anguish. The patient who had committed suicide was a highly disturbed young man, and the psychologist believed that the intern had acted appropriately in assessing the degree of dangerousness and fashioning a reasonable treatment plan. On further discussion, it appeared that the presence of a recent patient with suicidal ideation had triggered memories of her traumatic experience with the patient who did commit suicide.

The supervisor helped the intern process her experiences and reflect on her reactions. With his encouragement, she delayed her decision to leave the field and entered short-term individual therapy. Years later, when she received a prestigious award, she publicly thanked her supervisor. Only she, the supervisor, and a few close friends understood the depth of her appreciation.

Ensuring a Productive Relationship

The best way to ensure the quality of services is to ensure an honest and open relationship between the supervisor and supervisee. From the standpoint of the supervisee, the biggest dilemma is how to be honest and open to feedback while at the same time appearing competent. From the standpoint of the supervisor, the biggest dilemma is how to support the intern while at the same time correcting shortcomings and promoting professional growth. The difficulty of managing these dilemmas should not be underestimated. Many supervisees fear the evaluation or judgment of their supervisor. Defensiveness in supervision is especially problematic.

Supervisors can minimize the likelihood of an impasse in their competing obligations by screening intern applicants carefully, being direct and clear about expectations, and being supportive whenever possible. Supervisees can minimize the likelihood of an impasse by being honest about their abilities and limitations and not being afraid to tell supervisors about their uncertainties or clinical errors.

Trainee Ethical Errors

Trainees will make clinical errors and ethical misjudgments. Errors may become "teachable moments" as long as an open relationship exists between the supervisor and supervisee. Sometimes these errors involve violations of obvious rules, such as having multiple relationships with patients, or more subtle problems, such as defensiveness in supervision, poor clinical skills, or poor clinical judgment.

For example, we noted in chapter 6 (Multiple Relationships and Professional Boundaries) that all psychotherapists run a risk of eroticizing relationships. Supervisors who recognize this as a natural phenomenon are more likely to have interns who discuss these issues with them openly and seek guidance on how to handle these feelings in a manner that best promotes patient welfare. The last thing a supervisor should want is supervisees who harbor intense, forbidden, and hidden feelings.

Impaired Trainees

One of the goals of supervisors is to help interns understand personal issues that could harm the quality of their services (Vasquez, 1992). At times, supervisors may become aware of pervasive and substantial limitations that prevent the trainee from performing at minimally acceptable levels of behavior. The student may have done well academically, but only when in the practicum or internship setting can the supervisor see that the student lacks the qualities necessary for effective functioning as a mental health professional.

The internship year provides an important opportunity to identify and address impairment. The internship year is inherently stressful as it often involves relocation of one's family, minimal pay, and, in effect, starting a new "job." In their review of trainee impairment, Forrest, Elman, Gizara, and Vacha-Haase (1999) found that internship sites commonly encountered supervisees with depression, personality disorders, or other emotional problems. Looking at data across settings and with a different methodology, Forrest et al. estimated that the rate of impairment was between 4% and 5% of trainees. A retrospective study by Skorina, Bissell, and DeSoto (1990) found that most psychologists who became alcoholic identified 24 as the age at which they first concluded that drinking had begun to interfere with their lives. However, only 22% ever had a supervisor or employer discuss their alcoholism, and these occasions did not result in an effective intervention, and therefore, had little impact on them.

Training programs have a responsibility to deal with impaired trainees. Ideally the supervisor will establish clear goals for the trainee, give consistent feedback, document any problems, and give the trainee early warning to start addressing these issues and to respond to a remediation plan. The preferred goal is to have remediation programs in place so that students with personal needs can get assistance. In rare cases, students may have to be dismissed from the program.

Poor Judgment

The newspaper announced that an intern had been arrested for soliciting a prostitute. This was his first offense, and he was assigned to the Accelerated Rehabilitation Diversion program, which, if he successfully completed it, would enable the misdemeanor to be erased from his record after several years.

The supervisor later learned that the student was depressed following the breakup of his marriage. His behavior was very atypical for him, but he agreed to an evaluation by a psychologist not affiliated with the internship setting. The psychologist reported that he had an adjustment disorder with depressed mood and recommended treatment. The incident did not otherwise disrupt his internship. Fortunately, this setting had the authority to order the evaluation and treatment because the program had made it explicit at the outset of the supervision that it could require psychological or medical evaluations and therapy for any interns who appeared to have a condition likely to impair their ability to perform their professional duties competently.

Enhancing Supervisee Excellence

Usually training programs do a good job of preparing their interns for entry into the profession. From the acculturation model discussed in chapter 2 (Foundations of Ethical Behavior), one of the tasks of supervisors is to enhance the movement of trainees toward integration strategies of the model, where they can understand professional ethics and interpret them in light of a strong personal moral code.

Helping a Virtuous Intern Become a Virtuous Psychologist

An intern had worked as a counselor in a domestic abuse shelter before she entered graduate school in psychology. To her, being a good psychologist meant "going the extra mile" and "doing whatever it takes" to help her patients. However, under the firm but compassionate direction of her supervisor, she also came to understand the importance of professional boundaries with patients.

Additional models may be helpful to guide supervisors. First, it may be helpful for supervisors to think of one component of trainee competence in terms of virtue-based risk management (e.g., competence, knowledge, sensitivity, insight; see chap. 2, this volume). The goal of the supervisor is to ensure knowledge of ethics codes and professional data, technical competence, sensitivity, thoughtful reflectiveness, self-care, and careful documentation. In addition, it may be helpful for supervisors to think in terms of the long-term emotional health of trainees and of inoculating them against the personal and professional stressors and life events that could impair their ability to have a productive professional career (see chap. 5, this volume).

Encouraging Thoughtful Reflection

On the first day of their internships, a supervisor asked the interns to write down what they expected would be the most difficult (and most rewarding) situations they would face in their internship year. After they had done that, he gave them a list made by the prior year's interns on the last day of their internship listing the most difficult (and most rewarding) situations they faced during the last year. He then asked the interns what they could do to anticipate, prevent, or mitigate those negative situations and what they could do to foster those positive situations.

The supervisor was trying to encourage the virtue of thoughtful reflection as well as self-care. The exercise had a profound impact on the supervisees, who often referred to "the list" during their entire internship year.

Psychologists take reasonable steps to protect their supervisees from harm (Standard 3.04, Avoiding Harm) and exploitation (Standard 3.08, Exploitative Relationships) and do not have sex with them (Standard 7.07, Sexual Relationships with Students and Supervisees). Although supervisors may not have the same degree of control over supervisees as psychotherapists have over patients, there is still the potential for abuse.

A number of supervisees report having had sexual relationships with their supervisors sometime during their careers. These relationships diminish or eliminate the effectiveness of supervision because they threaten to reduce the objectivity of the supervising psychologist, and therefore, the quality of patient care.

Furthermore, there is a question as to whether the supervisee would be entering into the sexual relationship voluntarily given the power differential and the possibility of revenge if the supervisee said "no" (Slimp & Burian, 1994). In addition, many psychologists and supervisees who participated in these sexual relationships came to see them as increasingly negative over time, although more than half continued to view them as positive (Lamb & Catanzaro, 1998). Finally, these relationships may convey a message that boundary violations are acceptable and may increase the likelihood that the trainees will, as psychologists, engage in harmful boundary violations themselves. However, the data on this are mixed.

Lamb and Catanzaro (1998) suggested that the harmful impact of relationships between supervisors and supervisees could be minimized if the parties considered the length of their initial relationship and the circumstances of their termination, the power differential between the individuals (e.g., is the supervisor still expected to write letters of recommendation?), and the likely impact on the parties involved (e.g., is one of the individuals in crisis or a vulnerable life situation?). More information on multiple relationships with trainees can be found in chapter 6 (Multiple Relationships and Professional Boundaries).

However, multiple relationships between supervisors and supervisees involve other and more subtle boundary issues. The potential for harmful social relationships is probably not as great as it is for psychotherapy patients. Certainly social encounters can help make the work atmosphere more enjoyable for everyone. However, the objectivity of the supervisor may be compromised by a friendship, and the social relationship may not be entirely voluntary on the part of the supervisee.

The supervisor–supervisee relationship has some of the elements of a teacher–student relationship and some of the elements of a psychotherapeutic relationship (see Table 15.1). The educational relationship has a goal of promoting the competence of the student, usually requires no self-disclosure on the part of the student or self-disclosure limited to certain domains in the

TABLE 15.1
Comparison of Educational, Treatment, and Supervisory Relationships

Characteristic	Relationship		
	Educational	Treatment	Supervisory
Goals	Impart knowledge and skill	Foster behavioral, emotional, or cognitive change	Develop skills that involve both emotional and cognitive processes
Obligations	To both students and the public	Primarily to clients; some limited to the public	To both supervisees and the public
Requirement for self-disclosure	Limited for students	Extensive	Varies according to supervisory style, although may be relevant to performance

training program, and involves dual obligations to teach the student and to represent mastery of material accurately. The therapeutic relationship has a goal of promoting the well-being of the patient; requires extensive self-disclosure by the patient; and involves a primary obligation to the patient with limited exceptions, such as when a patient is an abused child. The supervisory relationship stands in the middle between the educational and therapeutic relationships. The goal is to promote the well-being of supervisees and to ensure their competence to practice. It involves dual obligations to supervisees and the public, and it may, depending on the supervisory style, require self-disclosure, although not to the extent found in the psychotherapeutic relationship.

Good supervisors create an atmosphere in which supervisees can engage in meaningful and honest self-exploration. They convey to the supervisee that the supervisory sessions are important to them. They are quick to praise supervisees for good work and honest effort. When it is necessary to criticize the supervisee, they do so tactfully and clearly prescribe alternative behaviors.

INFORMED CONSENT

The concept of informed consent can refer both to consent for the supervisee and consent for the patients being treated by the supervisee. We review the concept of informed consent for the supervisee first.

Informed Consent With Supervisees

Psychologists inform supervisees of the standards for feedback at the beginning of supervision, and they also give timely and specific feedback

(Standard 7.06a, Assessing Student and Supervisee Performance). Although it is not required by the APA Ethics Code, written agreements with supervisees minimize the risk of misunderstandings. The agreement should clearly specify the nature of the supervisory relationship, the type of services to be provided, the terms of termination of the supervisory relationship, record-keeping obligations of both parties, conditions governing the use of the supervisor's name, and a requirement that the supervisee follow the Ethics Code and relevant state laws and regulations. Also, it may include the means used to evaluate the supervisee, such as audio or video recordings, case summaries, case presentations, joint therapy with the supervisor, or other means. Such agreements should have some flexibility to account for the changing needs or skills of the supervisee.

Psychologists should also check with their malpractice carrier to be certain that their supervisory functions are covered. Supervisees should carry their own professional liability insurance as well.

Informed Consent With Patients of Supervisees

Supervisees must inform patients of the supervised nature of the relationship and provide the name of their supervisor (Standard 10.01c, Informed Consent to Therapy). In addition, psychologists need to ensure that supervisees do not engage in other activities that could mislead patients about their supervised status. For example, office stationary, professional business cards, billing statements, and other announcements should accurately reflect the supervised status of their trainees. Misleading stationery or public announcements can give patients the impression that the supervisee is providing services independently.

These practices protect the supervisee, the supervisor, and the public. Knowledge of the supervised status of the trainee also may protect the supervisor. It is preferable that the patient call the supervisor with a concern early in treatment rather than having the supervisor learn about the discontent through a formal complaint. Furthermore, the trainee or supervisee status may be relevant to the patient's ability to receive insurance reimbursement.

16

RESEARCH AND SCHOLARSHIP

Research in psychology has led to substantial advances in mental health treatment, educational practices, health care, child rearing, and other important domains of life. However, as important as the social utility of the findings are, the manner in which the research is conducted is important as well.

An Experiment Out of Control

A prison simulation experiment got out of control. The "guards" became increasingly callous and the "prisoners" became increasingly demoralized. The primary investigator became so engaged in his role that he initially failed to appreciate the harm his experiment could have on the participants. To his credit, he terminated the experiment and has subsequently used his experiences to teach about ethical issues in research. (Zimbardo, 1999)

Although most of the ethical issues that emerge during the conduct of psychological research are not as dramatic as those faced during the prison simulation experiment, they nonetheless do arise consistently. Psychologists are concerned that they treat their subordinates, colleagues, and research participants fairly and respectfully.

According to principle-based ethics, the moral principles most relevant in research or scholarship are respect for research participant autonomy[1] (e.g., through informed consent requirements, freedom from coercion, and limitations on when deception can be used) and integrity (e.g., standards require accuracy in awarding authorship and in reporting data). However, beneficence and nonmaleficence also apply here as well, especially if the researchers are providing health care treatment. Although beneficence and nonmaleficence are usually applied only to humans, the principles also could be interpreted to mean that psychologists have an obligation to treat animal subjects humanely. Justice could also be relevant to research ethics to the extent that research participants are recruited from all segments of society and treated fairly, such as through the use of linguistically appropriate informed consent forms.

Of course, principle-based ethics is not the only way to view ethical issues. Fisher (1994, 2000b) has seen benefits in viewing research ethics from a deontological perspective, in that psychologists should never treat research participants only as means to gather information, but should respect their intrinsic self-worth.

Standards governing the conduct of psychologists in research come from the Ethics Code (American Psychological Association [APA], 2002a). Other APA publications relevant to research are the *Publication Manual* (5th ed.; APA, 2001), *Guidelines for Ethical Conduct in the Care and Use of Animals* (APA, 1993a), and *Ethics in Research With Human Participants* (Sales & Folkman, 2000), which is not an official APA document but which reflects the work of an APA task force charged with addressing emerging ethical issues in research. Institutional policies, decisions by institutional review boards (IRBs), and federal regulations may apply to some research psychologists as well. Educational and other institutions establish IRBs to review and, if necessary, recommend modifications to research projects. Although their purpose is to protect the public, the extent to which they reach that goal reportedly varies (Fisher, 2000a). Members of IRBs sometimes lack knowledge about the techniques or procedures used by social science researchers and may require cumbersome informed consent forms because they lack a realistic appraisal of the actual risks (Azar, 2002).

Federal regulations on research, which apply to researchers using federal funds, are also important because federal funds support much basic and medical research. The federal regulations (Basic HHS Policy for Protection of Human Research Subjects, 1991) are based on the recommendations found in the *Belmont Report* (National Commission for the Protection of Human Subjects of Biomedical and Behavioral Research, 1979).

---

[1] In this chapter we modify the principle "respect for patient autonomy" to read "respect for research participant autonomy." Some research participants are patients, but many are not.

We have great respect for the scientific enterprise, but it is not a disembodied search for truth. Like all human activities, the enterprise of research includes a mixture of self-interest and altruism as well as arrogance and humility, with both risks and benefits to society and individuals. The reward structure of our social institutions promotes science and research. Psychologists who produce valued research can expect an increase in money, power, reputation, and fame. At times, these rewards can create apparent conflicts between the needs of researchers and research participants or between the needs of coauthors in a scholarly publication. The research enterprise requires a careful balance of scientific, legal, and ethical considerations.

In this chapter, we review the minimum ethical standards first. Then, we review aspirational standards for researchers and scholars.

MINIMUM ETHICAL STANDARDS IN RESEARCH AND SCHOLARSHIP

At a minimum, researchers and scholars show respect for research participants' autonomy and dispense with informed consent only in limited circumstances permitted by the APA Ethics Code. They should take special efforts to protect vulnerable populations. Minimum standards of conduct also exist concerning debriefing, deception in research, animal welfare, publishing and reporting research results, awarding authorship, deciding on student authorship, duplicate publications, plagiarism, and confidentiality in the peer review process.

Respect for Research Participant Autonomy

Research participants should give informed and voluntary consent. According to Standard 8.02a, Informed Consent to Research,

> When obtaining informed consent as required in Standard 3.10, Informed Consent, psychologists inform participants about (1) the purpose of the research, expected duration, and procedures; (2) their right to decline to participate and to withdraw from the research once participation has begun; (3) the foreseeable consequences of declining or withdrawing; (4) reasonably foreseeable factors that may be expected to influence their willingness to participate such as potential risks, discomfort, or adverse effects; (5) any prospective research benefits; (6) limits of confidentiality; (7) incentives for participation; and (8) whom to contact for questions about the research and research participants' rights.

Psychologists also provide prospective participants an opportunity to ask questions about their research participation and to receive answers.

From the standpoint of research participants, the benefits of research may be either intrinsic (e.g., if the participant is receiving treatment) or artificial (e.g., if the participant is receiving course credit or payment). A major purpose of university participant pools is to provide participants for the research projects of other students and faculty members. Often the use of college participant pools is justified in that the students are learning something by participating in the research. This may be especially true if the students receive meaningful debriefing after the experiment or discuss their research experiences during their class.

To protect research participants who are subordinates of psychologists, Standard 8.04a, Client/Patient, Student, and Subordinate Research Participants, states, "When psychologists conduct research with clients/patients, students, or subordinates as participants, psychologists take steps to protect the prospective participants from adverse consequences of declining or withdrawing from participation." Standard 8.04b states, "When research participation is a course requirement or an opportunity for extra credit, the prospective participant is given the option of equitable alternative activities."

These standards are designed to give students some leverage in the research process. Researchers know that students will decline to participate or will withdraw from experiments that are unnecessarily unpleasant. Furthermore, it may influence the nature of the results if participation is not uniformly voluntary.

Research participants have choice and control over any recording of their voice or image. This rule does not apply to naturalistic observations of behavior in public places or to research involving deception for which the psychologist obtains consent during the debriefing (Standard 8.03, Informed Consent for Recording Voices and Images in Research). Internet research presents unique challenges when obtaining informed consent. It could be argued that anything posted on the Internet constitutes public behavior and is, therefore, available for archival research. Researchers could, for example, report the data on the content of postings on an electronic mailing list or e-group even if they dealt with highly sensitive issues. However, the expectation of privacy on the part of the participants appears to be a salient factor in determining how to treat these communications, and those expectations of privacy may vary according to the nature of the communication (e.g., a message posted on a chat room vs. a one-to-one communication; Kraut et al., 2004). Researchers should consider precautions to limit the potential of harm to those unknowing participants. For example, they could seek their permission to gather data or heavily edit or disguise the responses (Pittenger, 2003).

Also, researchers have no way to verify the accuracy of the information given, such as the age of the participants. Even with adult participants, psychologists cannot guarantee that they actually have read the informed consent materials. Furthermore, some participants may log off of the experiment before they have had an opportunity to read the debriefing or dehoaxing information (Pittenger, 2003). To fulfill their ethical responsibilities, Internet researchers may need to take special steps, such as restricting their participant pool to those who have e-mail addresses given only to college students. They could also require participants to give them e-mail addresses before they start the experiment, thus ensuring that they would be sent the debriefing materials even if they logged off prematurely (Pittenger, 2003). The exact procedures to ensure informed consent may vary according to the degree of risk to the participants. When the risk of harm is high, researchers should take special protections or avoid using the Internet altogether (Kraut et al., 2004).

Dispensing With Informed Consent

Researchers can dispense with obtaining informed consent during "the study of normal educational practices, curricula, or classroom management methods conducted in educational settings" (Standard 8.05, Dispensing With Informed Consent for Research) or "the study of factors related to job or organization effectiveness conducted in organizational settings for which there is no risk to participants' employability, and confidentiality is protected" (Standard 8.05). In addition, psychologists may gather data from "anonymous questionnaires, naturalistic observations, or archival research" only if the "disclosure of responses would not place participants at risk of criminal or civil liability or damage their financial standing, employability, or reputation, and confidentiality is protected" (Standard 8.05). Prospective informed consent can also be waived in experiments involving deception (Standard 8.08, Debriefing; see section on deception later in this chapter).

Even when working with populations such as adolescents in situations in which informed consent may not be legally required, it may be desirable to get their assent. This shows respect for the adolescent and may help ensure fuller participation in the research process.

Participant Recruitment

According to Standard 8.06a, Offering Inducements for Research Participation, "Psychologists make reasonable efforts to avoid offering excessive or inappropriate financial or other inducements for research participation when such inducements are likely to coerce participation." Psychologists can reduce the likelihood of coerced participation by emphasizing the freedom of the person to decline participation, noting the availability of services elsewhere if participation is declined, and having a readable consent form. An example of an excessive or inappropriate inducement to research might be to give money to homeless persons who abuse alcohol or other drugs knowing that they are likely to use the money to buy alcohol or other drugs. An alternative may be to give the participant a voucher or gift certificate that can be redeemed at a restaurant or grocery store.

Federal regulations require researchers to attempt to recruit participants who represent a broad representation of society unless the study is directed toward a specific homogenous sample and a more diverse sample would undercut the purpose of the study. Even when it is not mandated, researchers should generally strive to have a diverse participant pool to improve external validity (Scott-Jones, 2000).

Recruiting diverse samples of research participants may not be easy. Many individuals from ethnic minority groups ascribe harmful motives to researchers (Alvidrez & Arean, 2002). In a survey on health care research, almost twice as many African Americans as Caucasian Americans feared that doctors would place the goals of a research proposal above their own welfare and use them as "guinea pigs" (Corbie-Smith, Thomas, & St. George, 2002). The perception of mistreatment is not without a factual basis.

A Serious Injustice

During the 1930s, a group of African American men with syphilis were followed longitudinally to observe the impact of that disease. At the time the study was started there were no effective treatments (antibiotics did not become available for the treatment of syphilis until 1943). However, these treatments were not provided even after they became available. A government panel reviewed the experiment in the 1960s and approved its continuation with minor changes. It was not until 1972 that the experiment was stopped following a media exposé. (Online Ethics Center, 1999b)

Unfortunately, a similar disregard for the welfare of research participants was found in other studies, albeit perhaps not as dramatically as in the Tuskegee study described in the previous paragraph.

In addition, members of minority groups often have had unpleasant or stressful encounters with health care personnel. Their encounters with physicians or other health care personnel may be sporadic or largely confined to emergency room visits. Consequently, special efforts may be required to address the fear of exploitation or the appearance of exploitation (Alvidrez & Arean, 2002).

Competence

Research psychologists must show minimal standards of competence (Standard 2.01, Boundaries of Competence). However, no predetermined sequence of courses or examination automatically qualifies or credentials an individual to conduct research, although universities usually assume that the attainment of a doctorate and success in getting one's research published are satisfactory evidence of competence. In addition, federal and state granting agencies, foundations, and other financial supporters of research provide external validation of researchers' ideas and work. Nonetheless, much of the responsibility for the quality of research rests with self-regulation. Of course, if the research entails the delivery of health care services, then researchers will be held to the standards of minimum competence required of all practitioners who deliver such services. Assistants working under the direction of psychologists should be competent to fulfill their responsibilities and follow applicable ethical standards (Standard 2.05, Delegation of Work to Others).

Research involving members of ethnic minority communities requires consideration of the characteristics of the population under study. Researchers need to ask themselves whether the study carefully describes the background of the participants (and avoids ethnic gloss), whether the assessment instruments have been standardized with the population under study (or if not, whether they accurately access the variables under study), and whether the informed consent procedures are linguistically and culturally appropriate (Fisher et al., 2002). If the population under study is a cultural or racial minority, then it is desirable to consider cultural factors throughout the entire research study from participant recruitment to interpretation (Tucker & Herman, 2002).

Standards Especially Important for Protecting Vulnerable Participants

The need for safeguards becomes heightened when experiments involve health care or involve vulnerable populations such as persons who lack financial resources (e.g., persons who are homeless), belong to a group that experiences social stigmas (e.g., persons who are lesbian, gay, bisexual, or transgendered), live in institutions (e.g., prisoners), or have mental limitations (e.g., those with serious mental illnesses, developmental disabilities, or dementias). It would be necessary to ask, for example, if it is ethical to assign individuals with suicidal ideation to a placebo group. Would it be ethical to assign individuals with a history of alcoholism to a controlled drinking treatment group? Could individuals with apparent dementia give informed consent? In these situations researchers should take greater efforts to protect the research participants because the potential for harm is greater. Some experiences in the recent past may be instructive for psychologists today.

During the 1940s and 1950s, neurosurgeons conducted thousands of surgical brain operations on patients with serious mental illness. They proclaimed great success in these operations, although the outcome evaluations were shoddy and superficial and often relied on brief secondhand reports from hospital personnel. Long-term follow-up evaluations were almost never conducted; however, today we see them largely as failures (Valenstein, 1986).

Can we be less critical of these experiments if we view them in their historical context? At that time, psychiatric hospitals were overcrowded, and the available treatments were poor or nonexistent. Probably some of the patients did benefit from the neurosurgery. Standards for outcome research were not as sophisticated as they are today. Nonetheless, Valenstein (1986) cautioned that the same forces that led to misuse of psychosurgery in the past exist to some extent today as well.

There are today no fewer desperate patients and desperate families; premature reports of spectacular cures with minimal risks are still accepted uncritically; the popular media promote innovative therapies even more enthusiastically; [and] economics is no less an influence on the selection of treatment. (p. 291)

Informed Consent With Vulnerable Participants

If research involves treatment for the research participants, then researchers need to adopt additional safeguards. As with nontreatment research, the informed consent of the participants is essential. Although informed consent does not ensure that the research will be ethical, it is nonetheless a critical safeguard of participant welfare (Woodward, 1999). When conducting intervention research involving the use of experimental treatments, psychologists should explain

(1) the experimental nature of the treatment; (2) the services that will or will not be available to the control group(s) if appropriate; (3) the means by which assignment to treatment and control groups will be made; (4) available treatment alternatives if an individual does not wish to participate in the research or wishes to withdraw once a study has begun; and (5) compensation for or monetary costs of participating including, if appropriate, whether reimbursement from the participant or a third-party payor will be sought. (Standard 8.02b, Informed Consent to Research)

Informing prospective participants of the possibility that they may be assigned to a control group is important. Assignment to a placebo or no-treatment group may benefit the researcher, but not the participant. Although not required by the APA Ethics Code, at times researchers may want to provide treatment later to those participants who were initially assigned to a control group.

The specifics of how to obtain informed consent with vulnerable populations is a topic of considerable study. For example, persons with mental retardation may or may not be able to understand the salient features of what is being asked of them. Many researchers have found the MacArthur Competence Assessment Tool for Treatment useful in assessing the competence of individuals to consent to experimental treatments (Grisso & Appelbaum, 1998). The mere presence of a mental disability does not automatically mean that an individual lacks the functional abilities necessary for competence. However, these disabilities may interfere with or impair those abilities.

Nonetheless, even persons with mental disabilities are often able to give informed consent if the concepts are explained to them adequately and they have the opportunity to have their questions answered. If the researcher suspects that an individual has an impaired ability to make a decision, then educational programs can be used to increase the competency to make a decision. These may include one-on-one educational sessions with teaching aids (e.g., videotapes, flip charts, diagrams), group instructional sessions, written materials, computer programs, using family members as educational aides, or involving the prospective participant in a dialogue over time (Roberts, 2000).

If vulnerable persons appear incapable of giving consent, then it may be desirable to rely on family members as a proxy, although this could create ethical problems if the family members do not act as a bona fide fiduciary for the research participant. One of the recommendations of the National Bioethics Advisory Committee (NBAC) is that the proxy base the decision "upon a best estimation of what the subject would have chosen if capable of making a decision" and that the proxy decision maker be "available to monitor the subject's recruitment, participation, and withdrawal from the study" (NBAC, 1998, p. 7).

Other Protections for Vulnerable Research Participants

The obligations to research participants do not end once they have enrolled in the study. Other ethical considerations include a fair process in the selection of treatment or control groups, a favorable benefit–risk ratio (i.e., a reasonable expectation that the benefits of treatment outweigh the risks), and respect for the research participants after they have enrolled in the study (Emanuel, Wendler, & Grady, 2000). Special scrutiny is required when placebo groups are being used, and consideration should be given to other comparison groups, such as "treatment-as-usual," dismantling, additive, or waiting-list controls. Heightened scrutiny should be given to studies that are designed to provoke symptoms, withdraw participants abruptly, or use placebo groups (NBAC, 1998).

Research participants should be debriefed after the study, have their welfare monitored throughout the study, and be given the opportunity to withdraw. Efforts should be made to protect participants from physical, psychological, or social (e.g., embarrassment) harm (Sieber, 2001).

At times, researchers may see the quality of their research at apparent odds with the welfare of the research participants. Consider the example of psychologists studying the natural development of girls (Fisher, 1994). In the course of their research, they learn that a girl may be in the early stages of developing anorexia. Should the researchers emphasize the welfare of the girl and intervene to get her a more thorough evaluation or medical services, or should they emphasize the integrity of the research study? Of course, the decision is influenced by the strength of the evidence suggesting a medical problem, the impact of such a medical problem on the long-term health of a child, the nature of the promises made to the child and parents about their participation, and other facts unique to the case.

Nonetheless, Fisher (1994) argued that a strictly act utilitarian analysis may lead to a solution contrary to the best interests of the research participant. According to an act utilitarian perspective, it could be argued that the social benefit of the particular research project would lead, in the longer run, to more benefit than caring for the needs of a particular research participant, which risks contaminating the study.

However, a rule utilitarian perspective would consider general rules of utility (see chap. 2, this volume, for a discussion of act utilitarianism, rule utilitarianism, and deontological theories). Accordingly, a utilitarian rule might be that researchers have an obligation to assist participants when necessary to protect them from serious harm. A deontological perspective would consider that research participants should never be used only as a means to an end but that their intrinsic worth needs to be considered. Consequently, rule utilitarian or deontological perspectives would give more weight to the needs of the participants and less to the social utility of the research project (Fisher, 1994).

Protecting the privacy of research participants is important as well. Ensuring privacy not only is fair to the participants but also enhances the credibility of the results by increasing the willingness of participants to give accurate information (Blanck, Bellack, Rosnow, Rotherman-Borus, & Schooler, 1992). Standard 6.02, Maintenance, Dissemination, and Disposal of Confidential Records of Professional and Scientific Work, requires psychologists to keep information on research participants private and to protect confidential information in databases. Identifying information as well as names should be removed or coded. Limitations of confidentiality should be discussed with participants, including mandated reporting laws. (Federal certificates of confidentiality can be obtained that would waive the requirements to respond to subpoenas on certain information, but these do not apply to mandated reporting laws; see National Institute of Mental Health, 2001.)

Consideration should be given to how data will be stored or shared, especially if they contain identifying information, such as information stored on videotapes or audiotapes. The research information should be kept in secure locations, and psychologists need to be aware of any limitations to the electronic storage of data (Standard 6.02, Maintenance, Dissemination, and Disposal of Confidential Records of Professional and Scientific Work).

Debriefing Research Participants

Psychologists give participants the opportunity to be debriefed or "to obtain appropriate information about the nature, results, and conclusions of the research" (Standard 8.08a, Debriefing). They also "take reasonable steps to correct any misconceptions that participants may have of which the psychologists are aware" (Standard 8.08a). However, Standard 8.08b acknowledges that at times debriefing may be delayed or withheld for scientific or humane reasons. If this occurs, then "psychologists take reasonable measures to reduce the risk of harm." If psychologists become aware that research participants have been harmed, then they "take reasonable steps to minimize the harm" (Standard 8.08c).

Ideally, debriefing should benefit both the researcher and the participant. In some studies, researchers have learned information during debriefing that assisted in interpreting the data and in planning for future research (Blanck et al., 1992).

If deception was used or a reasonable possibility exists that the participants might have misunderstood the nature or conclusions of the study, then psychologists need to attempt to correct these misconceptions. Of course, this does not need to be done if there are humane or scientific reasons for not doing so. This might occur, for example, when researching individuals who are near death or who could not comprehend the debriefing because of diminished mental capacity (Canter, Bennett, Jones, & Nagy, 1994). Finally, debriefing participants gives researchers an opportunity to determine whether harm has occurred and provides an opportunity to minimize the harm.

Brody, Gluck, and Aragon (2000) found wide variability in the content, format, and time allotted for debriefing (i.e., between 2 and 20 minutes; mode of 6 minutes). Participants often felt dissatisfied with the debriefing. Their results suggest the need to give greater attention to how debriefing could better fulfill its goal of educating participants concerning the nature or value of the research.

Deceiving Research Participants

Deception may mean different things, such as hiding the purpose of or deliberately misrepresenting facts about an experiment. Often deception ensures that the participants will not be influenced by knowledge of the real purpose of the study. For example, deception could be used in a memory experiment in which the participants are tested on their incidental learning during apparently unrelated tasks. This involves no harm to the participants, and it appears necessary to have some deception to study incidental learning.

A Deceptive Experiment
Psychologist Stanley Milgram recruited participant "teachers" for a series of purported studies of memory involving electrical shocks to another individual identified as a "learner." However, the teachers received instructions in which they perceived themselves as creating increasingly painful electric shocks for the learners. The teachers were not aware that the shocks were, in fact, not being administered; that obedience, not human memory, was being studied; and that the learners were confederates in the study. Despite the apparent anguish created in the participants, Milgram claimed that the social benefit of his study justified any problems created for the participants. (Milgram, 1975)

To his credit, Milgram provided to participants an extensive debriefing session that included a "friendly reconciliation with the unharmed victim and an extended discussion with the experimenter," and "in some instances, additional detailed and lengthy discussions of the experiment were also carried out with individual subjects" (Milgram, 1975, p. 24).

The study did produce socially useful information on why people can participate in atrocities such as political torture, which they ordinarily would not do. However, Milgram's experiment would be difficult to justify according to today's ethical standards. Other nondeceptive techniques could have been used to study obedience. In addition, termination of the experiment should have been considered when it became obvious that the participants were suffering. Despite the debriefing, some participants might have had more enduring psychological harm. The same obedience to authority displayed in the experiments may have led some participants to minimize the harm they experienced or their disapproval of the way in which they were treated.

Deception experiments today are usually far less dramatic than the ones conducted by Milgram. Nonetheless, even more benign forms of deception have been criticized on deontological grounds (it is intrinsically undesirable to deceive people) and utilitarian grounds (deception significantly influences the way participants act and undermines the trust that the public has in the discipline and profession of psychology; Kimmel, 1998; Ortmann & Hertwig, 1997). This "reputation spillover" may contaminate the participant pool, as more participants expect to be deceived in their experiments (Ortmann & Hertwig, 1998).

Accordingly, Standard 8.07, Deception in Research, limits the use of deception in research. Researchers must justify the use of deception and debrief research participants as soon as possible. This standard requires psychologists to weigh the costs and benefits of deception and consider other nondeceptive research designs, such as role plays, naturalistic observations, or self-report data. However, the cost–benefit analysis is only self-monitored, and researchers may overestimate the scientific importance of their work or may not be as scrupulous as they should be in considering nondeceptive alternatives.

Nonetheless, "psychologists do not deceive prospective participants about research that is reasonably expected to cause physical pain or severe emotional distress" (Standard 8.07b, Deception in Research). As early as is feasible, psychologists explain that deception is an integral feature of the design or conduct of an experiment. Preferably the debriefing occurs when the participants finish with the experiment, but no later than at the conclusion of the data collection. Psychologists also permit participants who were deceived to withdraw their data (Standard 8.07c).

Protecting Animal Welfare

Some wish to abolish animal research entirely. Others believe it is acceptable for limited purposes as long as basic protections are in place. All would agree that, especially in the past, protections for animals were not adequate.

Supporters of animal research argue that humans benefit from the knowledge gained by animal research, that animals do not experience discomfort or restrictions in freedom in the same manner as humans, and that they are not sentient beings that have basic rights. Opponents argue that the knowledge gained often has limited applicability to humans, that animals do have some sense of pain (although we cannot understand their subjective experience as well as we can understand that of humans), and that we have some obligations to animals, even if they do not have rights comparable to humans'. Furthermore, some opponents claim that a pattern of cruelty or insensitivity to animals may establish a precedence of cruelty or insensitivity to humans. Finally, some argue that animals do have some rights that need to be considered when making decisions about research (Beauchamp, 1997).

Practically speaking, more than 90% of psychological research with animals involves rodents (i.e., rats and mice) or birds (i.e., usually pigeons). Only about 5% of the research involves primates. Dogs and cats are rarely used in psychological research (American Psychological Association, n.d.).

Research on animals is governed by the APA Ethics Code (Standard 8.09, Humane Care and Use of Animals in Research) and various state and federal laws. In addition, a private organization, the American Association for the Accreditation of Laboratory Animal Care, sets standards for research facilities using animals. Researchers must ensure the welfare of animal subjects and may only inflict pain, stress, or privation on them when no alternative research procedure is available and can be justified by its prospective social value. When it is necessary to kill animals, it should be done rapidly with an effort to minimize pain. State and federal laws regarding the care of animals must be followed. More details on the specifics of protecting animal welfare can be found in *Guidelines for Ethical Conduct in the Care and Use of Animals* (APA, 1993a).

One original experiment on learned helplessness involved shocking dogs. The researcher conducted a thoughtful cost–benefit analysis before initiating the research. He sought consultation and was asked, "First, is there a reasonable chance that you will eliminate much more pain in the long run than the pain you cause in the short run? Second, can scientists ever generalize from animals to people?" (Seligman, 1991, p. 21).

Although some might not have reached the same answers as he did, the researcher asked the right questions about conducting research involving pain to animals. We would also add other questions, such as whether the information can be obtained through other means and whether efforts are being made to minimize the discomfort (or repair the harm) done to the animals.

The scientific enterprise assumes the accuracy of the data reported. The scientific discipline of psychology is harmed if researchers present inaccurate data, do not award credit for authorship accurately, or exploit student authors. The scholarship process is also harmed if psychologists publish information as original that has been published elsewhere, engage in plagiarism, deny access to data for reanalysis or verification, or do not respect the confidentiality of the peer review process.

Inaccurate Research Results

Despite efforts by conscientious researchers, mistakes in reporting data may creep into a publication. When that occurs, the authors should take steps to correct the errors (Standard 8.10b, Reporting Research Results).

Actual falsification of data is probably rare, but it does occur. Falsification of data can involve completely making up data or deleting participant responses to skew the data. Falsified data mislead future investigators and cause them to go down blind alleys and to follow bogus research leads. They also demean those who gather data honestly. Furthermore, falsification of data can directly harm the public.

Costly Misrepresentations

A psychologist falsified data dealing with the use of psychotropic medications with institutionalized persons with mental retardation. His publications could have led many physicians to alter their prescription habits on the basis of falsified research. Researchers who collaborated with him had their reputations tarnished by association. Doubts were cast on his other studies, even though allegations about fabrication of the data in those articles were never proven or admitted (Online Ethics Center, 1999a).

Awarding Authorship

Academic psychologists publish to receive academic advancement and to be competitive for grant funding. Senior authorship is especially important. However, the self-interest of individual psychologists is subordinate to the need to reflect contributions accurately. The integrity of the scientific or scholarly enterprise is protected when authors receive credit for the work they do and the ideas that they develop.

According to Standard 8.12b, Publication Credit, "Principal authorship and other publication credits accurately reflect the relative scientific or professional contributions of the individuals involved, regardless of their relative status." The criteria for authorship are described in more detail in APA's *Publication Manual* (5th ed.; APA, 2001). Some activities that could warrant authorship include developing the idea for a study, developing the design, conducting the literature review, performing a pilot study, coordinating the collection of the data, analyzing the data, writing a first draft, critically reading a manuscript, or making substantial contributions to the final draft. Other contributions probably would not warrant authorship except in unusual situations.

According to Standard 8.12b, Publication Credit, "Minor contributions to the research or to the writing for publications are acknowledged appropriately, such as in footnotes or in an introductory statement." Running participants and assisting with the statistical analyses typically do not warrant authorship in and of themselves. However, no algorithm can determine authorship in all situations, and authors may vary in their perception of the value of the different contributions. It shows foresight to talk about authorship issues early in the writing or research process to clarify expectations.

Standard 8.12b, Publication Credit, states, "Mere possession of an institutional position, such as department chair, does not justify authorship credit." This standard prohibits honorary authors (i.e., those who receive authorship because of their status but who did not do enough work to merit it) and ghost authors (i.e., those who receive no authorship credit but who did enough work to merit it). Determining authorship may be difficult when working with scholars from other disciplines who may have different standards for authorship.

Awarding Authorship to Students

According to Standard 8.12c, Publication Credit, students are usually listed as the "principal author on any multiple-authored article that is substantially based on the student's doctoral dissertation." In addition, advisors should "discuss publication credit with students as early as feasible and throughout the research and publication process as appropriate." This standard creates a presumption that the student will get first authorship. However, that presumption can be overturned by the facts of a given situation.

This rule protects students who are at a power disadvantage and at risk for having professors usurp authorship for their work (Sullivan & Ogloff, 1998). A recent graduate may depend on a dissertation advisor for a letter of reference or for other help in getting future employment and may fear reprisals for disagreeing with the authorship decision. In some situations, the student may have written the proposal, run the participants, analyzed the data, and written the report and article with little contribution from the advisor. The contribution of the advisors may warrant second authorship, if any.

In other situations, students depend much more on the knowledge, experience, and work of their advisors. For example, the advisors may identify key research areas, direct the students to the relevant sources (or even give them copies of key articles or chapters), direct or approve the research design, help solicit participants, and assist in writing the article. The contributions of the faculty members may be such that they deserve to be the primary authors. At other times, the students may lose interest in the topic after finishing the dissertation, and the faculty members become the primary force in preparing the article for publication and making necessary revisions. It is especially common in master's theses for advisors to contribute more to the research project and therefore become more deserving of primary authorship. In either case, it is desirable for collaborators to discuss their expectations for authorship well ahead of time.

Duplication in Publications

According to Standard 8.13, Duplicate Publication of Data, "Psychologists do not publish, as original data, data that have been previously published. This does not preclude republishing data when they are accompanied by proper acknowledgment." The usual assumption is that journal articles contain original data unless otherwise specified. This standard prohibits authors from publishing essentially the same article in two different publication outlets. However, this standard does not preclude using portions of the data in subsequent publications if appropriately noted.

Avoiding Plagiarism

Standard 8.11, Plagiarism, forbids plagiarism. Psychologists or psychology students should not appropriate sentences, charts, graphs, pictures, computer programs, innovative terminology, or original ideas of others without giving proper acknowledgment.

It is not necessary to footnote or reference information that is "common knowledge." Usually what constitutes common knowledge is obvious. For example, the fact that Wundt established a psychology laboratory in Leipzig, Germany, in 1879 is common knowledge. It can be found in literally thousands of sources and is taught to approximately 100,000 introductory psychology students every year. However, unique terminology or ideas that are not well known should be referenced.

Plagiarism has become especially problematic in recent years with the proliferation of documents available on the Internet. Some sources offer to sell papers to students on specific topics or prepare them for a fee. However, some plagiarism may be inadvertent.

A Highly Public Error

A famous historian had copied excerpts from other authors without giving proper acknowledgements (Lewis, 2002). It is very unlikely that this author, who knew that his work would be widely read, deliberately stole paragraphs from others. Perhaps he relied on professional researchers and never saw the original material, or perhaps the pressure of meeting time schedules caused him to be too lax when checking sources.

This comment is not made to excuse plagiarism but to indicate that it can happen to "good" people who failed to attend to the risk of accidental plagiarism.

Reanalyzing or Verifying Data

Psychologists do not withhold data needed for reanalysis or verification (Standard 8.14, Sharing Research Data for Verification). Although the APA Ethics Code does not set a specific time frame, APA's *Publication Manual* states that reviewers should keep data available for 5 years after publication of the research (5th ed.; APA, 2001). A prudent rule is to also keep treatment manuals and other information related to the research for 5 years after publication. The person requesting the information generally should bear whatever costs are involved in sharing the data. Although not required by this standard, it may be prudent to receive written approval to use the data for purposes other than reanalysis. The sole reliance on oral communications can sometimes lead to misunderstandings. Of course, the sharing of data assumes that the confidentiality rights of the participants and any proprietary rights of the funder of the research remain protected.

Ensuring Confidentiality in the Peer Review Process

Editors and authors may not reference works submitted for publication without the consent of the author until they are actually published (Standard 8.15, Reviewers). Manuscripts commonly change considerably from the time they are first submitted until the time they are published. It is not fair to the author to reference an earlier and less polished version of the work. Reviewers should also respect the originality of ideas found in the manuscripts or proposals that they review.

STRIVING FOR HIGHEST IDEALS AS A RESEARCHER

Striving for the highest ethics as a researcher means, of course, following the minimum standards required in the APA Ethics Code and federal regulations. It also means sensitivity to the ethical implications of one's own research and scholarly activities. Psychologists who strive for the highest ideals as researchers and scholars give research expertise away, are concerned about the social usefulness of their research, try to humanize the peer review process, and are sensitive to the impact of external sources on their research activities.

Giving Research Expertise Away

Of course, scientists and psychologists can give away their expertise by providing consultations to publicly oriented community agencies or by encouraging scientific activities such as science fairs. They can also direct their research activities toward issues involving members of historically underrepresented groups or toward issues involving health care services. They can share data, treatment manuals, and their expertise with other researchers.

Conducting Socially Useful Research

Probably all psychologists believe that their research programs have social significance. However, it may be useful to consider ways to make research even more socially significant. An example involving applied research concerns the way that psychotherapy researchers can incorporate practitioners and practitioners' insights into their research designs or protocols.

A pervasive problem across medicine is that practitioners are not always knowledgeable about the current knowledge base of medicine (Cabana et al., 1999). Professional psychology has a similar problem. Practitioners do not use research as much as they should, and researchers do not address the needs of practitioners as much as they should.

Finger-pointing (e.g., "If only the practitioners had paid more attention in graduate school" or "If only the researchers would learn to communicate their findings in an intelligible manner") ignores the complexity of the problems and does little to generate satisfactory solutions. Furthermore, finger-pointing ignores the underlying fact that both practitioners and applied researchers have the same goal: the development and implementation of treatments that produce the best results for their patients.

The optimal solution is to have ongoing dialogues and cooperation between applied researchers and practitioners. Practitioners can inform researchers of the issues that are most salient to them and help researchers identify and formulate research questions. Researchers can inform practitioners of the latest scientific evidence. Practice research networks that involve practitioners and scientists in collaborative projects may be one way to address this issue (Borkovec, Echemendia, Ragusea, & Ruiz, 2001).

Humanizing the Peer Review Process

Psychologist reviewers can try to make the peer review process more humane and helpful. Many psychologists have received gratuitous and destructive criticisms or ad hominem attacks in reviews of their writings (Hadjistavropolos & Bieling, 2000). The primary obligation to ensure the quality of journal articles can be accomplished by helping authors focus on ways to improve the article being submitted. Unnecessarily harsh reviews actually detract from substantive comments. Reviewers can improve the peer review process by completing their work within a specified time frame, refraining from personal attacks, and focusing on the merits of the article or the ways that it can be improved.

Sensitivity to the Impact of External Sources

Close consideration needs to be given to the impact of marketing or external funding on the scholarly or scientific process. Marketing tools such as pens, notepads, mugs, and educational programs reinforce awareness of particular drugs. No doubt much good has come out of the recent advances in psychopharmacology, and educational moneys from drug companies have helped psychologists and others learn about the benefits of certain drugs. However, these educational marketing techniques may overvalue the benefits of certain medications (Antonuccio, Danton, & McClanahan, 2003) and undervalue effective nonpharmacological interventions. Studies suggest that the educational marketing techniques do influence the prescription practices of physicians (Reist & VandeCreek, 2004).

Also, funding sources influence the nature of issues being studied and the extent to which research findings are publicized or disseminated to the professional community. This is particularly true of research with drug companies. According to DeAngelis (2000), when companies fund or have a financial interest in research, "the research is lower in quality, more likely to favor the sponsor's product, less likely to be published, and more likely to have delayed publication" (p. 2238). In a comprehensive review of 1,140 published studies, Bekelman, Li, and Gross (2003) found that "industry supported studies were significantly more likely to reach conclusions that were favorable to the sponsor than were nonindustry studies" (p. 463).

Although psychologists conduct less pharmaceutical research than physicians, they still face ethical challenges with funding sources. For example, a psychologist may accept money from a funding agency that requires "abstinence-only" perspectives to be taught in the HIV-prevention programs despite the fact that the evidence for the effectiveness of these programs is currently less promising than programs emphasizing discretion and judgment in sexual decision making.

These kinds of situations require careful ethical decision making. If the researcher believes that a properly presented abstinence-only HIV-prevention program (or "abstinence plus") can be successful in reducing HIV/AIDS risk, then it may be the most moral choice to accept the restrictions. However, interest in getting research money may cause the researcher to minimize the importance of other interventions. For example, the researcher may not investigate other more promising intervention strategies or may downplay their importance in the write-up of the program that was funded.

AFTERWORD

Our goal in writing this book was to help psychologists avoid misconduct and achieve their highest ethical aspirations. We do not dismiss or denigrate the remedial approach to ethics; indeed, we believe that disciplinary bodies have a role to play in protecting the public. However, we have tried to emphasize the limits of looking only to disciplinary bodies to guide our conduct. Throughout this book, we have emphasized the qualities or skills needed for psychologists to fulfill their ethical ideas. These are self-regulation models (e.g., virtue-based risk management, ethical decision making, self-care, and culture of safety) that psychologists can voluntarily adopt.

We are aware that we have only begun to identify all of the implications of positive ethics in the practice of psychology. We hope that other scholars will expand on and clarify the applications of positive ethics.

REFERENCES

Ackerly, G., Burnell, J., Holder, D., & Kurdek, L. (1988). Burnout among licensed psychologists. *Professional Psychology: Research and Practice, 19*, 624–631.

Ackerman, S., & Hilsenroth, M. (2001). A review of therapist characteristics and techniques negatively impacting the therapeutic alliance. *Psychotherapy: Theory, Research, Practice, Training, 38*, 171–185.

Acuff, C., Bennett, B., Bricklin, P., Canter, M., Knapp, S., Moldawsky, S., & Phelps, R. (1999). Considerations for ethical practice in managed care. *Professional Psychology: Research and Practice, 30*, 563–575.

Alvidrez, J., & Arean, P. (2002). Psychosocial treatment research with ethnic minority populations: Ethical considerations in conducting clinical trials. *Ethics and Behavior, 12*, 103–116.

American Educational Research Association, American Psychological Association, & National Council on Measurement in Education. (1999). *The standards for educational and psychological testing.* Washington, DC: American Educational Research Association.

American Psychiatric Association. (1994). *Diagnostic and statistical manual of mental disorders* (4th ed.). Washington, DC: Author.

American Psychological Association. (1992). Ethical principles of psychologists and code of conduct. *American Psychologist, 47*, 1597–1611.

American Psychological Association. (1993a). *Guidelines for ethical conduct in the care and use of animals.* Retrieved February 2, 2001, from http://www.apa.org/science/anguide.html

American Psychological Association. (1993b). Record-keeping guidelines. *American Psychologist, 48*, 984–986.

American Psychological Association. (1994). Guidelines for child custody evaluations in divorce proceedings. *American Psychologist, 49*, 677–680.

American Psychological Association. (1998). Proceedings of the American Psychological Association, 1997. *American Psychologist, 53*, 934–935.

American Psychological Association. (2000). Guidelines for psychotherapy with lesbian, gay, and bisexual clients. *American Psychologist, 55*, 1440–1451.

American Psychological Association. (2001). *Publication manual of the American Psychological Association* (5th ed.). Washington, DC: Author.

American Psychological Association. (2002a). Ethical principles of psychologists and code of conduct. *American Psychologist, 57*, 1060–1073; also available at www.apa.org/ethics/code2002.html

American Psychological Association. (2002b). *Guidelines and principles for accreditation of programs in professional psychology.* Washington, DC: Author.

American Psychological Association. (2003). Guidelines on multicultural education, training, research, practice, and organizational change for psychologists. *American Psychologist, 58*, 377–402.

American Psychological Association. (n.d.). *Research with animals in psychology*. Retrieved February 1, 2001, from http://www.apa.org/science/animal2.html

American Psychological Association, Ethics Committee. (2004). Report of the Ethics Committee, 2003. *American Psychologist, 59,* 434–441.

Ananth, J. (1998). Treatment-resistant depression. *Psychotherapy and Psychosomatics, 67,* 61–70.

Anderson, J., & Barret, R. (2001). *Ethics in HIV-related psychotherapy*. Washington, DC: American Psychological Association.

Anderson, S., & Kitchener, K. (1996). Nonromantic, nonsexual posttherapy relationships between psychologists and former clients: An exploratory study of critical incidents. *Professional Psychology: Research and Practice, 27,* 59–66.

Antonuccio, D., Danton, W., & McClanahan, T. (2003). Psychology in the prescription era: Building a firewall between marketing and science. *American Psychologist, 58,* 1028–1043.

Appleby, D. (2000, November). Academic community building. *Monitor on Psychology, 31,* 38–41.

Arnett, J. J. (2002). The psychology of globalization. *American Psychologist, 57,* 774–783.

Azar, B. (2002, February). Ethics at the cost of research? *Monitor on Psychology, 33,* 38–39.

Baer, B., & Murdock, N. (1995). Nonerotic dual relationships between therapists and clients: The effects of sex, theoretical orientation, and interpersonal boundaries. *Ethics and Behavior, 5,* 131–145.

Barnett, J. (1998). Should therapists self-disclose? Clinical and ethical perspectives. In L. VandeCreek, S. Knapp, & T. Jackson (Eds.), *Innovations in clinical practice: A sourcebook* (Vol. 16, pp. 419–428). Sarasota, FL: Professional Resource Press.

Barnett, J. (1999, November/December). My life as a small town psychologist. *The Maryland Psychologist, 45,* 20–21.

Barnett, J., & Hillard, D. (2001). Psychologist distress and impairment: The availability, nature, and use of colleague assistance programs for psychologists. *Professional Psychology: Research and Practice, 32,* 205–210.

Barrett, M., & Berman, J. (2001). Is psychotherapy more effective when therapists disclose information about themselves? *Journal of Consulting and Clinical Psychology, 69,* 597–603.

Basic HHS Policy for Protection of Human Research Subjects, 45 C. F. R. Pt. Subtitle A, 46-1.01-46.124 (1991). Protection of Human Subjects, National Institute of Health, Office for the Protection of Research Ethics.

Baur, S. (1997). *The intimate hour: Love and sex in psychotherapy*. Boston: Houghton-Mifflin.

Beahrs, J., & Guthiel, T. (2001). Informed consent in psychotherapy. *American Journal of Psychiatry, 158,* 4–10.

Beauchamp, T. (1997). Opposing views of animal experimentation: Do animals have rights? *Ethics and Behavior, 7,* 113–122.

Beauchamp, T., & Childress, J. (2001). *Principles of biomedical ethics* (5th ed.). New York: Oxford University Press.

Bedell, J., Hunter, R., & Corrigan, P. (1997). Current approaches to assessment and treatment of persons with serious mental illness. *Professional Psychology: Research and Practice, 28,* 217–228.

Behnke, S. (2003, July/August). Ethics records: Release of test data and APA's new Ethics Code. *Monitor on Psychology, 34,* 70–72.

Bekelman, J., Li, Y., & Gross, C. (2003). Scope and impact of financial conflicts of interest in biomedical research. *Journal of the American Medical Association, 289,* 454–465.

Belar, C., Brown, R., Hersch, L., Hornyak, L., Rozensky, R., Sheridan, E., et al. (2001). Self-assessment in clinical health psychology: A model for ethical expansion of practice. *Professional Psychology: Research and Practice, 32,* 135–141.

Bernard, J., & Jara, C. (1986). The failure of clinical psychology graduate students to apply understood ethical principles. *Professional Psychology: Research and Practice, 17,* 313–315.

Berry, J., & Kim, U. (1988). Acculturation and mental health. In J. Dasen, J. Berry, & N. Sartorius (Eds.), *Health and cross-cultural psychology: Forward applications* (pp. 207–236). Newbury Park, CA: Sage.

Bersoff, D. (1996). The virtue of principle ethics. *The Counseling Psychologist, 24,* 86–91.

Bersoff, D., & Koeppl, P. (1993). The relation between ethical codes and moral principles. *Ethics and Behavior, 3,* 345–357.

Betan, E., & Stanton, A. (1999). Fostering ethical willingness: Integrating emotional and contextual awareness with rational analysis. *Professional Psychology: Research and Practice, 30,* 295–301.

Biaggio, M., Paget, T. L., & Chenoweth, M. S. (1997). A model for ethical management of faculty–student dual relationships. *Professional Psychology: Research and Practice, 28,* 184–189.

Binder, R., & McNiel, D. (1996). Application of the *Tarasoff* ruling and its effect on the victim and the therapeutic relationship. *Psychiatric Services, 47,* 1212–1215.

Blanck, P. D., Bellack, A., Rosnow, R., Rotherman-Borus, M. J., & Schooler, N. (1992). Scientific rewards and conflicts of ethical choices in human subjects research. *American Psychologist, 47,* 959–965.

Blum, D. (1986). *Bad karma: A true story of obsession and murder.* New York: Jove Books.

Bongar, B., Maris, R., Berman, S. L., & Litman, F. E. (1992). Outpatient standards of care in the assessment, management and treatment of suicidal persons. *Suicide and Life Threatening Behavior, 22,* 453–478.

Borkovec, T., Echemendia, R., Ragusea, S., & Ruiz, M. (2001). The Pennsylvania Practice Research Network and future possibilities for clinically meaningful and scientifically rigorous psychotherapy effectiveness research. *Clinical Psychology: Science and Practice, 8,* 155–167.

Borum, R. (2000). Assessing violence risk among youths. *Journal of Clinical Psychology*, 56, 1263–1288.

Borys, D. (1994). Maintaining therapeutic boundaries: The motive is therapeutic effectiveness, not defensive practice. *Ethics and Behavior*, 4, 267–273.

Boyle, P. (1996). Managed care in mental health: A cure, or a cure worse than the disease? *St. Louis University Law Journal*, 40, 437–456.

Braaten, E., & Handelsman, M. (1997). Client preferences for informed consent information. *Ethics and Behavior*, 7, 311–328.

Bradford, D., & Muñoz, A. (1993). Translation in bilingual psychotherapy. *Professional Psychology: Research and Practice*, 24, 52–61.

Bransford, J., & Stein, B. (1993). *The ideal problem solver: A guide to improving thinking, learning, and creativity.* New York: Freeman.

Branstetter, S., & Handelsman, M. (2000). Graduate teaching assistants: Ethical training, beliefs, and practices. *Ethics and Behavior*, 10, 27–50.

Brems, C., Tryck, S., Garlock, D., Freemon, M., & Bernzott, J. (1995). Differences in family of origin functioning among graduate students of different disciplines. *Journal of Clinical Psychology*, 51, 434–441.

Brendel, D. (2003). Complications to consent. *The Journal of Clinical Ethics*, 14, 90–94.

Brenner, E. (2003). Consumer-focused psychological assessment. *Professional Psychology: Research and Practice*, 34, 240–247.

Bricklin, P. (2001). Being ethical: More than obeying the law and avoiding harm. *Journal of Personality Assessment*, 77, 195–202.

Bricklin, P., Knapp, S., & VandeCreek, L. (2001). *Educational modules on ethics.* Washington, DC: American Psychological Association Insurance Trust.

Bridges, N. (2001). Therapist's self-disclosure: Expanding the comfort zone. *Psychotherapy: Theory, Research, Practice, Training*, 38, 21–30.

Brittain, J., Frances, J., & Barth, J. (1995). Ethical issues and dilemmas in neuropsychological practice reported by ABCN diplomates. *Advances in Medical Psychology*, 8, 1–22.

Brody, J., Gluck, J., & Aragon, A. (2000). Participants' understanding of the process of psychological research: Debriefing. *Ethics and Behavior*, 10, 13–25.

Brown, L. (1994). Concrete boundaries and the problem of literal-mindedness: A response to Lazarus. *Ethics and Behavior*, 4, 275–281.

Brown, L. (2000). Feminist ethical considerations in forensic practice. In M. Brabeck (Ed.), *Practicing feminist ethics in psychology* (pp. 75–100). Washington, DC: American Psychological Association.

Buchanan, T. (2002). Online assessment: Desirable or dangerous? *Professional Psychology: Research and Practice*, 33, 148–154.

Burlingame, G., Fuhriman, A., & Johnson, J. (2001). Cohesion in group psychotherapy. *Psychotherapy: Theory, Research, Practice, Training*, 38, 373–379.

Cabana, M., Rand, C., Powe, N., Wu, A., Wilson, M., Abboud, P. A., et al. (1999). Why don't physicians follow clinical practice guidelines: A framework for improvement. *Journal of the American Medical Association*, 282, 1458–1465.

Canadian Psychological Association. (1986). *Code of ethics*. Ottawa, Canada: Author.

Canter, M., Bennett, B., Jones, S., & Nagy, T. (1994). *Ethics for psychologists*. Washington, DC: American Psychological Association.

Canterbury v. Spence, 464 F. Supp. 772 (D.C. Cir. 1972).

Cardemil, E., & Battle, C. (2003). Guess who's coming to therapy? Getting comfortable with conversations about race and ethnicity in psychotherapy. *Professional Psychology: Research and Practice, 34*, 278–286.

Carter, J. (2003). Looking into a distorted mirror. *The Journal of Clinical Ethics, 14*, 95–100.

Cates, J., & Graham, L. (2002). Psychological assessment of the Old Order Amish: Unraveling the enigma. *Professional Psychology: Research and Practice, 33*, 155–161.

Cerbin, W. (2001). *The course portfolio*. Retrieved April 23, 2001, from http://www.psychologicalscience.org/newsresearch/tips/040ltips.html

Chemtob, C., Bauer, G., Hamada, R., Pelowski, S., & Muraoka, M. (1989). Patient suicide: Occupational hazard for psychologists and psychiatrists. *Professional Psychology: Research and Practice, 20*, 294–300.

Cochran, S. (2001). Emerging issues in research on lesbians' and gay men's mental health: Does sexual orientation really matter? *American Psychologist, 56*, 931–947.

Committee on Ethical Guidelines for Forensic Psychologists. (1991). Specialty guidelines for forensic psychologists. *Law and Human Behavior, 15*, 655–665.

Corbie-Smith, G., Thomas, S., & St. George, D. M. (2002). Distrust, race, and research. *Archives of Internal Medicine, 162*, 2458–2463.

Corey, G., Williams, G., & Moline, M. (1995). Ethical and legal issues in group counseling. *Ethics and Behavior, 5*, 161–183.

Coster, J., & Schwebel, M. (1997). Well-functioning in professional psychologists. *Professional Psychology: Research and Practice, 28*, 5–13.

Cullari, S. (2001). The client's perspective of psychotherapy. In S. Cullari (Ed.), *Counseling and psychotherapy* (pp. 92–116). Boston: Allyn & Bacon.

Dattilio, F. (2000, January). Psychosocial evaluations: Cultural sensitivities in forensic psychological evaluations. *The Pennsylvania Psychologist, 60*, 5–6.

DeAngelis, C. (2000). Conflict of interest and the public trust. *Journal of the American Medical Association, 284*, 2237–2238.

deMayo, R. (2000). Patients' sexual behavior and sexual harassment: A survey of clinical supervisors. *Professional Psychology: Research and Practice, 31*, 706–709.

Dlugos, R., & Friedlander, M. (2001). Passionately committed psychotherapists: A qualitative study of their experiences. *Professional Psychology: Research and Practice, 32*, 298–304.

Dowd, E. T. (2003). Cultural differences in cognitive therapy. *The Behavior Therapist, 26*, 247–249.

Ei, S., & Bowen, A. (2002). College students' perceptions of student–instructor relationships. *Ethics and Behavior, 12*, 177–190.

Eisman, E., Dies, R., Finn, S., Eyde, L., Kay, G., Kubiszyn, T., et al. (2000). Problems and limitations in using psychological assessment in the contemporary health care delivery system. *Professional Psychology: Research and Practice, 31*, 131–140.

Elliott, D., & Guy, J. (1993). Mental health professionals versus non-mental-health professionals: Childhood trauma and adult functioning. *Professional Psychology: Research and Practice, 24*, 83–90.

Ellis, T., & Dickey, T. (1998). Procedures surrounding the suicide of a trainee's patient: A national survey of psychology internships and psychiatry residency programs. *Professional Psychology: Research and Practice, 29*, 492–497.

Emanuel, E., Wendler, D., & Grady, C. (2000). What makes clinical research ethical? *Journal of the American Medical Association, 283*, 2701–2711.

Emerich v. Philadelphia Center for Human Development, 720 A.2d 1032 (Pa. 1998).

Etzioni, A. (1996). *The new golden rule: Community and morality in a democratic society.* New York: Basic Books.

Feldman-Summers, S., & Pope, K. (1994). The experience of "forgetting" childhood abuse: A national survey of psychologists. *Journal of Consulting and Clinical Psychology, 62*, 636–639.

Finn, S., & Tonsager, M. (1997). Information-gathering and therapeutic models of assessment: Complementary paradigms. *Psychological Assessment, 9*, 374–385.

Fischer, C. (2004). Individualized assessment moderates the impact of HIPAA privacy rules. *Journal of Personality Assessment, 82*, 35–38.

Fischer, L. (1983). *The life of Mahatma Gandhi.* New York: HarperCollins.

Fisher, C. (1994). Reporting and referring research participants: Ethical challenges for investigators studying children and youth. *Ethics and Behavior, 4*, 87–95.

Fisher, C. (2000a, March/April). Preparing successful proposals for institutional review boards: Challenges and prospects for behavioral scientists. *Psychological Science Agenda, 13*, 12–13.

Fisher, C. (2000b). Relational ethics in psychological research: One feminist's journey. In M. Brabek (Ed.), *Practicing feminist ethics in psychology* (pp. 125–142). Washington, DC: American Psychological Association.

Fisher, C. (2003). *Decoding the APA ethics code.* Thousand Oaks, CA: Sage.

Fisher, C., Hoagwood, K., Boyce, C., Duster, T., Frank, D., Grisso, T., et al. (2002). Research ethics for mental health services involving ethnic minority children and youths. *American Psychologist, 57*, 1024–1040.

Fitzgerald, W. (1999). Legal and ethical considerations in the treatment of psychosis. *Journal of Clinical Psychiatry, 60*(Suppl. 19), 59–65.

Fly, B., van Bark, W., Weinman, L., Kitchener, K. S., & Lang, P. (1997). Ethical transgressions of psychology graduate students: Critical incidents with implications for training. *Professional Psychology: Research and Practice, 28*, 492–495.

Ford, M., & Hendrick, S. (2003). Therapists' sexual values for self and clients: Implications for practice and training. *Professional Psychology: Research and Practice, 34*, 80–87.

Forrest, L., Elman, N., Gizara, S., & Vacha-Haase, T. (1999). Trainee impairment: A review of identification, remediation, dismissal, and legal issues. *The Counseling Psychologist, 27*, 627–686.

Fortuny, L. A., & Mullaney, H. (1998). Assessing patients whose language you do not know: Can the absurd be ethical? *The Clinical Neuropsychologist, 12*, 113–126.

Friedrich, J., & Douglas, D. (1998). Ethics and the persuasive enterprise of teaching psychology. *American Psychologist, 53*, 549–562.

Gabbard, G. (1996). Lessons to be learned from the study of sexual boundary violations. *American Journal of Psychotherapy, 50*, 311–322.

Gentile, S., Asamen, J., Harmell, P., & Weathers, R. (2002). The stalking of psychologists by their clients. *Professional Psychology: Research and Practice, 33*, 490–494.

Glenmullen, J. (1993). *The pornographer's grief and other tales of human sexuality.* New York: HarperCollins.

Glickhauf-Hughes, C. (1998). Use of countertransference in answering client questions in psychotherapy. In L. VandeCreek, S. Knapp, & T. Jackson (Eds.), *Innovations in clinical practice: A sourcebook* (Vol. 16, pp. 55–64). Sarasota, FL: Professional Resource Press.

Goldfried, M. (2001). Integrating gay, lesbian, and bisexual issues into mainstream psychology. *American Psychologist, 56*, 975–988.

Gordon, R. (1993). Ethics based on protection of the transference. *Issues in Psychoanalytic Psychology, 15*, 95–105.

Gottlieb, M. (1993). Avoiding exploitative dual relationships: A decision-making model. *Psychotherapy: Theory, Research, Practice, Training, 30*, 41–48.

Gottlieb, M., Handelsman, M., & Knapp, S. (2004). *Ethical issues in informed consent.* Manuscript in preparation.

Greenberg, L., & Gould, J. (2001). The treating expert: A hybrid role with firm boundaries. *Professional Psychology: Research and Practice, 32*, 460–478.

Greenberg, L., Gould, J., Gould-Saltman, D., & Stahl, P. (2003). Is the child's therapist part of the problem? *Family Law Quarterly, 37*, 39–69.

Greenwald, A. (1997). Validity concerns and usefulness of student ratings of instruction. *American Psychologist, 52*, 1182–1186.

Grisso, T., & Appelbaum, P. (1998). *Assessing competence to consent to treatment: A guide for physicians and other health professionals.* New York: Oxford University Press.

Guthiel, T. (1985). Medicolegal pitfalls in the treatment of borderline patients. *American Journal of Psychotherapy, 142*, 9–14.

Guthiel, T. (1994). Discussion of Lazarus's "How certain boundaries and ethics diminish therapeutic effectiveness." *Ethics and Behavior, 4*, 295–298.

Guthiel, T., & Gabbard, G. (1993). The concept of boundaries in clinical practice: Theoretical and risk management dimensions. *American Journal of Psychiatry, 150*, 188–196.

Guthiel, T., & Gabbard, G. (1998). Misuses and misunderstandings of boundary theory in clinical and regulatory settings. *American Journal of Psychiatry, 155*, 409–414.

Guy, J. (1987). *The personal life of the psychotherapist.* New York: Wiley.

Guy, J. (2000). Holding the holding environment together: Self-psychology and psychotherapist care. *Professional Psychology: Research and Practice, 31*, 351–352.

Guy, J., Brown, C., & Poelstra, P. (1990). Who gets attacked? A national survey of patient violence directed at psychologists in clinical practice. *Professional Psychology: Research and Practice, 21*, 493–495.

Guy, J., Brown, C., & Poelstra, P. (1992). Safety concerns and protective measures used by psychotherapists. *Professional Psychology: Research and Practice, 23*, 421–423.

Hadjistavropolos, T., & Bieling, P. (2000). When reviews attack ethics, free speech, and the peer review process. *Canadian Psychology, 41*, 152–159.

Hall, G. C. N. (2001). Psychotherapy research with ethnic minorities: Empirical, ethical, and conceptual issues. *Journal of Consulting and Clinical Psychology, 69*, 502–510.

Hamanne v. Humenansky, C4-94-203 (Min. 2d J.D. 1995).

Hamilton, J., & Spruill, J. (1999). Identifying and reducing risk factors related to trainee–client sexual misconduct. *Professional Psychology: Research and Practice, 30*, 318–327.

Hammel, G., Olkin, R., & Taube, D. (1996). Student–educator sex in clinical and counseling psychology doctoral training. *Professional Psychology: Research and Practice, 27*, 93–97.

Handelsman, M. (2001). Accurate and effective informed consent. In E. R. Welfel & R. E. Ingersoll (Eds.), *The mental health desk reference* (pp. 453–458). New York: Wiley.

Handelsman, M., Gottlieb, M., & Knapp, S. (2005). Training ethical psychologists: An acculturation model. *Professional Psychology: Research and Practice, 36*, 59–65.

Handelsman, M., Knapp, S., & Gottlieb, M. (2002). Positive ethics. In C. R. Snyder & S. Lopez (Eds.), *Handbook of positive psychology* (pp. 731–744). New York: Oxford University Press.

Handelsman, M., Martinez, A., Geisendorfer, S., Jordan, L., Wagner, L., Daniel, P., & Davis, S. (1995). Does legally mandated consent to psychotherapy ensure ethical appropriateness? The Colorado experience. *Ethics and Behavior, 5*, 119–129.

Hansen, N. D., Pepitone-Arreola-Rockwell, F., & Greene, A. (2000). Multicultural competence: Criteria and case examples. *Professional Psychology: Theory and Practice, 31*, 652–660.

Harris, E. (2003, Winter). HIPAA update: Resolving areas of continuing confusion. *Massachusetts Psychological Association Journal*, 19–29.

Härtel, C., & Härtel, G. (1997). SHAPE-assisted intuitive decision making and problem solving information-processing-based training for conditions of cognitive busyness. *Group Dynamics: Theory, Research, and Practice, 1*, 187–199.

Heinssen, R., Levendusky, P., & Hunter, R. (1995). Client as colleague: Therapeutic contracting with the seriously mentally ill. *American Psychologist, 50*, 522–532.

Heppner, P., & Lee, D. (2002). Problem-solving appraisal and psychological adjustment. In C. R. Snyder & S. Lopez (Eds.), *Handbook of positive psychology* (pp. 288–298). New York: Oxford University Press.

Hess, A. (1998). Accepting forensic case referrals: Ethical and professional considerations. *Professional Psychology: Research and Practice, 29*, 109–114.

Hickson, G., Federspiel, C., Pichert, J., Miller, C., Gauld-Jaeger, J., & Bost, P. (2002). Patient complaints and malpractice risks. *Journal of the American Medical Association, 287*, 2951–2957.

Hill, C., & Knox, S. (2001). Self-disclosure. *Psychotherapy: Theory, Research, Practice, Training, 38*, 413–422.

Hinnefeld, B., & Newman, R. (1997). Analysis of the Truth and Responsibility in Mental Health Practices Act and similar proposals. *Professional Psychology: Research and Practice, 28*, 537–543.

Housman, L., & Stake, J. (1999). The current state of sexual ethics training in clinical psychology: Issues of quantity, quality, and effectiveness. *Professional Psychology: Research and Practice, 30*, 302–311.

Howe, E. (2001a). How to determine competency. *The Journal of Clinical Ethics, 12*, 3–16.

Howe, E. (2001b). To teach ethics better—Lie. *The Journal of Clinical Ethics, 12*, 97–110.

Huber, M., Balon, R., Labbate, L., Brandt-Youtz, S., Hammer, J. H., & Mufti, R. (2000). A survey of police officers' experience with *Tarasoff* warnings in two states. *Psychiatric Services, 51*, 807–809.

Institute of Medicine. (2000). *To err is human: Building a safer health system.* Washington, DC: National Academies Press.

Jackson, H., & Nuttall, R. (2001). A relationship between childhood sexual abuse and professional sexual misconduct. *Professional Psychology: Research, and Practice, 32*, 200–204.

Jackson, L. (1999). Ethnocultural resistance in multicultural training: Students and faculty. *Cultural Diversity and Ethnic Minority Psychology, 5*, 27–36.

Jacob-Timm, S. (1999). Ethically challenging situations encountered by school psychologists. *Psychology in the Schools, 36*, 205–217.

Jaffee v. Redmond, 135 L.Ed.2d 337 (1996).

Jensen, J., McNamara, J. R., & Gustafson, K. (1991). Parents' and clinicians' attitudes toward the risks and benefits of child psychotherapy: A study of informed-consent content. *Professional Psychology: Research and Practice, 22*, 161–170.

Jobes, D., & Berman, A. (1993). Suicide and malpractice liability: Assessing and revising policies, procedures and practice in outpatient settings. *Professional Psychology: Research and Practice, 24,* 91–99.

Johnson, H., Cournoyer, D., & Bond, B. (1995). Professional ethics and parents as consumers: How well are we doing? *Families in Society: The Journal of Contemporary Human Services,* 408–420.

Johnson, W. B., & Wilson, K. (1993). The military internship: A retrospective analysis. *Professional Psychology: Research and Practice, 24,* 312–318.

Johnston, S., & Farber, B. (1996). The maintenance of boundaries in psychotherapeutic practice. *Psychotherapy: Theory, Research, Practice, Training, 33,* 391–402.

Joint Committee on Testing Practices. (1998, August). *The rights and responsibilities of test takers; Guidelines and expectations.* Retrieved December 24, 2003, from http://www.apa.org/science/ttrr.html

Jordan, A., & Meara, N. (1990). Ethics and the professional practice of psychologists: The role of virtues and principles. *Professional Psychology: Theory and Practice, 21,* 107–114.

Kalb, P. (1999). Health care fraud and abuse. *Journal of the American Medical Association, 282,* 1163–1168.

Kamphuis, J., & Emmelkamp, P. M. G. (2000). Stalking—A contemporary challenge for forensic and clinical psychiatry. *British Journal of Psychiatry, 176,* 206–209.

Kant, I. (1988). *Fundamental principles of the metaphysics of morals* (T. K. Abbot, Trans.). Amherst, NY: Prometheus Books. (Original work published 1785)

Keith-Spiegel, P., Tabachnick, B., & Allen, M. (1993). Ethics in academia: Students' views of professors' actions. *Ethics and Behavior, 3,* 149–162.

Keith-Spiegel, P., Whitely, B., Balogh, D. W., Perkins, D., & Wittig, A. (2002). *The ethics of teaching: A casebook* (2nd ed.). Mahwah, NJ: Erlbaum.

Kelly, J., & Kalichman, S. (2002). Behavioral research in HIV/AIDS primary and secondary prevention: Recent advances and future directions. *Journal of Consulting and Clinical Psychology, 70,* 626–639.

Kier, F., & Molinari, V. (2004). Do-it-yourself testing for mental illness: Ethical issues, concerns, and recommendations. *Professional Psychology: Research and Practice, 35,* 261–267.

Kimmel, A. (1998). In defense of deception. *American Psychologist, 53,* 803–804.

Kirkland, K., Kirkland, K. L., & Reaves, R. (2004). On the professional use of disciplinary data. *Professional Psychology: Research and Practice, 35,* 179–184.

Kitchener, K. S. (1984). Intuition, critical evaluation and ethical principles: The foundation for ethical decisions in counseling psychology. *The Counseling Psychologist, 12,* 43–55.

Kitchener, K. S. (2000a). *Foundations of ethical practice, research, and teaching in psychology.* Mahwah, NJ: Erlbaum.

Kitchener, K. S. (2000b). Reconceptualizing responsibilities to students: A feminist perspective. In M. Brabeck (Ed.), *Practicing feminist ethics in psychology* (pp. 37–54). Washington, DC: American Psychological Association.

Kleespies, P., & Dettmer, E. (2000). The stress of patient emergencies for the clinician: Incidence, impact, and means of coping. *Journal of Clinical Psychology, 56,* 1352–1369.

Kleespies, P., Penk, W., & Forsyth, J. (1993). The stress of patient suicidal behavior during clinical training: Incidence, impact, and recovery. *Professional Psychology: Research and Practice, 24,* 293–303.

Knapp, S. (1999). Utilitarianism and the ethics of professional psychologists. *Ethics and Behavior, 9,* 383–392.

Knapp, S., & DeWall, T. (2003). Ethics of government advocacy. *The Pennsylvania Psychologist, 63,* 4.

Knapp, S., & Keller, P. (2004, January). Survey reveals stressful events for psychologists. *The Pennsylvania Psychologist, 64,* 6, 8.

Knapp, S., & Slattery, J. (2004). Professional boundaries in nontraditional settings. *Professional Psychology: Research and Practice, 35,* 553–558.

Knapp, S., & VandeCreek, L. (1987). *Privileged communications in the mental health professions.* New York: Van Nostrand Reinhold.

Knapp, S., & VandeCreek, L. (2003a, Fall). Do psychologists have supererogatory obligations? *Psychotherapy Bulletin, 38,* 29–31.

Knapp, S., & VandeCreek, L. (2003b). *A guide to the 2002 revision of the APA Ethics Code.* Sarasota, FL: Professional Resource Press.

Knapp, S., & VandeCreek, L. (2004). A principle-based analysis of the 2002 American Psychological Association ethics code. *Psychotherapy: Theory, Research, Practice, Training, 41,* 247–254.

Knapp, S., & VandeCreek, L. (2005). Ethical and patient management issues with older, impaired drivers. *Professional Psychology: Research and Practice, 36,* 197–202.

Koocher, G. (2003). Ethical issues in psychotherapy with adolescents. *Journal of Clinical Psychology, 59,* 1247–1256.

Koocher, G., & Keith-Spiegel, P. (1998). *Ethics in psychology* (2nd ed.). New York: Oxford University Press.

Kozlowski, N., Rupert, P., & Crawford, I. (1998). Psychotherapy with HIV-infected clients: Factors influencing notification of third parties. *Psychotherapy: Theory, Research, Practice, Training, 35,* 105–115.

Kramen-Kahn, B., & Hansen, N. D. (1998). Rafting the rapids: Occupational hazards, rewards, and coping strategies of psychotherapists. *Professional Psychology: Research and Practice, 29,* 130–134.

Kraut, R., Olson, J., Banaji, M., Bruckman, A., Cohen, J., & Couper, M. (2004). Psychological research online: Report of Board of Scientific Affairs' Advisory Group on the Conduct of Research on the Internet. *American Psychologist, 59,* 105–117.

Krishnamurthy, R., VandeCreek, L., Kaslow, N., Tazeau, Y., Miville, M., Kerns, R., et al. (2004). Achieving competence in psychological assessment: Directions in education and training. *Journal of Clinical Psychology, 60,* 725–739.

Kroll, J. (2000). The use of no-suicide contracts by psychiatrists in Minnesota. *American Journal of Psychiatry, 157*, 1684–1686.

Krumboltz, J. (2002). Encouraging research: Make it collegial, enjoyable, and relevant. *American Psychologist, 57*, 931–940.

Lam, A., & Sue, S. (2001). Client diversity. *Psychotherapy: Theory, Research, Practice, Training, 38*, 479–486.

Lamb, D., & Catanzaro, S. (1998). Sexual and nonsexual boundary violations involving psychologists, clients, supervisees, and students: Implications for professional practice. *Professional Psychology: Research and Practice, 29*, 498–503.

Lamb, D., Catanzaro, S., & Moorman, A. (2003). Psychologists reflect on their sexual relationships with clients, supervisees, and students: Occurrence, impact, rationales, and collegial interventions. *Professional Psychology: Research and Practice, 34*, 102–107.

Lamb, D., Catanzaro, S., & Moorman, A. (2004). A preliminary look at how psychologists identify, evaluate, and proceed when faced with possible multiple relationships. *Professional Psychology: Research and Practice, 35*, 248–260.

Lamb, D., Strand, K., Woodburn, J., Buchko, K., Lewis, J., & Kang, J. (1994). Sexual and business relationships between therapists and former clients. *Psychotherapy: Theory, Research, Practice, Training, 31*, 270–278.

Lambert, M., & Barley, D. (2001). Research summary on the therapeutic relationship and psychotherapy outcome. *Psychotherapy: Theory, Practice, Research, Training, 38*, 357–361.

La Roche, M. (1999). Culture, transference, and countertransference among Latinos. *Psychotherapy: Theory, Research, Practice, Training, 36*, 389–397.

La Roche, M., & Maxie, A. (2003). Ten considerations in addressing cultural differences in psychotherapy. *Professional Psychology: Research and Practice, 34*, 180–186.

Lasser, J., & Gottlieb, M. (2004). Treating patients distressed regarding their sexual orientation: Clinical and ethical alternatives. *Professional Psychology: Research and Practice, 35*, 194–200.

Lehman, N. C. (2002, February). Cultural consultation service bridges mental health divide. *Psychiatric News, 37*, 7, 27.

Levinson, W., Roter, D., Mullooly, J., Dull, V., & Frankel, R. (1997). Physician–patient communication: The relationship with malpractice claims among primary care physicians and surgeons. *Journal of the American Medical Association, 277*, 553–559.

Lewis, M. (2002, February). *Did Ambrose write Wild Blue, or just edit it?* Retrieved December 27, 2002, from http://www.forbes.com/2002/02/27/0227/ambrose-print.html

Liddle, B. (1997). Gay and lesbian clients' selection of therapists and utilization of therapy. *Psychotherapy: Theory, Research, Practice, Training, 34*, 11–18.

Lopez, S. (1997). Cultural competence in psychotherapy: A guide for clinicians and their supervisors. In C. E. Watkins (Ed.), *Handbook of psychotherapy supervision* (pp. 570–588). New York: Wiley.

Lowery, J. (2001, August). Successful supervision: Supervisor and supervisee characteristics. In J. Barnett (Chair), *Supervision: Ethical, legal and clinical issues*. Symposium conducted at the annual meeting of the American Psychological Association, San Francisco, CA.

Mahalik, J., Van Ormer, E. A., & Simi, N. (2000). Ethical issues in using self-disclosure in feminist therapy. In M. Brabeck (Ed.), *Practicing feminist ethics in psychology* (pp. 189–202). Washington, DC: American Psychological Association.

Malony, H. N. (2000). The psychological evaluation of religious professionals. *Professional Psychology: Research and Practice, 31*, 521–525.

Martin, M. (2000). *Meaningful work: Rethinking professional ethics*. New York: Oxford University Press.

Martino, C. (2001, August). Secrets of successful supervision: Graduate students' preferences and experiences with effective and ineffective supervision. In J. Barnett (Chair), *Supervision: Ethical, legal and clinical issues*. Symposium conducted at the annual meeting of the American Psychological Association, San Francisco, CA.

McCarthy, P., Kulakowski, D., & Kenfield, J. (1994). Clinical supervision practices of licensed psychologists. *Professional Psychology: Research and Practice, 25*, 177–181.

Meara, N., Schmidt, L., & Day, J. (1996). Principles and virtues: A foundation for ethical decisions, policies, and character. *The Counseling Psychologist, 24*, 4–77.

Meer, D., & VandeCreek, L. (2002). Cultural considerations in release of information. *Ethics and Behavior, 12*, 143–156.

Meyer, G., Finn, S., Eyde, L., Kay, G., Moreland, K., Dies, R., et al. (2001). Psychological testing and psychological assessment. *American Psychologist, 56*, 128–165.

Milgram, S. (1975). *Obedience to authority*. New York: Harper & Row.

Mill, J. S. (1987). Utilitarianism. In A. Ryan (Ed.), *John Stuart Mill and Jeremy Bentham: Utilitarianism and other essays* (pp. 272–338). New York: Penguin. (Original work published 1861)

Monahan, J. (1993). Limiting therapist exposure to *Tarasoff* liability: Guidelines for risk containment. *American Psychologist, 48*, 242–250.

Monahan, J., Steadman, H., Appelbaum, P., Robins, P., Mulvey, E., Silver, E., et al. (2000). Developing a clinically useful actuarial tool for assessing violence risk. *British Journal of Psychiatry, 176*, 312–319.

Montgomery, L., Cupit, B., & Wimberly, T. (1999). Complaints, malpractice, and risk management: Professional issues and personal experiences. *Professional Psychology: Research and Practice, 30*, 402–410.

Moreland, K., Eyde, L., Robertson, G., Primoff, E., & Most, R. (1995). Assessment of test user qualifications: A research-based measurement procedure. *American Psychologist, 50*, 14–23.

Moursund, J. (2001). Getting started. In S. Cullari (Ed.), *Counseling and psychotherapy: A practical guide for students, trainees, and new professionals* (pp. 29–58). Boston: Allyn & Bacon.

Murphy, R., & Halgin, R. (1995). Influences on the career choice of psychotherapists. *Professional Psychology: Research and Practice, 26*, 422–426.

Myers, D. (1992). *The pursuit of happiness: Who is happy and why.* New York: Morrow.

National Association for Consumer Protection in Mental Health Practices. (1994, August). *A proposal to finance preparation of model legislation titled Mental Health Consumer Protection Act.* Unpublished manuscript.

National Bioethics Advisory Commission. (1998). *Research involving persons with mental disorders that may affect decision making capacity.* Executive summary. Retrieved December 29, 2002, from http://www.georgetown.edu/research/nrcbl/nbac/capacity/Executive.htm

National Commission for the Protection of Human Subjects of Biomedical and Behavioral Research. (1979). *The Belmont report: Ethical principles and guidelines for the protection of human subjects of research* (HHS Pub. No. 8887-809). Washington, DC: U.S. Government Printing Office.

National Institute of Mental Health. (2001, April). *Certificates of confidentiality: Privacy protection for research subjects.* Retrieved October 25, 2001, from http://www.nimh.nih.gov/research/confidentfaq.cfm

Norcross, J. (2000). Psychotherapist self-care: Practitioner-tested, research-informed strategies. *Professional Psychology: Research and Practice, 31*, 710–713.

Online Ethics Center. (1999a). *Case Study #1: Overly ambitious researchers: Fabricating data.* Retrieved January 5, 2003, from http://onlineethics.org/edu/precol/classroom/cs1.html

Online Ethics Center. (1999b). *Case Study #3: The Tuskegee syphilis study.* Retrieved January 5, 2003, from http://onlineethics.org/edu/precol/classroom/cs3.html

Ortmann, A., & Hertwig, R. (1997). Is deception acceptable? *American Psychologist, 52*, 746–747.

Ortmann, A., & Hertwig, R. (1998). The question remains: Is deception acceptable? *American Psychologist, 53*, 806–807.

Osheroff v. Chestnut Lodge Inc., 490 A.2d 720 (Md. App. 1985).

Palmiter, D., & Renjilian, D. (2003). Clinical web pages: Do they meet expectations? *Professional Psychology: Research and Practice, 34*, 164–169.

Paxton, C., Lovett, J., & Riggs, M. (2001). The nature of professional training and perceptions of adequacy in dealing with sexual feelings in psychotherapy: Experiences of clinical faculty. *Ethics and Behavior, 11*, 175–189.

Pearlman, L. A., & MacIan, P. (1995). Vicarious traumatization: An empirical study of the effects of trauma work on trauma therapists. *Professional Psychology: Research and Practice, 26*, 558–565.

Peterson, Z. (2002). More than a mirror: The ethics of therapist self-disclosure. *Psychotherapy: Theory, Research, Practice, Training, 39*, 21–31.

Pipes, R. (1997). Nonsexual relationships between psychotherapists and their former clients: Obligations of psychologists. *Ethics and Behavior, 7*, 27–41.

Pitta, P. (1996, Winter). An integrated supervisory model. *The Family Psychologist, 12*, 16–18.

Pittenger, D. (2003). Internet research: An opportunity to revisit classic ethical problems in behavioral research. *Ethics and Behavior, 13*, 45–60.

Plante, T. (1996). Ten principles of success for psychology trainees embarking on their careers. *Professional Psychology: Research and Practice, 27*, 304–307.

Pope, K. (1994). *Sexual involvement with therapists: Patient assessment, subsequent therapy, forensics.* Washington, DC: American Psychological Association.

Pope, K., & Brown, L. (1996). *Recovered memories of abuse: Assessment, therapy, forensics.* Washington, DC: American Psychological Association.

Pope, K., Sonne, J., & Holroyd, J. (1993). *Sexual feelings in psychotherapy: Explorations for therapists and therapists-in-training.* Washington, DC: American Psychological Association.

Pope, K., & Tabachnick, B. (1993). Therapists' anger, hate, fear, and sexual feelings: National survey of therapist responses, client characteristics, critical events, formal complaints, and training. *Professional Psychology: Research and Practice, 24*, 142–152.

Pope, K., Tabachnick, B., & Keith-Spiegel, P. (1987). Ethics of practice: The beliefs and behaviors of psychologists as therapists. *American Psychologist, 42*, 993–1006.

Prilleltensky, I. (1997). Values, assumptions, and practices: Assessing the moral implications of psychological discourse and action. *American Psychologist, 52*, 517–535.

Prilleltensky, I., Rossiter, A., & Walsh-Bowers, R. (1996). Preventing harm and promoting ethical discourse in the helping professions: Conceptual, research, analytical, and action frameworks. *Ethics and Behavior, 6*, 287–304.

Procidano, M., Busch-Rossnagel, N., Reznikoff, M., & Geisinger, K. (1995). Responding to graduate students' professional deficiencies: A national survey. *Journal of Clinical Psychology, 51*, 416–433.

Ragusea, A., & VandeCreek, L. (2003). Suggestions for the ethical practice of online psychotherapy. *Psychotherapy: Theory, Research, Practice, Training, 40*, 94–102.

Ragusea, S. (2002). A professional living will for psychologists and other mental health professionals. In L. VandeCreek & T. Jackson (Eds.), *Innovations in clinical practice: A sourcebook* (Vol. 20, pp. 301–305). Sarasota, FL: Professional Resource Press.

Rave, E., & Larsen, C. (Eds.). (1995). *Ethical decision making in therapy: Feminist perspectives.* New York: Guilford Press.

Reist, D., & VandeCreek, L. (2004). The pharmaceutical industry's use of gifts and educational events to influence prescription practices: Ethical dilemmas and implications for psychologists. *Professional Psychology: Research and Practice, 35*, 329–335.

Richards, P. S., & Bergin, A. E. (Eds.). (2004). *Casebook for a spiritual strategy in counseling and psychotherapy.* Washington, DC: American Psychological Association.

Richards, P. S., & Potts, R. (1995). Using spiritual interventions in psychotherapy: Practices, successes, failures, and ethical concerns of Mormon psychotherapists. *Professional Psychology: Research and Practice, 26*, 163–170.

Richardson, F., Fowers, B., & Guigon, C. (1999). *Re-envisioning psychology: Moral dimensions of theory and practice.* San Francisco: Jossey-Bass.

Riggs, D., Caulfied, M., & Street, A. (2000). Risk for domestic violence: Factors associated with perpetration and victimization. *Journal of Clinical Psychology, 56,* 1289–1316.

Roberts, L. W. (2000). Evidence-based ethics and informed consent in mental illness research. *Archives of General Psychiatry, 57,* 540–543.

Roberts, L. W., Battaglia, J., & Epstein, R. (1999). Frontier ethics: Mental health care needs and ethical dilemmas in rural communities. *Psychiatric Services, 50,* 497–503.

Rodolfa, E., Hall, T., Holms, V., Davena, A., Komatz, D., Antunez, M., & Hall, A. (1994). The management of sexual feelings in therapy. *Professional Psychology: Research and Practice, 25,* 168–172.

Rønnestad, M., & Skovholt, T. (2001). Learning arenas for professional development: Retrospective accounts of senior psychotherapists. *Professional Psychology: Research and Practice, 32,* 181–187.

Ross, W. D. (1998). What makes right acts right? In J. Rachels (Ed.), *Ethical theory* (pp. 265–285). New York: Oxford University Press. (Original work published 1930)

Rotgers, F., & Barrett, D. (1996). *Daubert v. Merrell Dow* and expert testimony by clinical psychologists: Implications and recommendations for practice. *Professional Psychology: Research and Practice, 27,* 467–474.

Roy v. Hartogs, 366 N.Y.S.2d 297 (1975).

Ruiz, M., Drake, E., Glass, A., Marcotte, D., & van Gorp, W. (2002). Trying to beat the system: Misuse of the Internet to assist in avoiding the detection of psychological symptom dissimulation. *Professional Psychology: Research and Practice, 33,* 294–299.

Sales, B., & Folkman, S. (Eds). (2000). *Ethics in research with human participants* (2nd ed.). Washington, DC: American Psychological Association.

Samuel, S., & Gorton, G. (1998). National survey of psychology internship directors regarding education for prevention of psychologist–patient sexual exploitation. *Professional Psychology: Research and Practice, 29,* 86–90.

Sandifer, B. (1989, September). Dual relationships: Ethical hazards in small-town practice. *Mississippi Psychologist, 7.*

Schank, J., & Skovholt, T. (1997). Dual-relationship dilemmas of rural and small-community psychologists. *Professional Psychology: Research and Practice, 28,* 44–49.

Schneider, M., Brown, L., & Glassgold, J. (2002). Implementing the resolution on appropriate therapeutic responses to sexual orientation: A guide for the perplexed. *Professional Psychology: Research and Practice, 33,* 265–276.

Schoener, G. (1999). Preventive and remedial boundaries training for helping professionals and clergy: Successful approaches and useful tools. *Journal of Sex Education and Therapy, 24,* 209–217.

Schoener, G. (2002, September). *Sexual exploitation: Interviewing victims, profiling offenders, and remedies*. Paper presented at the annual meeting of the Council on Licensure, Enforcement, and Regulation, Las Vegas, NV.

Schoenfeld, L., Hatch, J., & Gonzalez, J. (2001). Responses of psychologists to complaints filed against them with a state licensing board. *Professional Psychology: Research and Practice, 32,* 491–495.

Scott-Jones, D. (2000). Recruitment of research participants. In B. Sales & S. Folkman (Eds.), *Ethics in research with human participants* (2nd ed., pp. 27–34). Washington, DC: American Psychological Association.

Seligman, M. (1991). *Learned optimism.* New York: Knopf.

Seligman, M., & Csikszentmihalyi, M. (2000). Positive psychology: An introduction. *American Psychologist, 55,* 5–14.

Sharkin, B., & Birky, I. (1992). Incidental encounters between therapists and their clients. *Professional Psychology: Research and Practice, 23,* 326–328.

Sharpe, R. (2002, January 24). Suicide at MIT raises parents' ire. *USA Today.* Retrieved August 14, 2003, from http://www.usatoday.com/news/nation/2002/01/25/usat-mit.html

Sherman, M., & Thelen, M. (1998). Distress and professional impairment among psychologists in clinical practice. *Professional Psychology: Research and Practice, 29,* 79–85.

Shidlo, A., & Schroeder, M. (2002). Changing sexual orientation: A consumers' report. *Professional Psychology: Research and Practice, 33,* 249–259.

Shuman, D., & Greenberg, S. (2003). The expert witness, the adversary system, and the voice of reason: Reconciling impartiality and advocacy. *Professional Psychology: Research and Practice, 34,* 219–224.

Sieber, J. E. (2001). Planning research: Basic ethical decision making. In B. Sales & S. Folkman (Eds.), *Ethics in research with human participants* (2nd ed., pp. 13–26). Washington, DC: American Psychological Association.

Simon, R. (1992). *Clinical psychiatry and the law* (2nd ed.). Washington, DC: American Psychiatric Press.

Skorina, J., Bissell, L., & DeSoto, C. (1990). Alcoholic psychologists: Routes to recovery. *Professional Psychology: Research and Practice, 21,* 248–251.

Slimp, P. A. O., & Burian, B. (1994). Multiple role relationships during internship: Consequences and recommendations. *Professional Psychology: Research and Practice, 25,* 39–45.

Smith, B., & Evans, F. B. (2004). The end of the world as we know it (and I feel fine): Comment on Erard. *Journal of Personality Assessment, 82,* 39–43.

Sommers-Flanagan, R., Elliott, D., & Sommers-Flanagan, J. (1998). Exploring the edges: Boundaries and breaks. *Ethics and Behavior, 8,* 37–48.

Sperry, L., & Shafranske, E. P. (2005). *Spiritually oriented psychotherapy.* Washington, DC: American Psychological Association.

Stake, J., & Oliver, J. (1991). Sexual contact and touching between therapist and client: A survey of psychologists' attitudes and behavior. *Professional Psychology: Research and Practice, 22,* 297–307.

Sternberg, R., Grigorenko, E., & Kalmar, D. (2001). The role of theory in unified psychology. *Journal of Theoretical and Philosophical Psychology, 21,* 99–117.

Stevenson, L., & Haberman, D. (1998). *Ten theories of human nature* (3rd ed.). New York: Oxford University Press.

Stuart, R. (2004). Twelve suggestions for achieving multicultural competence. *Professional Psychology: Research and Practice, 35,* 3–9.

Sullivan, L., & Ogloff, J. (1998). Appropriate supervisor–graduate student relationships. *Ethics and Behavior, 8,* 229–248.

Sullivan, T., Martin, W., & Handelsman, M. (1993). Practical benefits of an informed-consent procedure: An empirical investigation. *Professional Psychology: Research and Practice, 24,* 160–163.

Swanson, J., Swartz, M., Essock, S., Osher, F., Wagner, H. R., Goodman, L., et al. (2002). The social–environmental context of violent behavior in persons treated for severe mental illness. *American Journal of Public Health, 92,* 1523–1531.

Tabachnick, B., Keith-Spiegel, P., & Pope, K. (1991). Ethics of teaching: Beliefs and behaviors of psychologists as educators. *American Psychologist, 46,* 506–515.

Tarasoff v. Regents of the University of California et al., 551 P.2d 334 (Cal. S. Ct. 1976).

Tesler, P. (1999). Collaborative law: A new paradigm for divorce lawyers. *Psychology, Public Policy, and Law, 5,* 967–1000.

Thompson, V. S., Bazile, A., & Akbar, M. (2004). African Americans' perceptions of psychotherapy and psychotherapists. *Professional Psychology: Research and Practice, 35,* 19–26.

Thoreson, R., Budd, F., & Krauskopf, C. (1986). Alcoholism among psychologists: Factors in relapse and recovery. *Professional Psychology: Research and Practice, 17,* 497–503.

Thoreson, R., Miller, M., & Krauskopf, C. (1989). The distressed psychologist: Prevalence and treatment considerations. *Professional Psychology: Research and Practice, 20,* 153–158.

Tjeltveit, A. (1999). *Ethics and values in psychotherapy.* New York: Routledge.

Tryon, G., & Winograd, G. (2001). Goal consensus and collaboration. *Psychotherapy: Theory, Research, Practice, Training, 38,* 385–389.

Tucker, C., & Herman, K. (2002). Using culturally sensitive theories and research to meet the academic needs of low-income African American children. *American Psychologist, 57,* 762–773.

Turner, S., DeMers, S., Fox, H. R., & Reed, G. (2001). APA's guidelines for test user qualifications: An executive summary. *American Psychologist, 56,* 1099–1113.

U.S. Department of Health and Human Services. (2002, August 14). Standards for privacy of individually identifiable health information. *Federal Register, 67,* 53182–53277.

Vacha-Haase, T., Davenport, D., & Kerewsky, S. (2004). Problematic students: Gatekeeping practices of academic professional psychology programs. *Professional Psychology: Research and Practice, 35*, 115–122.

Valenstein, E. (1986). *Great and desperate cures.* New York: Basic Books.

Van Horne, B. (2004). Psychology licensing board disciplinary actions: The realities. *Professional Psychology: Research and Practice, 35*, 170–178.

VandeCreek, L., & Knapp, S. (2001). *Tarasoff and beyond: Legal and clinical considerations in the treatment of life endangering patients* (3rd ed.). Sarasota, FL: Professional Resources Press.

VandeCreek, L., Knapp, S., & Rosas, G. (2003, August). *Ethics literacy in professional psychology.* Poster session presented at the annual meeting of the American Psychological Association, Toronto, Ontario, Canada.

Vasquez, M. (1992). Psychologist as clinical supervisor: Promoting ethical behavior. *Professional Psychology: Research and Practice, 23*, 196–202.

Vasquez, M. (1998). Latinos and violence: Mental health implications and strategies for clinicians. *Cultural Diversity and Mental Health, 4*, 319–334.

Vasquez, M. (2002). Complexities of the Latina experience: A tribute to Martha Bernal. *American Psychologist, 57*, 880–888.

Watkins, C. E. (1997). Defining psychological supervision and understanding supervisor functioning. In C. E. Watkins (Ed.), *Handbook of psychotherapy supervision* (pp. 3–10). New York: Wiley.

Weinberger, L., & Sreenivasan, S. (1994). Ethical and professional conflicts in correctional psychology. *Professional Psychology: Research and Practice, 25*, 161–167.

Weiss, A. (2001). The no-suicide contract: Possibilities and pitfalls. *American Journal of Psychotherapy, 55*, 414–419.

Whitley, B., Perkins, D., Balogh, D. W., Keith-Spiegel, P., & Wittig, A. (2001). *Fairness in the classroom.* Retrieved April 23, 2001, from http://www.psychologicalscience.org/newsrearchtips0700tips.html

Williams, M. (1996). Boundary violations: Do some contended standards of care fail to encompass commonplace procedures of humanistic, behavioral, and eclectic psychotherapy? *Psychotherapy: Theory, Research, Practice, Training, 34*, 238–249.

Williams, M. (2000). Victimized by "victims": A taxonomy of antecedents of false complaints against psychologists. *Professional Psychology: Research and Practice, 31*, 75–81.

Wiseman, H., & Schefler, G. (2001). Experienced psychoanalytically oriented therapists' narrative accounts of their personal therapy: Impacts on professional and personal development. *Psychotherapy: Theory, Research, Practice, Training, 38*, 129–141.

Wood, B., Klein, S., Cross, H., Lammers, C., & Elliott, J. (1985). Impaired practitioners: Psychologists' opinions about prevalence, and proposals for intervention. *Professional Psychology: Research and Practice, 16*, 843–850.

Woodward, B. (1999). Challenges to human subject protections in US medical research. *Journal of the American Medical Association, 282*, 1947–1952.

Woody, R. H. (1997a). Dubious and bogus credentials in mental health practice. *Ethics and Behavior, 7,* 337–345.

Woody, R. H. (1997b). *Legally safe mental health practice: Psycholegal questions and answers.* Madison, CT: Psychosocial Press.

Woody, R. H. (1998). Bartering for psychological services. *Professional Psychology: Research and Practice, 29,* 174–178.

Woody, R. H. (1999). Domestic violations of confidentiality. *Professional Psychology: Research and Practice, 30,* 607–610.

Yarhouse, M., & Throckmorton, W. (2002). Ethical issues in attempts to ban reorientation therapies. *Psychotherapy: Theory, Research, Practice, Training, 39,* 66–75.

Younggren, J., & Gottlieb, M. (2004). Managing risk when contemplating multiple relationships. *Professional Psychology: Research and Practice, 35,* 255–260.

Zeddies, T. (1999). Becoming a psychotherapist: The personal nature of clinical work, emotional availability, and personal allegiances. *Psychotherapy: Theory, Research, Practice, Training, 36,* 229–235.

Ziegler, R. (1999). The formation and transformation of moral impulse. *Journal of Moral Education, 28,* 445–457.

Zimbardo, P. (1999). *Stanford prison experiment: A simulation study of the psychology of imprisonment.* Retrieved December 24, 2003, from http://www.prisonexp.prg/

INDEX

and virtue ethics on ethical dilemmas,
18
See also Role conflicts
Confucian tradition, 56–57
Confucius, 17
Consent forms, 108
Consequentialism, 20
Consultation, 138
and billing, 151
competence through, 53
and confidentiality, 116
as duty, 194–196
and ethical decision making, 45, 47
peer, 53, 217
for publicly oriented community agencies, 247
as social support, 71
on suicidal patients, 223
vs. supervision, 54
vs. supervision (clinical), 151, 217
Consumer-focused assessments, 183
Context, and morality of specific behaviors,
47
Continuing education (CE), 6
in advertising by psychologists, 158
as condition of licensure renewal, 53
as impairment prevention, 73
Contracting, therapeutic, 102
Controls
after-the-fact, 5, 6–9
before-the-fact, 5, 6
Controversial topics, teaching of, 207–208
Coordinating of joint treatments, 192–194
Coping models, 68
Copyright laws, and test security, 188, 190
Correctional facility, psychologist in, 200
Countertransference, 138
eroticized, 97
need for graduate-program teaching
about, 93
and supervision, 223
Court-ordered treatment, 167–168
and HIPPA, 171
multiple relationships from, 88
Court orders, 122–123
Coverage, responsibilities for, 198
Credentials
and advertising, 158–159
proficiency, 62
in forensic psychology, 163
vanity, 159
Criminal laws, and psychologists, 7

Crisis. *See* Emergency or crisis
Cultural diversity, 13
and assessment, 177
and teaching of psychology, 208
Cultural and linguistic minorities, competence with, 54–59
Culture of safety, 35–36
and communication between health-
care professionals, 193
confidentiality in, 115
and informed consent, 100
and self-disclosure, 84
as self-regulation, 251

Dangerousness prediction scales, 134
Data
reanalyzing or verifying of, 247
standardization lacking for, 8
Dating relationships, and threat of violence,
134
Debriefing of research participants, 240–241
Debts of patients, 152–153
Deception in research, 241–242
and APA Ethics Code, 34–35
and participants' control over voice or
image, 234
Decision making, ethical. *See* Ethical decision making
Decision making, shared, 99. *See also* Informed consent; Participatory model
Democracy, 155–156
Demographic match, question of significance
of, 56
Deontological (duty-based) ethics, 18–19
vs. consequentialism, 20
and deceptive experiments, 242
and supererogatory obligations, 25
and welfare of research participants, 240
Desensitization, in vivo, 78
Diagnosis
in cultural competence, 57–58
and third-party reimbursement, 150–
151
See also Assessment
*Diagnostic and Statistical Manual of Mental
Disorders* (4th ed.), and diagnosis for
insurance reimbursement, 151
Didactic training
and sexual exploitation issues, 94–96
use of confidential information for, 127–
128
Dietary supplements, 64

Disaster relief services, 157

Disciplinary codes, 4, 25. *See also* Remedial ethics

Disciplinary complaints, 9

Disciplinary mechanisms, 7

Disposal of records, 124–125

Distributive justice, 22

Diversity, sensitivity to, 207–208

Documentation

    in forensic setting, 171

    for hospitalized patients, 137–138, 138

    incomplete (as negligence), 36

    in risk management, 37

    for supervisory sessions, 222

Domestic abuse, and threat of violence, 134

Dual relationships, 78, 88. *See also* Multiple relationships

Duty-based perspective, 12–13

Duty to consult or refer, 194–196

Duty-to-warn-or-protect, 131, 133

    and HIV/AIDS or other STDs, 143

Educational relationship, compared with treatment and supervision, 227–228

Electronic communication, APA Code silent on, 40–41

e-mail therapy, 64–65

Emergency or crisis

    ethical decision making in, 49

    and exceptions to competency requirements, 65

Emergency phone calls, 149

Emerging or experimental treatments, 63

Emerich v. Philadelphia Center for Human Development, 134–135

Emotional balance, 37

Emotional competence, 12, 51–52, 65–66, 214

    assessment of, 213

    and personal stressors, 66–68

    and professional stressors, 68–72

Empowered consent, 12

Ethical acuity, 16

Ethical decision making, 39

    areas of particular need for, 39–42

    balancing of competing demands in, 14, 119, 132

    in emergency or crisis, 49

    five-step model of, 42–49

        and aggressive patients, 133–137

        and child abuse, 144

        for HIV or other infections diseases, 141–144

and suicidal patients, 137–141

and philosophical systems, 16

as self-regulation, 251

Ethical errors, trainee, 224–225

Ethical ideals, in career choice, 15

Ethical intuitions, 21

    as intuitive moral sense, 15–16

Ethical misconduct (unethical conduct)

    identification of, 201–202

    by students, 215

Ethical Principles of Psychologists and Code of Conduct, APA, 3. *See also* Ethics Code, APA

Ethics, 3

    minimalist (rigid prohibitions or commandments), 9–10

    positive (active), 4, 9–11, 251

        benefits of, 13–14

        and integration of professional and personal ethics, 25–29, 36

        as moral maximalism, 25

        precursors of, 11–13

        vs. remedial, 12

        (*see also* Aspirational principles)

    practical (applied), 3

    remedial, 3, '4, 251

        vs. positive, 12

    self-regulation models of, 251

    See also at Moral

"Ethics-across-the-curriculum" model, 210

Ethics code(s)

    aspirational principles of, 32

    moral values behind, 13

    virtue ethics on, 17–18

Ethics Code, APA, 3, 7, 31–32

    and advertising or public statements, 157

    on web sites, 160

    on animal research, 243

    aspirational (General) principles of, 3–4, 31, 32

        and positive ethics, 10

        on self-care and competence, 66

        and supererogatory obligations, 41–42

    and assessment, 175

        and sharing evaluation results, 182

        and test security (changes), 184–188, 190

        for unfamiliar cultures, 177

    and assimilated group, 95

    and boundaries, 76

and boundary crossings, 83
as clinically indicated, 78
Homophobia, internalized, 60
Homosexuality, 59–60
Honor codes, 211
Hospitalization, involuntary, threats of to be avoided, 137
Hugging, 86
Hybrid roles, 167, 168
Hypothetical imperative, 19

IDEAL system, 42
Identification of ethical misconduct, 201–202
Identification of problem, in ethical decision making, 43
and aggressive patients, 133–135
and HIV or other infectious diseases, 142–143
and suicidal patients, 137–138
Immigrants
and demographic match, 56
information to be documented on, 59
Impaired professional program, 72–73
Impaired psychologists, 72–73
and behaviors to prevent impairment, 69
Impaired trainees, 225–226
Impairment as source of complaints, 8
Implementation of ethical decisions, 47. See also Acting on ethical decisions
Incompetence, as source of complaints, 8
Infectious diseases, patients with, 141–144
Informed consent, 99
and academic research psychologists, 8
and adolescents, 102
for research, 235
APA Ethics Code on, 40, 99–100, 104–106
and research, 233
in assessments, 182–184
exceptions to, 182–184
in clinical supervision, 228–229
on financial matters, 148–150
of forensic clients, 169–170
and therapy with patients involved in litigation, 169
information needed for, 104–107
letter vs. spirit of law on, 4
and "Mental Health Bill of Rights," 108–109
models of

medicolegal, 100–101
participatory, 100, 101–102, 107–108
patients eligible to give, 102–104
in psychology training programs, 213–214
readability of forms for, 108
in religious-based psychotherapy, 61
and remedial vs. positive ethics, 12
and research, 235
with vulnerable participants, 238
Infractions, data on, 8–9
Innovative therapies, and informed consent, 105
Institutional policies, confronting of, 199–201
Institutional review boards (IRBs), 232
Insurance contracts
and fee disputes, 148–149
and problems-in-living, 151
and services by trainees or unlicensed employees, 151
Integrated group, 27, 28
Integration of professional and personal ethics, 25–29
and boundaries, 94
and virtue-based risk management, 36
Integrity, as virtue, 17
in research or scholarship, 232, 244
Internalized homophobia, 60
Internet research, 234
and plagiarism, 246
Interns
in alcoholism example, 43, 45, 46–47, 48
suicides among patients of, 223
See also Supervisees; Trainees
Internship year, 225, 226
Interpreters, 58. See also Translation
Intervention, and cultural competence, 58–59
Intrusive advocacy, 82, 87
Intuitive sense of morality, 15–16, 21
In vivo desensitization, 78
Involuntary hospitalization, threats of to be avoided, 137

Jaffee v. Redmond, 121
Joint treatments, coordinating of, 192–194
Journal club, 54
Judgment
in implementing moral principles, 17

professional
in implementing standards, 40
in selecting and using tests, 177–178
Judicial process, 162
adversarial process in, 162, 165
Justice, 21, 22
distributive, 22
formal (procedural), 22
vs. unfair discrimination, 33

Kant, Immanuel, 18–19, 25
Key (foundational) standards in APA Ethics Code, 33
clarification, amplification or application of, 33, 34
exceptions to, 33, 34
Kohlberg, Lawrence, 208

Language, and assessment, 178
Latino patients, and cultural competence, 58
Laws
in conflict with APA Ethics Code, 41
ignorance of (example), 146
and remedial approach, 3
Laws, federal (and APA Ethics Code), 32
Laws, state
on child protection (need to be aware of), 144
and identification of ethical misconduct, 201
and length of time for keeping records, 124
and patient privacy, 113
and psychotherapy notes, 114
record-keeping required by, 125–126
Layered notice, 114
Legal issues, and ethical issues, 11
Letters of reference, 211
LGBT (lesbian, gay men, bisexual, transgendered) people, 59–60
Liability, vicarious, 221
Licensing boards, 6, 8
and advertising or public statements, 157
and APA Ethics Code, 32
and bill collection, 153
and civil liberty protections, 6–7
complainants' burden in, 7
complaints over court testimony to, 162
and interpretation of Ethics Code, 14
and lack of competence, 52

and length of time for keeping records, 124
and negligent assessment, 176
number of psychologists responding to, 8–9
and sexual exploitation, 91
and supervision, 218
and teaching psychologists, 203
Life-endangering patients, 129–130
child abusers, 144–146
with HIV or other infectious diseases, 141–144
suicidal, 137–141
and termination, 199
threatening harm to others, 130–137
Limit setting, positive, 78
Linguistic minorities, competence with, 54–59
Litigation. *See* Forensic psychology

MacArthur Competence Assessment Tool for Treatment, 238
Malpractice
and expert witnesses, 162
percentage of psychologists sued for, 9
teacher–student relationship exempt from, 203
Malpractice carriers, information from, 8
Malpractice charges or complaints
and bill collection, 153
and boundary violations, 76
four *D*s of, 7
sensitivity as protection against, 37–38
sexual relationships as grounds for, 89–90
Malpractice courts, 7
and confidentiality, 111
and informed consent, 100
and multiple relationships, 78
and supervision, 218
Malpractice suits
from death of patient or third party 129–130
four *D*s of, 197
and negligent assessment, 176
statute of limitations on, 124
Managed care, 153–155
and psychological assessments, 175
Marginalized group (integration of professional and personal), 27, 28
and boundaries, 95–96
Marginalized groups (societal), studying accounts of, 13

Massachusetts Institute of Technology (MIT), suicidal student at, 139
Master Kong-Fut-zi (Confucius), 17
McArthur Violence Risk Assessment Scale, 134
Means, using others as, 19
Media presentations, 159–160
Medical errors, 192–193
Mennonites, 61
"Mental Health Bill of Rights," 108–109
Milgram, Stanley, obedience experiment of, 241–242
Military, psychologists in, 200
Mill, John Stuart, 20
Minorities
    characteristics of considered by researchers, 237
    cultural and linguistic, 54–59
    ethnic, 55, 55–56, 236, 237
    religious, 60–62
    and researchers, 236
    sexual, 59–60
Misconduct. See Ethical misconduct
Moral bases of rules, 13
Morality, and context, 47
Moral maximalists, 25. See also Aspirational principles; Positive ethics
Moral principles
    and aspirational approach, 3–4
    infringing on, 23, 48, 119, 132
    Ross on, 23
    See also Ethics
Moral reasoning, cultural differences in, 208
Moral vision, enhancing of, 13
Multiple relationships, 76, 77
    concurrent, 77–79
    consecutive, 79–80
    in forensic psychology, 88, 166–169
    and friends–professionals exercise, 96
    as not necessarily harmful, 77–78
    as source of complaints, 8
    with students, 91
    with supervisees, trainees, or students, 88–89, 227–228
    in teaching of psychology, 208–210, 214–215
        and therapy for students possibly to be evaluated, 214
    unavoidable, 80–81
        and "you first" rule, 81
    See also Boundaries
Mutual consultation groups, 53

Negligence, six Is of, 36
New or experimental therapies, and informed consent, 105
No-harm agreement, 139–140
Nondiscrimination, and remedial vs. positive ethics, 12
Nonmaleficence, 21, 22, 33
    and boundaries, 77
    and competence standards, 51
    and confidentiality rules, 112
    and cultural sensitivity, 55
    and research or scholarship, 232
    and supervising psychologists, 218
No-suicide agreement, 139–140

Obedience experiment of Milgram, 241–242
Online assessments, 178–179
Online therapy, 64–65
Optimizing of treatments, and sexual exploitation, 93–97
Options, evaluating or analyzing of, 43, 46–47
Organizational standards, APA Ethics Code in conflict with, 41
Osheroff v. Chestnut Lodge, 195
Other health care professionals. See Colleagues

Participant recruitment, for research, 235–236
Participatory model, 100, 101–2, 107–8
    in assessment, 182–184
Partner abuse, and threat of violence, 134
Partner notification programs, 144
Past records, obtaining of, 127
Patient access to records, 123–124
Patient autonomy, respect for, 21, 22, 33
    and beneficence, 196
    in billing and collecting of fees, 148
    and boundaries, 77
    and informed consent, 99
    and other cultures, 56
    in participatory model, 107
    and supervising psychologists, 218
    vs. threats to self or identifiable third parties, 129
Patients
    eligible to give informed consent, 102–104
    receiving services from others, 191–192
    treatment-resisting, 196
Patients, life-endangering. See Life-endangering patients

Therapy, by telephone or other electronic means, 64–65
Third-party reimbursement
    and diagnosis, 150–151
    and psychotherapy notes, 114
    and termination, 196
Titrating, of information given patients, 103
Touching, 86
Trainees
    ethical errors of, 224–225
    impaired, 225–226
    multiple relationships with, 88–89
    preparing for salient professional stressors, 222–24
    See also Supervisees
Transference, need for graduate-program teaching about, 93
Translation
    and assessment, 178
    See also Interpreters
Traumatization, vicarious, 69
Treatment-resistant patients, 196
Treatment(s)
    compared with education and supervision, 227–228
    court-ordered, 167–168
    emerging or experimental, 63
Tuskegee study on syphilis impact, 236

"Underground curriculum," 216
Unethical conduct. See Ethical misconduct
Unethical institutional policies, confronting of, 199–201
Utilitarianism, 20–21
    and deception experiments, 242

and privileged communication, 120–121
    rule utilitarianism, 20–21, 240
    and supererogatory obligations, 25

Vanity credentials, 159
Verifying of data, 247
Vicarious liability, 221
Vicarious traumatization, 69
Vignettes, disguising of patient identities in, 127
Violence, predictions of, 164
Violent behavior, indicators of, 134
Virtue ethics, 17–18
    and risk management, 35–38
        and boundary crossings, 77
        and insight into emotional fatigue, 68
        and life-endangering patients, 130
        as self-regulation, 251
        and trainee competence, 226
Voyeurism, psychological, 82, 87

Waiting room
    and cultural attitudes, 59
    noise seepage in (example), 35
    radio kept playing in, 116
Web site(s), 160
    privacy notice on, 114
    test designed for (example), 181
Withdrawal from treatment on part of psychologist, 38. See also Termination
Wrongful-death suit, in Tarasoff case, 131

You-first rule, 81

ABOUT THE AUTHORS

Samuel J. Knapp, PhD, is the director of professional affairs for the Pennsylvania Psychological Association. He has authored or edited about 15 books and approximately 100 articles and made more than 200 professional presentations on ethics and other professional issues. He is a fellow of Division 31 (State, Provincial, and Territorial Psychological Association Affairs).

Leon D. VandeCreek, PhD, is a professor in the School of Professional Psychology at Wright State University. He has authored or edited more than 20 books and about 200 articles and professional presentations. He holds the Diplomate in Clinical Psychology from the American Board of Professional Psychology, and he is a fellow of several divisions of the American Psychological Association. In 2005 he served as president of Division 29 (Psychotherapy).